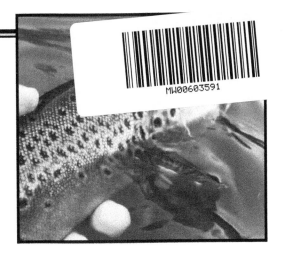

CHATTAHOOCHEE
TROUT

The definitive guide to
fishing for trout in Georgia's
Chattahoochee River

By Steve Hudson

Chattahoochee Trout

The definitive guide to fishing for trout in Georgia's Chattahoochee River

By Steve Hudson

Published by

Chattahoochee Media Group
121 Wills Lane
Alpharetta, GA 30009
770 329 7642

Contact us via email
Info@chattahoocheemedia.com

Visit us on the web
www.chattahoocheemedia.com

Like us on Facebook
facebook.com/chattahoocheemedia

ISBN 978-1-941600-21-4

Manufactured in the United States

For John,
a true fishing buddy

CONTENTS

Preface

Chattahoochee Trout

Like many Georgia anglers, I cut my trout-fishing teeth in the waters of the Chattahoochee River. Sure, I'd fished for bass and bream for years. That was part and parcel of growing up in the south

But trout? Trout were exotic, mysterious and unknown – until that fateful day back in the late 1960s when my enlightened buddy Randy offered to show me how this thing called "trout fishing" was done. I think I was about 14 years old.

So off we went to some little mountain stream. Which one was it?

Truth be told, I'm not sure I remember. Maybe it was a tributary of the Chattahoochee.

What I do remember, though, is that sparkling little gem of a rainbow trout that came out from under a log and finally found its way to my net. I don't think it was a very big fish, but I do remember that it was big enough to change my life forever.

Since that first little rainbow, I've landed who knows how many trout. A lot of them have come from the Chattahoochee, and in fact,the Hooch remains my go-to trout stream.

There are other places I could fish, of course. Georgia is abundantly blessed with hundreds upon hundreds of miles of trout water.

But more often than not, when the trout bug bites, I end up back on some part of "the Hooch." In this book, I'll try to tell you why.

Though I've been fishing the Chattahoochee for many decades, writing this book made me realize anew that you can never know all there is to know about anything. That is certainly the case with the Chattahoochee River, as I discovered on an almost daily basis while working on this book. I gained fresh insights every time I interviewed an outfitter, talked with a guide, or chatted with a fellow angler streamside. I kept notes, sketched maps, and drew diagrams.

The notebooks started piling up until, pretty soon, the stack was close to a foot high.

And then it was time to write. With Ellie the puppy curled up under the desk, the work began. Slowly it all took shape, and the result is the book you now hold in your hands.

Chattahoochee Trout doesn't tell you which rock or log to cast to. That wouldn't be any fun (and besides, there are too many rocks and logs to cover them all). Instead, it divides the trout water into manageable bits with plenty of detail and first-hand insights on each. It's exactly what you will need to figure out the river and its trout, and I think that the result is a practical and eminently useful fishing guide.

But I hope that you find this to be more than just another guidebook. I hope that it also captures the essence of Chattahoochee trout fishing and that it gives you a sense of how rewarding that fishing can be.

Sometimes, of course, fishing is just fishing. But other times it's a path to renewal or a way to figure things out – or even a sort of mirror that lets us see ourselves in new and revealing ways.

I suppose we could talk about fishing as metaphor and rivers as symbols. But that seems so academic and sounds like a lot of work too. It's better, I think, just to wade on in (pardon the expression) and see where it all leads. The river becomes the pathway, and the trout become the reason (or excuse, if you need one) for being there.

"There," in fact, is where I'm heading in just a few minutes. I've got my rod ready and my flies picked out.

Won't you join me? Let's go see if we can find some of those Chattahoochee trout.

Steve Hudson

Meet the Hooch

1

Meet the Hooch

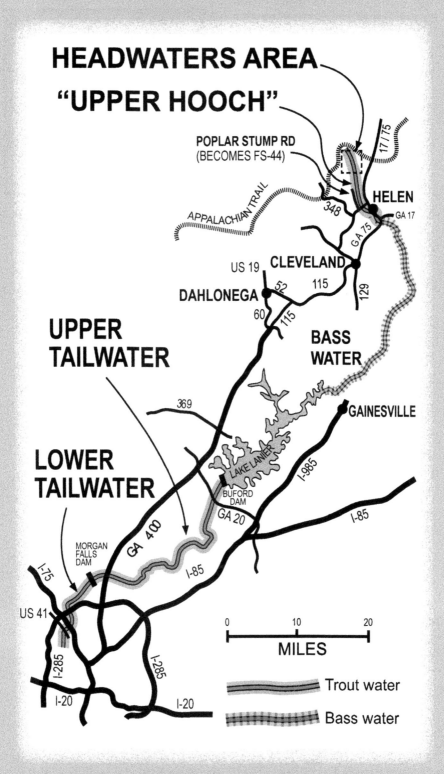

The river...

From Atlanta north, Georgia's Chattahoochee River is a trout angler's dream come true.

"Is the Chattahoochee really that good?"

I first heard that question one day a few years ago as I was wrapping up a program on trout fishing in the south. In fact, I hear that question quite a bit. It's a fair one to ask too.

So what about it? How good is the Hooch? Let's take a look and see.

The upper Chattahoochee

The Chattahoochee is born in White County near Chattahoochee Gap (at an elevation of about 3,600 feet) as a tiny flowing spring that burbles out of the rocks a few hundred yards off the Appalachian Trail. It ends more than 430 river miles later when it merges with the waters of the Flint River to form Lake Seminole near the Georgia/Florida line.

At the point where it comes out of the ground, the river is only a few inches wide. You can cross it in a single step without getting water on your shoes.

But then, right away, it takes off south.

The first several miles of its journey are a fast downhill run as the fledgling river splashes its way down the mountainside, losing elevation and gaining volume as it goes. In the first 11 or so miles from the spring to the ALT-75 bridge at Robertstown near Helen, it drops more than 2,000 feet. Along the way it picks up water from several tributaries, and by the time it reaches Helen it's a respectable middle-sized mountain stream.

Anglers call this the "upper Hooch," and it's one of two sections of the river of interest to trout enthusiasts. It's an exciting stretch of water that offers a variety of fishing opportunities – hunting native brook trout in remote headwaters, pursuing wild and stocked rainbows and browns through the Chattahoochee Wildlife Management Area, fishing for stocked fish literally in downtown Helen, and perhaps even trying for the trout of a lifetime on private trophy water at Nacoochee Bend.

And all that's in the first 11 miles. It's no surprise that this whole upper section is, for many, near the top of the "must-fish" list.

The tailwater

What happens then? Downstream from Helen the river's water warms quickly (especially during the summer). During the summer it's too warm for trout, though bass like it fine. The river stays that way down to Lake Lanier.

And below the lake?

Below the lake (specifically, below Buford Dam) the trout water comes back. That's the legendary 48-mile "Chattahoochee tailwater," and there is no doubt that it is a trout fishing treasure. It lures anglers from all over the country, and the fishing can be unforgettable.

Has the tailwater always held trout? No. In fact, it wouldn't support trout at all were it not for Buford Dam and Lake Lanier. Some old-timers remember the pre-dam days and talk about fishing for catfish, bream and bass. But they did not catch trout.

The thing that turned this stretch of river into a world-class trout fishery is the simple fact that water released from Buford Dam comes from the *bottom* of Lake Lanier. That water is really cold too – usually around 50 degrees.

Buford Dam was by no means the first dam built on the Chattahoochee. Long before Lake Lanier was ever even thought about, Native Americans built stone dams called fish weirs (V-shaped structures which helped them catch fish) at several places in the river. The first

What's in a name?

My linguist friends tell me that the name *Chattahoochee* comes from the Creek Indian words *chatto* (stone) and *hoche* (marked) – "marked rocks," in other words. Exactly what that refers to is uncertain, though it appears that the rocks in question were apparently found on what we would call the "lower Chattahoochee" today in what would have then been Creek Indian territory.

The headwaters, on the other hand, were in Cherokee territory. The Cherokee referred to the river as *Chota*.

What you had, then, was a river with two names, depending on what part of the river you were talking about. In Creek territory, it was the Chattahoochee. In Cherokee territory, however, it was Chota River or Chota Creek – and that's where the trout are found.

So why isn't this book called "Chota Trout"? With the removal of the Cherokee from their traditional homelands, many Cherokee place names began to fade from memory. Surveyors mapping the river continued to reference the Creek name for it until, today, the whole thing is known as the Chattahoochee.

"modern" dam on the river, Nora Mill Dam, was built near Helen in 1824.

Over the years, many dams have been constructed on the Chattahoochee, most of them downriver from Atlanta. The most recent one was West Point Dam, finished in 1974 – and interestingly enough, even in these supposedly enlightened times, the urge to dam the Chattahoochee has not gone away. Case in point: In 1986, in an effort to address metropolitan Atlanta's ever-growing water needs, the Army Corps of Engineers received authorization to build a new "re-regulation" dam at a site on the upper tailwater about two and a half miles upriver from the McGinnis Ferry bridge. Fortunately that project never got beyond the planning stage. Instead, the decision was made to allocate more water from Lake Lanier to ever-thirsty Atlanta, a decision which fueled the now infamous (and still ongoing) water wars between Georgia and neighboring states which also rely on the Chattahoochee as a source of water. There were (and are) hard feelings, but river users applauded the decision to abandon plans for that dam.

No matter what you think about dams, however, the fact is that the Chattahoochee near Atlanta would never have become a trout fishery if it was not for the construction of Buford Dam.

When cold water began flowing from Lake Lanier in the mid-1950s, the river below the dam almost instantly went from a warmwater river to one that was really and truly cold. Trout were eventually introduced and found the river to be much to their liking. Trout fishermen found that they liked it, too, and the rest (as they say) is history.

So how good is it?

Because the Chattahoochee River is right in our backyards, it's easy to take it for granted and forget what a real treasure it is. Sometimes I'm as guilty of that as anybody.

But then I remember just how multi-faceted the Chattahoochee trout water really is. For example: If I'm hankering for a road trip and some backcountry adventure, the Hooch can provide it. Or maybe it's one of those days when I want to fish closer to home. This river lets me do that too.

Some days I get the urge to go for wild browns or native brookies. Other days I want to take a new angler, or maybe a grandkid, to catch stocked rainbows. The Hooch has me covered.

Some days I want to wade; other days I want to float. Some days I want to fish with others, and other times I want the blessed solitude of having what seems like the whole river to myself.

I can find it all, and so much more, on the Chattahoochee.

Yes, it's really that good. ☐

...and its trout

Rainbows, browns and brookies too wait for you somewhere on the Chattahoochee River

Before we look more closely at the river, let's consider the trout that live there. This certainly isn't a science book, so I don't want to get bogged down in biology. But to catch trout, it definitely helps to know something about how the river's trout live. So let's take a look at the lifestyles of Chattahoochee trout, starting with the now-ubiquitous rainbows.

Rainbows: The fish from the Pacific rim

When most folk think about trout fishing in Georgia, they think of rainbow trout (*Oncorhynchus mykiss*). These adaptable fish, which have a definite preference for fast-flowing water, are able to handle warmer or less-than-pristine environs better than either brook trout or browns. They grow large and eagerly take flies and lures, too, all of which make them popular with anglers.

Rainbows are attractive fish with that distinctive reddish-pink stripe along each flank. That trademark swath of color can be especially vivid in wild fish.

Loading trout from the Buford Hatchery for a trip to the Hooch tailwater.

They're native to the Pacific Rim. Their home range extends from Russia's Kamchatka Peninsula around through Alaska and British Columbia to the western United States and even down into Mexico. But they've been transplanted all over the place and now occur just about everywhere that trout are found.

How did they get to Georgia? Most say that the first rainbows were stocked in Georgia waters in the 1880s as a potential replacement for the fast-disappearing brook trout (more on that later). The new residents thrived in the state's cold, clear waters, and

A stocked rainbow (above) and a wild stream-born brown (below), both from the Chattahoochee tailwater below Buford Dam.

it wasn't long until many Georgia streams had self-sustaining populations of wild rainbow trout.

Huge numbers of rainbows are stocked in Georgia each year, many into the Chattahoochee. Typically, these fish are in the 9- to 10-inch range (they're referred to as "SNITs," or "standard 9-inch trout"). But larger fish may be in the mix too. Some waters, including the upper Chattahoochee in the Chattahoochee Wildlife Management Area, are designated as big-fish waters and receive some larger fish of 12 to 14 inches in addition to the SNITs. Now and then an even bigger one finds its way onto the stocking truck too. You never know!

What about wild rainbows in the Hooch? They're certainly present in the upper Hooch above Helen. Most wild fish tend to be in the 4- to 7-inch range, usually with parr marks (large dark blotches in a row down the fish's side) clearly visible. But wild 'bows of 8 to 10 inches are present in the headwaters, too, and even larger wild fish are out there if you take the time to find them and are skilled enough to fool them. If you catch one of the wild ones, you'll immediately see the difference in coloration between wild and stocked fish.

It also appears that there may be limited rainbow reproduction in parts of the Chattahoochee tailwater below Buford Dam. Rainbows spawn in creeks in early to late spring, however, and conditions in most of the tailwater's feeder streams are not ideal for rainbow spawning. But nature is persistent.

Fortunately for anglers, rainbows are not particularly picky eaters. Though they'll cheerfully chow down on minnows (and minnow imitations), they're usually thought of as insect eaters. Even large fish can be caught on small insect imitations – and (to the delight of fly fishers) they will hammer a dry fly.

Sometimes Chattahoochee rainbows become selective. That can happen (for example) on the tailwater during the springtime caddis hatch, when the fish sometimes turn up their collective noses at anything except an adult Caddis of some sort or a Soft-Hackle Caddis Emerger. But more often the key is simply to choose a buggy-looking fly of the fly size right and then present it so as to get a natural (drag-free) drift and without letting the fish know you're there. With rainbows, that's not hard to do since they like to hang out in broken water. The same rippled surface that keeps predators from seeing them will also keep them from seeing you.

Browns: The European delegation

Browns originated in Europe. Their native range includes Iceland and northern Norway, tributaries to the White Sea in Russia, and streams in the Atlas Mountains of northern Africa – and even parts of Pakistan and Afghanistan.

Like rainbows, brown trout have been transplanted all over the world. Some of the earliest stocking of browns took place in Australia in the 1860s. They were brought to Newfoundland a couple of decades later, in the 1880s, which is about the time they were introduced into Georgia streams.

Young browns start out eating insects and other small foods, but their tastes may shift toward meat as they become larger. Bigger browns have certainly made that transition and definitely prefer eating fish. What size fish do the big browns go for? "Anything they can get their jaws around" is how one seasoned Chattahoochee angler described it.

Where do the biggest browns hang out? In the headwaters, look for them in deeper and more sheltered spots (pools, undercut banks and so on). On the tailwater, they tend to prefer slower, deeper places with cover (such as logjams) nearby. But slow water gives them plenty of time to inspect your offerings, so presentation becomes critical. Wherever you look for them, remember that less bright (cloudy) days are often best.

One of the most exciting things about brown trout in the Chattahoochee is that there's now a healthy and self-sustaining population of wild browns in the tailwater below Buford Dam. Biologists began to suspect that browns might be reproducing there when small fish (smaller than any being stocked) began to show up in the late 1990s. Monitoring over the next few years suggested that the browns were indeed reproducing, and as a result the stocking of brown trout in the upper tailwater was discontinued in 2004. Today, any brown you land in the upper tailwater is a wild and streamborn fish.

How large do Georgia's browns get? The current state record (which came from the Chattahoochee tailwater downriver from Buford Dam) is 20 lb. 14 oz. and 30.5 inches long. It was caught by angler Chad Doughty in 2014. But there are lots of other big ones in there too. Since Doughty's record-setting catch, a number of other browns topping the 30-inch mark have been caught and released. Presumably they're still in there...growing bigger...maybe just waiting for you to show up.

Brook trout: The headwaters comeback kids

Let's wrap up this section with a look at the finned gems of this river – the beautiful brook trout that inhabit the upper headwaters.

Technically, brook trout *(Salvelinus fontinalis)* are not really trout but are "char." Among other things, char tend to have a darker base color with lighter spots, while true trout have a lighter base color with darker spots. But calling them "brook *trout*" is okay. Brook char just doesn't have the same ring.

Brook trout are beautiful fish with olive-to-dark-green backs covered with darker wormlike markings. Their sides tend to be some shade of green (accented by vivid red spots with electric blue borders) above a red-to-orange belly. The lower fins are orange with brilliant white leading edges next to a streak of black.

Until browns and rainbows came onto the scene in the 1880s, brookies were the only trout (okay, char) in the Chattahoochee. They enjoyed the good life too – cold clear water, a sheltering forest canopy, and clean gravel streambeds which they depended on for food and as nurseries. But by the mid-1800s, logging was stripping the hillsides. With the trees gone, the water began to warm up and streambeds began to silt up. Brook trout populations began to fall.

> ## Help out the brook trout!
>
> Habitat enhancement work continues on the Chattahoochee headwaters. Stream "work days" are staffed by the Forest Service, Georgia DNR and volunteers from the trout fishing community and are publicized in advance through organizations such at Trout Unlimited and North Georgia Trout Online. Be a part of a work day, and you'll know that you're doing your part to help keep the Chattahoochee headwaters brook trout fishery viable for years to come.

In Georgia, the final blow came in the 1880s when well-meaning groups (who by then were missing their brook trout) decided to fix the fishing by stocking streams with more durable rainbows and browns. Those newcomers adapted well to their new homes. In fact, they soon went wild, and there are now self-sustaining brown and (especially) rainbow populations in many Georgia streams. Nowadays, in fact, the browns and rainbows are considered "naturalized" species – that is, non-native species which have settled in and become a permanent part of the landscape – and they're managed as such.

But what about the brookies?. How did they fare against the introduced browns and rainbows? Alas, not too well. In fact, when browns or rainbows encountered brookies, they often simply ate 'em.

With their range slashed, their habitat badly degraded, and their new status as the blue plate special, brook trout faced an iffy future.

By the late 1960s wildlife officials were looking at ways to save brook trout in Georgia, starting in some high-elevation streams where brookies had once thrived. Among the criteria used to choose those streams were whether the watershed was on public land (so it could be managed) and whether there was a "barrier falls" (to keep rainbows and browns from moving up into what was about to become brook trout water).

One stream that made the cut was the headwaters portion of the Hooch. After some prep work, native brook trout from a nearby stream were

Easing up on a brook trout pool on the upper headwaters of the Hooch.

transplanted into the new water. Then everyone waited to see how it would go.

What happened was that the brook trout settled right in. Today there is a solid brook trout fishery in the uppermost Chattahoochee headwaters.

Trout tend to grow to fit the stream where they live, and wild brookies are no exception. Those headwaters brookies don't get very big. A 5- or 6-inch fish is worth telling your friends about, and an 8-incher earns bragging rights.

Are brook trout hard to catch? Not really. They tend to be enthusiastic eaters and love any form of insects. A suitable nymph can be very effective. However, Hooch headwaters brookies eagerly go for topwater offerings too. A carefully placed dry may be all it takes to tempt a wild native brookie to leave the safety of the depths and commit with a splashy strike.

But never keep one. Take a picture instead. Most who fish for these headwaters jewels practice catch-and-release fishing, and I urge you to do so too.

The bottom line?

The bottom line is this: there's a lot of variety, trout-wise, in the Hooch. In the upper reaches, above Upper Chattahoochee Falls, it's the realm of the brook trout. Below that falls down to Helen, and again for many miles downstream of Buford Dam, expect to find rainbows and browns.

All three species – and years of fishing enjoyment – await you on north Georgia's Chattahoochee River. ☐

The Upper Hooch

2

The Upper Hooch

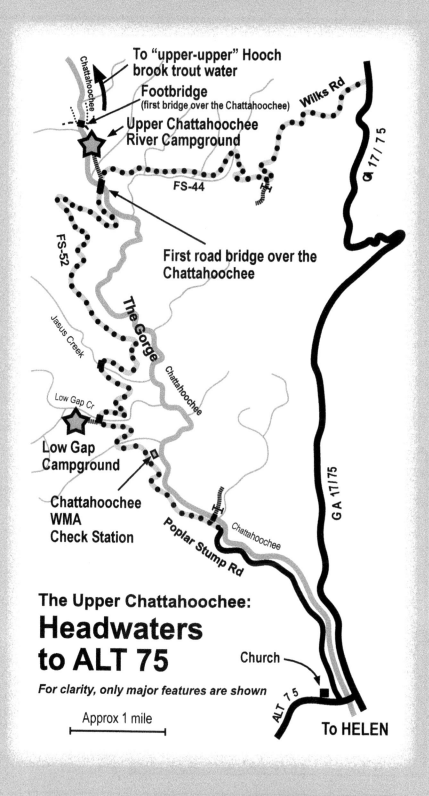

To "upper-upper" Hooch brook trout water

Footbridge
(first bridge over the Chattahoochee)

Upper Chattahoochee
River Campground

Chattahoochee

Wilks Rd

GA 17 / 75

FS-44

First road bridge over the
Chattahoochee

FS-52

The Gorge

Jasus Creek

Chattahoochee

Low Gap Cr

Low Gap
Campground

Chattahoochee
WMA
Check Station

GA 17/75

Poplar Stump Rd

Chattahoochee

The Upper Chattahoochee:
Headwaters
to ALT 75

Church

For clarity, only major features are shown

ALT 75

To HELEN

Approx 1 mile

Getting to know the Upper Hooch

There's something for everyone on the upper Hooch above Helen.

The Chattahoochee River is really several rivers in one.

Best known is the wide and wonderful tailwater section below Buford Dam. It provides world-class trout fishing that draws anglers from all over the country. We'll look at it in detail later on.

And yet the tailwater is only part of the picture. There's another side to the Hooch, too – the upper portion above the town of Helen.

Helen, in north Georgia's White County, marks the point where the

river begins to warm too much for trout. Not far below Helen it shifts from a trout fishery to one more suited to bass. But if you go the other way from Helen – if you go upriver instead of down – you'll enter that magical realm

The upper part of the Chattahoochee offers trout fishing adventure for any angler, whether you're a seasoned veteran or a newcomer to the sport.

known simply as "the headwaters."

The headwaters section of the Hooch, which we will arbitrarily say starts at the ALT-75 bridge on the upriver side of the mountain town of Helen, is one of my favorite trout fisheries anywhere. Why? Maybe because it offers so many different fishing experiences from which to choose. From stocked and easily accessible water to off-the-beaten-track wild-trout fishing – and everything in between – this piece of the Chattahoochee lets me pick my destination according to my mood and inclination on any given day.

On mountain water like the upper Hooch, you never know what the next cast will bring.

For example, say that you have young anglers in your group and want to introduce them to trout fishing on a mountain stream. The portion of the river in the lower part of the Chattahoochee Wildlife Management Area is perfect for that, offering easy access to water that is stocked weekly between March and Labor Day. It's a great place for anyone to learn trout fishing.

Or say you want solitude and don't mind hiking to get it. The Gorge section of the river, upstream from the area just mentioned, offers miles of remote trout water for you to explore.

What if you want to combine camping and fishing? Forest Service campgrounds at Low Gap Creek and at Upper Chattahoochee River Campground are great places to pitch a tent or set up a camper. There are undeveloped primitive sites in the area too.

And what if you want real backcountry adventure, perhaps with some brook trout fishing thrown in? You'll find that on these headwaters too.

In this section of this guide, we'll take a detailed look at the trout fishing opportunities that await you along the headwaters portion of the river. We'll start with a look at some of the gear you will need to fish there. Then we'll dive into the experience itself, starting with my own search for Chattahoochee Spring, the place where the river begins.

I love this part of the river, and I think that you will too. ☐

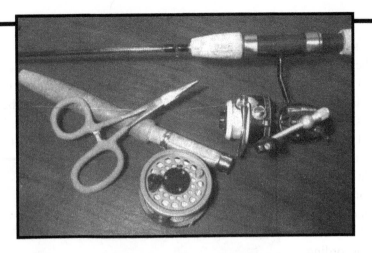

Gearing up for the Upper Hooch

Some thoughts on choosing the right gear for trout fishing on the upper Hooch

One key to getting the most from fishing the upper Hooch is to have the right gear. Every angler has preferences, of course. But there are some things to keep in mind when choosing gear for this part of the river.

Fly gear for the upper Chattahoochee

Rods: Your choice of rods will be determined primarily by where on the river you're fishing. For example, the lower part of the upper Hooch (from the WMA check station downstream) is relatively open and suitable for longer rods. Many who fish that water choose 3- to 5-weight rods in the 7.5 to 8 foot range. My personal favorite is a 7.5 foot 4 weight – short enough for casting in tight spots but with enough punch for longer casts when needed. That rod will also handle indicator-based nymph rigs, though if I'm focusing on nymphing I'll choose a longer rod for the greater reach it provides.

Upstream from the check station, conditions are a bit tighter and casts are often shorter. Thus, shorter rods become more useful. Consider a 2- to 4-weight rod with a length of 6.5 to 7.5 feet. My personal choice is a 6 ft. 6

in. 2-weight rod; it suits me well since I enjoy using a single dry or a dry/
dropper combo. Again, if I plan on mostly nymphing I'll use something a
little longer – perhaps a 7 ft. 6 in. 4-weight instead.

What about the reel? Pick one for the line size you're using, and make
sure it isn't too heavy for your rod. And the drag? Any drag system is fine.

Line and backing: A weight-forward floating line works great.

As you move on up into the headwaters, casts will become shorter and
you'll may not even have much fly line outside your guides. For that reason,
some folks fishing the uppermost areas prefer double-tapered lines because
the line can be flipped end-for-end when one end becomes worn. That
works because the first several yards of a double-tapered line are essentially
identical to the first several yards of a weight-forward line; when making
short casts, both cast about the same at the distances we're considering here.

Backing? You won't need it as far as the fishing is concerned. However,
it increases spool diameter and can reduce kinking of your line.

Leaders: How long should the leader be? Longer (9-ft.) leaders keep fly
line away from the fish if you have room to use them, but shorter (7.5 ft.)
leaders may be more practical and less prone to tangle in tight quarters.

Still further upstream, conditions get tighter as the stream gets smaller.
There'll be times when you're only casting a few yards. Sometimes, in fact,
you'll be casting mostly leader with little or no fly line in play. In those cases, some prefer a furled leader. Such a leader is extremely supple and turns
over beautifully all by itself, even with little or no fly line extending beyond
the tip of your rod. It makes casting in tight quarters elegantly feasible, and
that's why I use a furled leader for most of my smaller-water fishing.

Flies for the upper Hooch

Trout in the upper Hooch, even wild ones, are not too picky if you give
them more or less what they expect to see.

Imagine you're a trout sitting there waiting for breakfast. As the current
carries a potential entree into view, your eat/don't-eat call has to be made
quickly or the food will be gone. You may only have a second or two to
decide – so if something looks good to eat then odds are you'll go for it.

Yes, at times the fish become selective and key on a specific pattern. But
that's not the norm here. These fish are opportunistic and will usually eat
whatever happens along unless to give 'em a reason to say no.

Your job is to encourage them to say "yes."

The chart on page 29 will help; it gives you a month-by-month listing of
some of the adult (flying) insects that you (and the trout) might see during
each month, along with suggestions on some dry patterns to use to imitate

What do they look like?

Identify the type of bug you're seeing. Then use the bug chart at right to help you pick a suitable dry fly imitation.

Mayfly
(upwings, tapered body, prominent tail)

Caddisfly
(delta wings, moth-like)

Stonefly
(wings held flat against body)

Midge
(appearance may vary but very small)

those insects.

What about nymphs? When you see adult insects, it's a sure bet that subsurface forms (nymphs and emergers) are also active. Rather than carry dozens of different nymph imitations, keep it simple with basic buggy patterns such as the Pheasant Tail Nymph, Gold Ribbed Hare's Ear, or a Soft-Hackled Emerger. Size 'em one size larger than the adults you're seeing (because nymphs are usually a little larger than the adults) – and note that nymphs often work even when you are not seeing adult insects flying around the stream.

Here are some other things to keep in mind:

•   As you move away from stocked water and into more wild-trout water (for example, the Gorge or the upper headwaters), it becomes more important to more closely imitate the *size* of the insects you see on the stream.

•   When using nymphs, use enough weight to get them down near the bottom. All other things being equal, using too little weight is almost certainly the number one problem among nymph fishers who are having trouble connecting with fish.

•   When fishing dries, attractors such as Stimulators and Royal Wulffs can be effective if you're not sure which pattern to use. Match the size of the flies you see or choose size based on the "Bug Chart" on page 29.

•   If fish rise to the fly but refuse it at the last second, it may be that you've got the pattern right but your fly is too large. Downsize and try again.

The upper Chattahoochee "bug chart"

For a while now, I've been asking every expert I can find this one question: What's your favorite dry (surface) fly on the upper Chattahoochee? Here's what they told me:

"If you see these ... then use these..."

JAN	Small mayflies	Blue Winged Olive, Parachute Adams (16-20)
FEB	Small black stoneflies Small caddisflies Small mayflies	Black Elk Hair or Foamback Caddis (18-20) Brown Elk Hair or Foamback Caddis (18-20) Blue Winged Olive, Parachute Adams (16-18)
MAR	Very small brown caddisflies Small tan/cream caddisflies Small brown mayflies	Brown Elk Hair or Foamback Caddis (16-18) Tan Elk Hair or Foamback Caddis (12-14) March Brown, Parachute Adams (12-14)
APR	Small tan/cream caddisflies Very small gray caddisflies Small brown mayflies Light-colored mayflies	Tan Elk Hair or Foamback Caddis (12-14) Gray Elk Hair or Foamback Caddis (16-18) March Brown, Parachute Adams (12-14) Light Cahill (12-14)
MAY	Very small gray caddisflies Small brown mayflies Light or sulphur mayflies Greenish mayflies	Gray Elk Hair or Foamback Caddis (16-18) March Brown, Parachute Adams (12-14) Light Cahill (12-14), Sulphurs (14-18) Green Drake (8-10)
JUN	Small gray caddisflies Sulphur mayflies Terrestrials	Gray Elk Hair or Foamback Caddis (16-18) Sulphurs (16-18) Ants, beetles, etc. (size varies)
JUL	Light mayflies Stoneflies Terrestrials	Light Cahill (12-14) Yellow Stimulator (8-12) Ants, beetles, etc. (size varies)
AUG	Light mayflies Stoneflies Terrestrials	Light Cahill (12-14) Yellow Stimulator (8-12) Ants, beetles, etc. (size varies)
SEP	Small caddisflies Large tan caddis Terrestrials	Brown Elk Hair or Foamback Caddis (18-20) Ginger Elk Hair or Foamback Caddis (8-10) Ants, beetles, etc. (size varies)
OCT	Large tan caddis Small mayflies	Ginger Elk Hair or Foamback Caddis (8-10) Blue Winged Olive, Parachute Adams (16-18)
NOV	Small mayflies Small caddisflies	Blue Winged Olive, Parachute Adams (16-18) Brown Elk Hair or Foamback Caddis (18)
DEC	Small mayflies	Blue Winged Olive, Parachute Adams (16-18)

NOTE: Midges may be present at any time of the year. Imitate these midges with a small Blue Winged Olive or Griffith's Gnat (18-20). Good midge emerger imitations include the Zebra Midge or Blue Assassin (16-18).

Streamers for the upper Hooch

Whether targeting stocked or wild trout, streamers can be effective in the upper Chattahoochee. Here are four favorites:

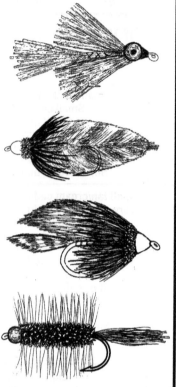

Rolex – A flashy streamer...think of it as the fly rod equivalent of a Mepps Spinner. Try size 8 or 10 in gold/silver, red/gold, or all silver. Work this fly through deep pools or strip fast through runs.

Hudson Streamer – A good streamer when fishing for stocked trout, this pattern also works well on wild fish. The barred (shown here) or mottled flank wings enhance the "sizzle" of the fly.

Weighted Muddler Minnow – A good imitation of sculpins and other mottled minnows. Fish weighted versions or add split shot. Can be very effective in moderate riffle water on stocked as well as wild fish.

Black or Olive Sparkle Bugger – When tied with softer hackle and stripped instead of drifted, a Sparkle Bugger makes a good minnow imitation. Olive, green or black are favorites. Bead heads add weight and flash, enhancing effectiveness.

- Dry/dropper combos can be effective. Choose a dry fly to match the adult insects that you are seeing...and pair it with an emerger or nymph dropper one size larger.
- During summertime, ants (wet or dry) can be exceptionally effective. Match the size of the ants you see crawling on your lunch!
- If you're fishing a stretch where the banks are thickly overgrown, consider terrestrials such as beetles or hoppers.
- Here's a real upper Hooch secret: tiny popping bugs tied on size 14 or 16 hooks sometimes work wonders. Don't feel bad; I didn't believe it either.

When targeting recently stocked fish: The river below the check station, as well as the section through Upper Chattahoochee River Campground, is regularly stocked from sometime in March through Labor Day – and newly stocked fish are not yet experts on the natural food forms available to them. They tend to operate on instinct, so patterns such as egg imitations (Y2Ks,

3-D Sucker Spawn, Yarn Eggs, etc.) are effective. Flashy streamers such as the Rolex work well too. Worm patterns (in shades of red, pink or chartreuse) are also good producers on recently stocked fish.

Sometimes (especially a month or two after stocking begins) you'll find yourself fishing water that simultaneously holds newly-stocked fish as well as more experienced fish. The new stockers are running on instinct, but the more seasoned fish have learned that the river holds lots of good things to eat. One strategy for such water is a multi-fly rig which pairs (say) a gaudy egg imitation such as a Y2K with a more natural-looking fly such as a buggy Gold

Egg imitations such as (from top) the Y2K, 3-D Sucker Spawn, and Yarn Egg, can work well on stocked trout on the upper Hooch. Be sure to add enough weight to get them down deep.

Ribbed Hare's Ear or other nymph or emerger. That gives the fish a choice and allows you to interest fresh stockers as well as more established residents. You'll learn a lot more about this strategy in the section on fishing the Delayed Harvest portion of the lower tailwater below Morgan Falls Dam.

Spinning gear for the upper Hooch

Spin fishing is popular on the upper Chattahoochee. In fact, in some spots, spinning gear may be the only feasible way to fish.

What's the best spinning outfit for headwaters trout? To answer that one, let's start not with the rod but with a look at spinning lures.

Lures: In the upper Hooch, smaller lures are generally the rule. Depending on the water you're fishing, lure weights up to about 1/8 oz. work well. Go with the "heavy" end of that range on bigger water (say, closer to Helen) or in deep pools, shifting to smaller lures on smaller sections upstream. Tiny 1/24 or 1/32 oz. spinners can work very well in the extreme headwaters.

What's the best color? Now there's a question sure to cause discussion! Lure manufacturers understand that color and pattern are big selling points and constantly introduce new color combinations – and who's to say that the newest offering is not the one we've been waiting for all along? I suppose that the only way to find out is to purchase a few and give 'em a try!

When it comes to succumbing to the lure of lures, I'm as guilty as anyone and have boxes full of lures to prove it. However, when I fish the upper Chattahoochee, it seems that I keep returning to a simple white inline spinner with a silver or gold blade. Black and silver works well too. These are widely available, do a great job of imitating minnows, and (most importantly) consistently catch fish.

Many manufacturers make in-line spinners. Names like Blue Fox, Mepps, Roostertail, and Panther Martin come to mind. But be careful about bargain-box look-alikes. Some of 'em don't like to spin.

Another popular lure is the Little Cleo spoon. It can be great for probing the deeper pools you'll find.

Painted jig heads with curlytail grubs can work well too. Try a 1/16 oz. white jig head with a white grub tail. Yellow also works, and black is good if the water is a little off-color or if the sky is cloudy.

Finally, don't overlook small crankbaits. Shallow-running or diving crankbaits, especially in rainbow trout patterns, can be effective in pools or when fished across runs.

Line: Just as important as the lure is the line to which you tie it. Most spin fishers on the upper Hooch use monofilament (nylon or fluorocarbon). Clear or green are favorites. Also consider abrasion resistance; it can be important in the rock-strewn upper Hooch.

As for strength, 4-lb. test seems to be the unofficial standard. But serious upper Hooch spin fishers sometimes go with 2-lb. line. It's so small as to be essentially invisible, and that can pay off if the fish are pressured or the water is low. Certainly that 2-lb. test line is a dream to cast. Just don't use a 4-lb. hookset while fishing with 2-lb. line!

My personal line choice for upper Hooch spin fishing is one of the small-diameter 4-lb. fluorocarbons. It costs a bit more, but it's much less visible to fish – and that (at least in my mind) gives me an edge. If I'm not using fluorocarbon, then I tend to favor one of the current crop of low-diameter, abrasion resistant 4-lb. nylon lines.

And that brings us, at last, to choosing the right spinning rod.

Spinning rods for headwaters trout: Though some upper Hooch trout anglers start with the same gear they use down at the bass pond, the fact is that bass gear is rarely the best choice for trout. Bass rods are designed to throw heavier lures, but the trout angler needs something which will handle precision casting with lightweight lures and relatively small-diameter line.

What sort of spinning rod is best for the upper Chattahoochee? A moderate-action ultralight in the 5-foot range is ideal. Pair it with a well-designed open-face reel (a good closed-face reel is fine too) and you're good to go.

My personal spinning outfit for these waters is a neat little 5-foot ultralight rod with an open-face reel filled with 4-lb. test fluorocarbon. It will make long casts when needed, handles close-in casts with ease, and is short enough to use in tight places too. It's given me years of pleasurable fishing on the upper Chattahoochee.

Bait: Regulations permit the use bait in the upper Chattahoochee, and it's a favorite technique on the stocked water of the WMA. Simply set up a rig with a bobber, a sinker, and a hook. Then drift it through pools and runs, holding your breath in anticipation. It's a great way to introduce kids to trout fishing because it's easy – and fun.

What bait is best? Every fisherman has a favorite – salmon eggs or corn, a little blob of cheese, a pinch of marshmallow, or even a ball

An ultralight spinning rig can be a great tool for trout fishing on the upper Chattahoochee.

of bread. Red wigglers are trout-approved. So are nightcrawlers or crickets. All will work, and sometimes they are the *only* things that work. I'll bet I'm not the only fly fisher who has covertly slipped a bit of nightcrawler onto the hook of a Pheasant Tail Nymph!

Powerbait can be a good choice too and is widely available in a variety of colors and forms. The round orange or yellow ones, which resemble fish eggs, can be especially effective.

Other gear you'll want to have

Whether fly or spin fishing, there's more to add to your "gear list.

Wading gear: Many anglers like to use waders on upper Hooch trips. Breathable waders are much better than vinyl or neoprene (which may leave you overheated in summer or damp and chilled in winter). I use breathable chest waders or wading pants most of the year, but during the heat of summer I'll often wade "wet" with wading boots but no waders.

What about hip boots? "Hippers," as they're called, come up to mid-thigh and are great for shallow water. But you may encounter places where the water is too deep for hippers to be used.

Your wading footwear is also important. In mountain streams, expect rocky streambeds. Those rocks can move underfoot, so good ankle support is important. You also want soles that grip well on the rocks – and that means felt or studs. Avoid footwear such as sandals or "water shoes," which offer little protection and no support

Wading staff: If your knees or balance not what they once were, a wading staff can steady you on uneven stream bottoms and provides a great sense of security as you move around the stream.

Back-up fly or lure box: I learned the importance of this one the hard way. I was far up the upper Hooch fishing for brook trout when I suddenly realized I no longer had my fly box! That was the end of that trip. Nowadays I carry a small back-up box in a zippered pocket – just in case.

Change of clothes: Changing weather is always a possibility in the mountains. Temperatures can drop suddenly, even in summer. If you get wet from unexpected rain or from a fall in the river, there's a risk of hypothermia. Have a spare set of clothes just in case.

Polarized sunglasses: These will protect your eyes from glare and will help you see the bottom of the stream as you wade. They're essential.

And a few more things...

If you're going to be fishing off the beaten track (for example, in the extreme headwaters) there are some other things to consider as you plan.

Navigation aids: This can be as simple as a printed topo map or as sophisticated as a handheld GPS. But just having it is not enough. Be sure you know how to use it in the field.

Flashlight: This one is so obvious that people forget it all the time. Last time I forgot mine, I'd lost track of time and had fished too late and found myself hiking out at dusk. No problem. But then dusk turned to dark...a *big* problem since I had no light. What should have been a 20-minute walk back to the car turned into an hour-plus can't-hardly-see-a-thing adventure. I don't mind admitting it was scary.

When I told my wife about it later, her first words were, "Didn't you carry that little flashlight I gave you?" Those conversations never turn out well, so I just hung my head in shame and put the light in my day pack where it should have been all along.

Day pack: Speaking of day packs, should you carry one? If you're hiking very far, it's not a bad idea. It can hold snacks, extra fly boxes, and so on. You can always set it down if you want to be unencumbered while fishing a particular pool or riffle and then pick it up when you're done.

Rain jacket: If there's any chance of rain, put a lightweight rain jacket into your day pack. It just might keep you from getting soaked. You won't appreciate it until you experience just how cold you can get in an unexpected rain, even in summer. It happened to me once when a 30-minute rainstorm soaked me to the skin. The temperature dropped at the same time, and I was shivering by the time I got back to the car and some dry clothes.

First aid kit: A basic first aid kit lets you deal with minor scrapes and similar problems. Many outfitters sell small packaged first-aid kits that weight very little and take up next to no space.

Bug spray: Out in the woods, bugs are a fact of life. In particular, be on guard for unexpected yellow jacket or hornet nests. If you're allergic to stings, always carry your epi pen.

Along the upper Chattahoochee, the bug you hear about most often is the tick. Yellowjackets are at least upfront with you. But ticks are devious and sneaky. Indiana Jones hated snakes; I feel the same way about ticks. Various tick repellents are available on the market, and every outdoors person seems to have a personal favorite. But sometimes it seems that a repellent just weeds out the weak ones.

Always check yourself for ticks at the end of the day.

Bear spray? Although bears are certainly present here, the fact is that bear encounters are rare. Most anglers go for years and never see one (though many secretly wish they would, since many consider a bear sighting to be a highlight of any trip).

Here, as elsewhere, the best way to deal with bears is to avoid surprising them. As you fish, make some noise so that any bear which happens to be in the neighborhood knows you're there.

Whistle: I learned the value of this from a friend who spends lots of time backcountry hiking. "I always carry a whistle," he said. "It doesn't weigh hardly anything, but it makes a lot of noise if I ever need to be found."

Three blasts on a whistle is a universal call for help, and the whistle's piercing sound carries a long way. Put one in your vest right now. Then forget about it unless you need it someday.

Flight plan: A flight plan lets others know where you are and can help rescuers find you if the need ever arises. Mine is a map printout that I leave with my wife with the area I'll be fishing marked clearly. That way she knows where I am in case I don't return when expected. I also leave a copy of that map on the seat of my car. Cars are easier to find than are misplaced anglers, and that would allow rescuers to know where to start searching.

Hopefully my flight plans will never be needed. But if something should happen (and it's an uncertain world) then it's nice to know that someone would know where to look. □

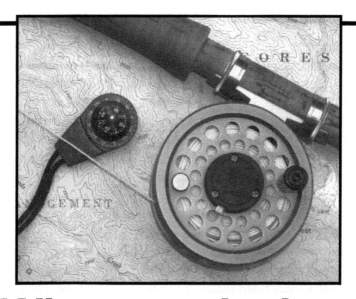

Where and when on the Upper Hooch

Picking the right time and place for trout fishing on the upper Chattahoochee

The upper part of the Chattahoochee River is a many-faceted fishery that offers a bit of everything from casual roadside fishing to much more ambitious hike-in angling adventures. Thus, when you're planning a trip on this section of the river, the first step is to look at what you want to get out of the experience. That helps you figure out the "where."

For example, if you are seeking solitude or a more backcountry type of experience, you might want to consider the Gorge or perhaps some of the more remote brook trout water.

On the other hand, if you are looking for trout for dinner then you may want to focus on the stocked water in the WMA.

Or maybe you want to combine camping and fishing? Then a few days at the Upper Chattahoochee River or Low Gap Campground may be ideal.

Clearly, there are lots of options to choose from.

As you consider the possibilities, however, be honest with yourself about your physical abilities and fishing skills. For example, if your plans involve hiking, are you physically up to the task? If you have decided to tackle the more remote brookie water, are you up to precision tight-quarters casting?

Think about the others in your group too. If you're taking kids along with you, for instance, remember that they'll want to catch fish and may become bored very quickly if they do not. That might nudge you away from some of the more remote or more technical sections and push you toward the easily accessible stocked water below the WMA check station. Young anglers often do well on that water, especially with bait such as worms, crickets, Powerbait or salmon eggs.

What time of day is best?

One question that I hear a lot is this: Is it better to fish in the morning, or at midday, or in the afternoon and evening?

Picking the right time of day can make a definite difference on the upper Hooch. You want a time when the fish are active, and fish activity depends on water temperature as much as anything. Thus, to position yourself for best success, you want to find times when the water temperature is most to the liking of the fish.

Without getting too technical and delving into specific temperature ranges, let's break it down seasonally.

During the summertime, the water in the river will be at its warmest from midday into the afternoon. Those midday temperatures may be too high for trout to be comfortable, and the fish may thus hunker down somewhere cool and not move. You won't catch those fish because they don't want to be bothered. But those same fish may be active at other times of day when the water is cooler. Thus, during the warmer months of the year, you'll probably do best planning your fishing early or late in the day.

There are exceptions, of course. Cloudy days keep water temperatures down and can extend the sweet spot. But as a general rule the best warm-weather times are early or late.

One of the most pleasant seasons to fish here is the fall. Temperatures are agreeable (to fish and fishers alike), there's usually some insect activity, and (assuming that there's been rain and that there's enough water in the streams) life is good all around. In fact, one of the few drawbacks to fall fishing is what I call the "leaf hatch." As the autumn leaves turn and begin to drop, a lot of them end up in the water. When they do, you'll sometimes find that you catch more leaves than fish.

What about winter fishing? The same idea applies, but the bottom line is pretty much opposite what it is during the summer. During wintertime, the water can be so cold in the morning that the fish are simply not active. But as the sun rises and touches the streambed, the water may warm enough to wake 'em up and get 'em moving.

Rarely will winter fishing be at its best before 10 or 11 a.m. That means you can sleep in a bit or have that extra cup of coffee. Similarly, things will begin to slow down about 3 or 4 in the afternoon as the sun drops lower in the sky – and that means you'll be home in plenty of time for supper.

Other seasonal considerations

The upper Chattahoochee is definitely a mountain stream. Mountain weather can be unpredictable at times, so weather thus becomes a factor in trip planning.

Winter weather can be especially problematic. It can be fun to fish in the snow, and I love to do so. But it's important to be sure you stay warm when

enjoying wintertime fishing. That usually means layering your clothing so you can shed outer layers as the day warms. Pay particular attention to keeping your hands, head and feet warm at this time of year.

Also be aware that winter weather can adversely impact roadways. Roads can ice quickly in the mountains and can make travel a dicey undertaking. Consider the forecast when scheduling a winter trip.

Weather can

Fall fishing can be good on the upper Chattahoochee River...but fall means falling leaves. During the peak of leaf season, don't be surprised if you catch as many leaves as you do fish.

be a factor in the summertime too. There's the matter of heat, of course, but a bigger issue is usually the possibility of unexpected summer storms. One potential result of such storms is fast-rising water following even a brief summer rain event, and such downpours happen fairly often when the forecast calls for "scattered pop-up storms."

It can be surprising how quickly a summer storm somewhere in the watershed can bring up the river. On one occasion, while fishing the Gorge section near the WMA check station, my buddy and I were caught on the wrong side of the river after an unanticipated cloudburst dropped enough rain to temporarily raise the river's level by about two feet. There was nothing to do but wait for the water to come down.

Fortunately, after one of those weather events, the river does tend to come down relatively quickly.

If there has been a period of extended rain, the river through the WMA may simply be too high to fish. In that case, stay at home and tie some flies.

Working around hunting seasons

Since the upper Hooch is located within the Chattahoochee Wildlife Management Area, you'll be sharing the woods with hunters during the fall, winter and early spring.

Hunting within the Chattahoochee WMA begins as early as mid-August with the opening of squirrel season, and small game hunting continues on and off through the end of February. On the big-game side, the archery deer season opens in early September, with firearms hunts scheduled at various times through the fall and early winter. Turkey season comes in the spring, starting in March and continuing till mid-May.

Except for possible issues with traffic, hunting won't impact fishermen very much on the roadside section of river downstream from the WMA check station.

However, since Georgia's trout season is now year-round, it's possible that backcountry anglers might cross paths with backcountry hunters. For that reason, during hunting season, it's a good idea to wear fluorescent orange when fishing in the backcountry or in areas where hunting might be going on. Orange camo is good if you can find it.

You can check the exact dates when there will be hunting on the Chattahoochee Wildlife Management Area by visiting Georgia DNR's online regulations site at **georgiawildlife.com/hunting/regulations**

The biggest potential impact is during the firearms part of deer season. During scheduled firearms deer hunts, I'd fish elsewhere or (as when it's been raining a lot) simply stay home and tie flies. It's safer that way. ☐

Where the river begins

It's always good to start at the beginning, and that means finding the spring at Chattahoochee Gap.

It's Thursday morning, lightly overcast with the air temperature in the 60s. There's no rain in the forecast, and though it's almost the start of thunder-and-lightning season the nearest storm is hundreds of miles away.

That's good, because I'm a man on a mission and I don't want bad weather to get in the way.

My mission – my goal, if you will – is to find the place where the Chattahoochee begins. That seems a necessary first step. I suppose it's the same as beginning at page one of a book, for the very beginning of the story is what I want to understand. I don't just want some far-upriver stretch of stream, no sir. Instead, I want the place where water comes out of the ground and begins its long, long run down to the Gulf of Mexico.

Can that point of origin be found? Yes, it can.

So last week I set out to find it: the place where the river begins.

The generally agreed-upon head of the Chattahoochee is a flowing spring (known as Chattahoochee Spring) up near Chattahoochee Gap just off the Appalachian Trail. Though not celebrated with billboards or signs, the spring is actually not too hard to find. You can make your way to Chattahoochee Gap either via the AT or via the Jack's Knob Trail, a connector trail which links Brasstown Bald with the AT by way of Jack's Knob. It's about 5 miles from the Jacks Knob Trail trailhead near the summit of Brasstown Bald to the Appalachian Trail.

Brasstown Bald, with a peak that's 4,784 feet above sea level, is Georgia's highest peak. From its summit, on a clear day, you can see four states – not only Georgia but North Carolina, South Carolina, and Tennessee too – with ease. Visitors delight in the panorama, and you can even enjoy the view from home thanks to a pair of webcams operated by the U.S. Forest Service. You can access those webcams at www.fs.usda.gov/detail/conf/home/?cid=fsm9_029190.

In Cherokee, Brasstown Bald is *itse'yi* ("place of fresh green"), a reference to its grassy (as opposed to timbered) summit. The name "Brasstown" came about when early settlers mistook that Cherokee name for a similar word meaning "brass," while a "bald" is a common Appalachian word for a mountain summit which offers a 360-degree unobstructed view.

How did the summit become bald? According to Cherokee legend, there was once a great flood that swept across the earth. Almost all of the people perished in that flood; the only survivors were members of a few Cherokee families who sought safety in a giant canoe. Eventually, it is said, the canoe ran aground on the summit of a

The author, ever-hopeful with flyrod in hand, at the start of the hike to Chattahoochee Spring. Note that at this point in the hike he's still smiling...

forest-covered mountain. However, there was no wild game on the summit for the people to hunt...and because of the trees, there was no place to plant crops either. That could have been bad, but the Great Spirit intervened, removing all the trees from the top of the mountain so the survivors would have a place to plant their crops. The people lived there that way, surviving on what they could grow, until the waters of the flood finally subsided.

The Jacks Knob Trail starts near the summit of Brasstown Bald, working its way down the mountain and eventually crossing GA 180 after about 2.5 miles of fairly tough hiking. From there, it continues another 2.4 miles to its intersection with the Appalachian Trail.

The entire Jacks Knob Trail is a great hike if you have the time. But you can shorten the hike to Chattahoochee Gap by about half (that is, to 2.4 miles) if you start at the parking area where the trail crosses GA 180.

In the interest of time, and because I was on an urgent journalistic mission, I decided to take that option and so started where the trail intersects 180. There, you'll find a small parking area near a large informational sign; the trail itself is about 75 yards to the left along GA 180 back toward GA 75 and Helen. The trailhead is pretty easy to spot; just look for a marker post on the south side of the road.

I'd gotten a late start, so I wasted no time before taking to the trail. It let me know who was boss right away with a leg-stretching steady climb, but about the time I started to think "I hope the whole thing isn't like this," it moderated into a gently rolling and more-or-less level path that continued that way for quite a while. The trail through this stretch takes you by a number of spots that offer unobstructed wintertime views across the mountains, but during the warmer months you may see little besides a visually impenetrable wall of green leaves.

The relatively easy grade of this part of the trail allowed me to make good time. *I should be able to do this before it gets dark,* I said to myself. *Piece of cake.* But then, just about the time I was getting into the rhythm of things, and just at the precise moment when I was telling myself that maybe I really was God's gift to hiking after all, the trail reminded me otherwise.

That reminder was gentle at first, a slight but noticeable uphill. Then I was climbing sure enough. It was getting steep. And my legs were beginning to hurt.

But being known to some as "Steve of the Wilderness," and not wanting to give up all the glory and fame that comes with a moniker like that, I had no choice but to push on. Besides, I figured that the climb couldn't go on forever. I could make it. I could –

But the trail didn't seem to care and continued to ascend. Legs ached more...climbing, climbing...breath coming harder...climbing still!

But I can make it –

Or you could stop right here, said a helpful voice from somewhere in my head. *Just give it up here and enjoy the view and then turn around and enjoy that easy downhill stroll back to the car...*

I thought about that as I stopped to lean against a tree, trying to catch my breath. Then I thought about it some more...

And then I turned around. The trail had won, and I had given up without even much of a fight.

As I began that somewhat deflated walk back to the car, I thought about what had just happened. Looking at my watch, I tried rationalizing things by telling myself that it was really a matter of the time of day. It was late –

Sure! said that voice. *Not enough time. You had no choice but to give it up and turn back. No choice at all. It was the smart thing to do.*

I hoped so, because "turn back" is what I had done.

It was blessedly downhill most of the way back, and I was out of the woods and back at the car two hours before dusk. Yeah, I would have had plenty of time. No comfort there. The fact is that the trail had won, which is the same thing as saying that I had lost.

And as I unlocked the car door, that voice poked me again:

You didn't quite finish, it said. *You didn't reach the source. You gave up.*

"Not quite finishing a hike" is kind of like telling the kids on a soccer team that they didn't quite win. That's what I used to do years ago when my boys were little and I was coaching five-year-old soccer. It happened at the end of just about every game (okay, so they weren't quite ready for the World Cup), and usually it would go like this:

"Coach Steve! Coach Steve!" one of the kids would ask. Sometimes several would ask it in unison. "Did we win the game?"

Well," I'd answer, with great drama, "almost. We *came in second!*"

"Second!" they'd all say. "Wow!" And then, to anyone within earshot, one and all would proclaim, *"We came in second!"*

That minor shading of facts worked until the following season, when they started understanding the world at a first-grade level. Once they reached that exalted plane of perception, I had to start telling it like it was. Second out of two, they learned, was the same as "losing." They might not like it, but that was life and that's how life is.

That's kind of how I felt that first time I tried to find the headwaters – like I'd come in second out of two. I'd set out to finish a hike, to reach a

The vistas across the mountains can be spectacular from the Jacks Knob Trail as you hike to Chattahoochee Spring, especially during winter when there are no leaves on the trees to block the view.

destination, to put the period at the end of an expeditionary sentence…but I hadn't made it. I'd tried to tell myself that I'd simply started too late in the day. I even believed that for a little while. But the truth (and I knew it was the truth) was that I wasn't quite up to the challenge, modest though the challenge was. Some might even suggest that I'd been spending too much time in "stationary" mode and not enough time in "active" mode. That's fancy sounding language, but you get the general idea.

No matter how you parse it, the fact was that the trail had won.

I'm not used to being defeated by the out-of-doors, so I decided to fix the problem with a couple of weeks of "watching what I eat" and "power walking" and all those other things that are not as much fun as they sound like that but that promise, in the end, to make me a better person and help make sure I don't come in second any more.

And so, some 14 days later, I find myself back in the car and driving north once again to continue my search for the source of my river. I am ready for a rematch with the Jack's Knob Trail.

I start at the same place as before, at the parking area off Georgia 180 near the big Brasstown Bald info sign. Opening the car door, I'm greeted by the soft whisper of wind through the limbs of a million trees. I like that sound; it reminds me that there are still places like this and that I am, at least now and then, on hand to immerse myself in that reality.

I go over the contents of my day pack. Water bottle? Check. Trail snacks? Check, with a silent thank-you to my wife. Camera? Check (and fully charged). GPS? Yes, and spare batteries as well.

Oh – and a fly rod. I've brought what I call my "baby rod," a microscopic little 5-foot two-weight that's exquisite perfection on tiny creeks. It has a 7-foot leader on the reel, and there's a tiny little size 16 Foamback Caddis tied to the leader's end. I don't really know what I think I'm going to do with it, but a hike such as this one begs to be done with a fly rod in hand.

Inventory complete, I set out at last. Crossing GA 180, I walk to the trailhead and begin that first long uphill climb. It's just like before...or is it maybe a little easier?

Next comes the long and level stretch (also like before) but this time I seem to have upped my pace. *I think,* I say out loud, *that I might make this after all.*

But then (yes, exactly and distressingly like before) there is The Big Climb. In front of me the trail turns upward, up and up and up some more.

Abandon all hope, ye who enter here...

There's that voice again. This time it's reminding me that this isn't even much of a climb as mountain trails go. My buddy Ray, who recently completed the entire Appalachian Trail, could probably do it in his sleep without even breaking a sweat.

But I tell myself that I'm a Writer, a Deskbound Worker of Words who spends too much time sitting in front of a keyboard and not enough time doing stuff like this. So cut me some slack, okay?

Sure, that voice reminds me, *but don't forget that Ray's a writer too...*

The wind picks up a half a click, and the rustle of the breeze edges up a few decibels. For an instant it drowns out the voice, and that is enough. I wrestle my focus back to the trail, which continues on...getting steeper...

Steeper...

I push my legs to pick up the pace –

It gets worse...

– to leave that voice behind.

It's just going up and up and up and up, it whispers.

Legs are getting tired...

They're aching...throbbing...

Heart beats faster.

Can you get enough air...?

I stop and lean against a tree, breathing hard, thinking about that...

You can stop any time and go back, it says.

Yes. But then the Start of Things would remain unseen.

So what? Who would know? Who would tell?

Part of my mind continues this conversation even as another part recalls something that hiker extraordinaire Kimberly Maxwell said to me one day. Kimberly is another of those rare folks who have hiked the entire Appalachian Trail, and I once asked her what she did when she felt like giving up. At such moments, she told me, she simply didn't. Instead, she hiked on…because she knew that she could.

So I hike on too. One foot in front of the other. Again. One more step, and one beyond that, then a yard more, each following the one before it.

And then the trail levels and levels some more and at once, just like that, I am at the top. How about that?

A providentially placed log provides a place to sit and a chance for breath and allow the ol' heart rate return to some semblance of normal. How far have I gone? Five hundred miles?

The sound of – singing? – coming from behind me announces the approach of another hiker.

"On Jordan's stormy banks I stand…"

I turn and look and sure enough, a lone figure is climbing the trail toward me at an astonishing rate of speed, singing at the top of his lungs as he power walks up the same slope that only moments before had just about done me in.

"…and cast a wishful eye…"

As he gets closer and I get a good look, I realize (and must have said out loud) that he looks to be in his 70s.

"Nope, closer to 82!" the man says. "Great day to be out! Do this a couple of times a week! Keeps me young!"

He doesn't break cadence as he strides on past, and as the trail turns and carries him out of sight I hear the refrain drifting through the trees again…

"…bound for the Promised Land…"

I shake my head slowly and say, for the umpteenth time, that I really do have to get in better shape.

After a while I continue on. A long descent…and then another climb…and then, eventually, one final downhill delivers me, at last, to Chattahoochee Gap and the intersection with the Appalachian Trail.

So I've made it. How about that.

By trail standards, this coming together of trails at Chattahoochee Gap is an interchange of Interstate proportions. A wooden post to the left of the trail helps sort it all out with a sign pointing out the white-blazed AT crossing left-to-right and the blue-blazed Jacks River Trail via which I've just arrived.

But I'm more interested in a third signpost, this one with the word "WATER" carved into it. It points left to what appears to be a moderately steep trail which curves off down the mountainside, presumably the trail to the spring where the river begins. I see blue blazes painted on the trees.

I know then that I'm close. The accounts I'd read said that from Chattahoochee Gap, it's only a couple of hundred yards down "a blue-blazed side trail" to the flowing spring where the river begins.

So off I go, following blue blazes through gray and green trees.

The trail I'm following works its way along the hillside, eventually turning to the right and almost doubling back on itself. The path is a good one at first. But then it begins to deteriorate a bit and seems to heading toward a certain dead-end.

Is there really a spring down here? I begin to wonder.

The first bit of reassurance that I'm on the right track is what appears to be a patch of damp ground ahead of me and a bit off the trail to the right. Picking my way among the trees, I go to have a closer look. The hillside is slick with fallen leaves, and I move carefully as I step over a downed limb here and a moss-covered rock there and then another limb or two. And then there I am, face to face with a dimple in the hillside from which an occasional drop of water lets go to disappear among the leaves and loam at my feet.

Is it the spring? No, not really. Instead, it's what the mountain folks call a seep – a place where water oozes from the ground.

I stop there for a moment, long enough to watch as a drop takes shape, lets go and then falls. It's water, yes, but it is not a flowing spring.

From the look of things I am not the first person to stand there and ponder the steady drip-drip-dripping of the water. The ground in the immediate vicinity bears the unmistakable signs of a landscape that has been walked on by a few too many feet.

Had they, like me, come to find the source? Maybe so. Had they found it? I suppose that one could convince oneself that this seep is, in fact, where the river begins. Those drops must surely go somewhere, and if you trace them downhill far enough then one of those drops must inevitably connect with the flow which miles later becomes the river.

Is this where it starts? Somehow I don't think so.

I take a few pictures, just in case, but it doesn't feel right. It doesn't have the aura of the start of a river, hydrologic considerations notwithstanding. And besides, everybody had said that I was looking for an honest-to-goodness flowing spring.

So what am I to do? I see that the footpath pretty much ends in the vicinity of the seep. But I have a notion that I am not there yet, wherever exactly "there" might be.

I decide that I'll just have to keep looking.

The wristwatch tells me I have an hour or two before I need to start back. Will that be enough time?

I hope so, I tell myself, already beginning to search, working my way downhill along the little draw below the seep.

And then, unexpectedly, the wind which has been my companion up to that point suddenly stops. I mean it stops like it never was there at all, and its whisper through the trees is replaced by an unmistakable and unavoidable absence of sound.

But the silence is not quite total. There is now a new sound, a sound that has been with me all along but which had apparently been masked by the wind in the trees.

Gurgling water.

To gurgle, water must have a certain minimum flow. I'll bet some scientist somewhere has studied that very matter, perhaps quantifying exactly how much flow it takes to create an audible gurgle that can be heard in the Georgia woods.

The sound seems to come from downhill, so downhill I go. The little draw I am following curves around a tree, curves a little more, and then (wonder of wonders) there it is: a tiny but relentless flow of water coming out of the ground.

It really is a neat sight. Surrounded by stones and ferns, a steady flow of water issues from the earth. It collects itself in a tiny little pool just a foot or so across, then spills over rocks and begins its descent toward whatever awaits it far below. Toward the river...?

Only it *is* the river. I am seeing it, I realize with a start, at the very beginning of things, at the point where the flowing Chattahoochee is born.

What does one do with the spring where a river begins? I ask myself, and since I'm not sure how to answer that question I simply sit down on the leaf-covered ground a yard from the gently flowing water and just look at it. It's rare to observe the real start of anything, but when you get the opportunity it's something to savor.

So savor it I do for quite a while – for longer, in fact, than I should have – and it is soothing and restful.

Eventually I glance at the watch and see that (uh-oh) time has marched on faster than I had planned. It will, I realize, be a close thing getting out of these woods before the light begins to fade and afternoon turns into twilight and twilight itself at last goes away. *I'd better get a move on,* I say to myself, *or I'll be finishing this hike in the dark.*

But before I leave, there are some things I have to do.

One is to taste the water. I know, I know…but I dip my finger into the spring pool anyway and bring a drop to my lips. The water is sweet. A second drop is even sweeter.

And then...

Then I have to take a photo of my fly rod, placing the rod carefully on the ground so that it straddles the fledgling river from one bank to the other. Try *that* in Atlanta.

And finally, because fishing really is just a metaphor for life (or is it the other way around?) and because I also just happen to have that fly rod with me, I step back a few feet and pull out a couple of yards of line and with a single cast drop that tiny little Caddis onto the surface of the pool. It lands with barely a ripple, right there at the spring where the river is born.

Did I get a hit? Of course not. It's only two inches deep. But I can now say that I've fished the very uppermost pool of the Chattahoochee River.

I stay one minute more, enjoying the sense of place that unique places like that one always provide. And is that a wisp of distant singing drifting on the wind? Then I turn back up the trail, heading for the car again, accompanied by the barely audible murmur of the flowing spring…and this time there's a different voice in my head,

This one is saying, *"Way to go, buddy. This time you came in first."* □

At the end of all the hiking, you will come at last to the gently flowing water of Chattahoochee Spring – the place where the river begins.

Access:

Finding the place where the river begins

If you don't mind some walking, it's easy to find Chattahoochee Spring.

Chattahoochee Spring, the place that's generally considered to be the start of the Chattahoochee River, is a year-round flowing spring located near Chattahoochee Gap not far from the Appalachian Trail. Making the trip to this spring is a sort of must-do pilgrimage for any real fan of the Chattahoochee River. After all, as someone wiser than me once put it, only by seeing the beginning is it possible to fully understand what something eventually becomes.

You can access Chattahoochee Spring from the Appalachian Trail or from the Jacks Knob Trail. Either way, you'll have do a bit of fairly strenuous hiking to get there. But it's worth the effort, for Chattahoochee Spring is where it all begins.

Since the Jacks Knob Trail approach is shorter, that's what we'll profile here.

Finding the trailhead: From Hiawassee, take US-76 east to GA 17/75 and turn right (south). Continue for 6.3 miles to GA 180. Turn right (west) and follow 180 for about 5.3 miles to the intersection with GA 180 Spur, the road to the top of Brasstown Bald. Park in the small parking area at the 180/180 Spur intersection.

The hike: From the parking area at the 180/180 Spur intersection, walk a few yards to Highway 180 and turn left (east). Continue for about 75 yards, looking for the Jacks Knob Trail pathway which heads off to your right. The trail intersection is marked by a post.

Your hike begins with a moderate ascent which carries you up one side of Henry Knob. Soon, however, the trail levels out at an elevation of about 3200 feet as it follows the flank of Henry Knob generally southeast and into the Mark Trail Wilderness Area.

A bit more hiking brings you to another gap. The trail once

again begins to climb, this time toward a peak known locally as Brookshire Top. You'll skirt the summit (it's to your right) at about the 1-mile point.

Following a brief descent to yet another gap, you'll begin a long but gentle climb along Hiawassee Ridge toward Eagle Knob. Near the 2-mile point (at an elevation near 3600 feet) you'll be passing the summit of Jacks Knob, which will be to your left (that is, off to the east).

As you swing around Jacks Knob, the trail descends. That descent ends at the intersection with the Appalachian Trail at Chattahoochee Gap. There, a sign indicates the Jacks Knob Trail and the Appalachian Trail – and a third arrow on the sign points along a blue-blazed spur trail toward "WATER." That's the way to the spring.

The blue-blazed spur trail descends moderately steeply through a switchback

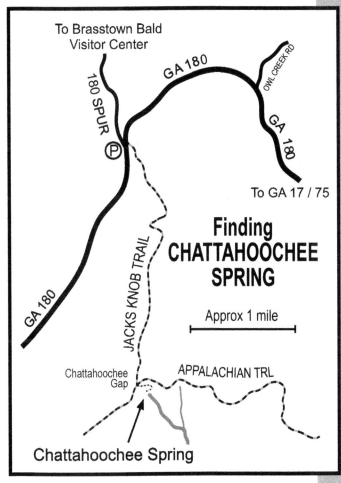

Finding CHATTAHOOCHEE SPRING

for about 200 yards. You'll spot that seep first, but the actual spring is a still a few more yards farther down the hill. Follow the shallow gully downhill to find it. Watch your footing, as there are loose rocks that can cause you to stumble. ☐

Bluelining
on the
upper-upper Hooch

Finding big adventure and small wild trout far up the Chattahoochee River.

"Don't get eaten by a bear!" my wife Ann said to me as I left the house that morning.

Don't get eaten by a bear? Well, yeah.

Actually, that was the second time she'd said that to me that morning. We'd been talking about bears at breakfast. I'd told her I was hoping to do a little small-stream fishing that afternoon somewhere on the backcountry waters of the upper-upper Hooch.

I'd also told her that I was going to be fishing an area where bears were not uncommon.

Why did I feel the need to mention bears at all? Maybe because bears are always a good topic of conversation. Or maybe I said it because I wanted to impress the lady in my life with my extreme bravery out there in the middle of all that raw and untamed wilderness.

"Think of it!" I said. "Me and the woods!"

"Um-hm," she replied. "Have fun." And then she said it again:

" Don't get eaten by a bear."

There's a footbridge over the river at Upper Chattahoochee River Campground, and upstream from it you're in the realm of the most dedicated of fishermen – the blueliner. Bluelining is the art of finding and fishing small streams that may be known only as blue lines on maps. Such water is remote and often all but unfished, and the experience can be incredible.

Bluelining is good here. Near the bridge you'll find mostly wild rainbows with an occasional brown in the mix. But above the falls, above a waterfall known as Upper Chattahoochee Falls, it's the realm of the brook trout.

Let's note from the start that this is not the place to go for big trout or for fish for the frying pan. The stocking truck never gets up this far. This is small water – and the trout it holds are correspondingly small too. Certainly, it's a place where catch-and-release is the norm.

Step one is to get to Upper Chattahoochee River Campground. This requires traversing several miles of gravel road. Give yourself plenty of time to make the trip, for this is one drive that will take longer than you think.

Even after you reach the campground, though, you're just getting started. You've still got some hiking to do. At first, the trail's not too bad. But if you *really* want to taste the upper-upper Hooch, you've got to get much farther back in the woods. Fallen trees block your way. Loose rock and wicked roots try to trip you. You may encounter yellow jackets, hornets, and ticks. And spiders. And copperheads. Wild hogs wander through now and then, and they're mean. Skunks pass this way as well, and they – well, they stink.

And just to make sure you don't get bored, every now and then you'll even encounter a bear.

Last time I ran across a bear, I was fishing this very area a ways upstream above the campground area. The solitude was exquisite, and the fishing was good enough.

What's it like to fish this kind of water? To be honest, it can be a little bit intense. For one thing, there's all that streamside vegetation – a rather tame-sounding phrase that conjures images of wildflowers waving in a gentle breeze. But on a mountain stream like this one the laurel and rhododendron

At top left is Upper Chattahoochee Falls, the 30-foot barrier falls which marks the start of the upper-upper Hooch brook trout water. It's upstream from the day use parking area at Upper Chattahoochee River Campground.

can be as thick and impenetrable as a fence made of spring steel.

Sometimes the creek will unexpectedly narrow, too, with rock crowding in from both sides. Getting past rocky outcrops can be a challenge. You'll have to clamber over them (dangerous if they're steep or wet) or detour around them (did I mention yellow jackets?) while always watching where you put your hands and feet (and snakes?) until, finally, breathing hard, you make your way around the obstacle and can fish a little ways further before you have to do some version of it all over again.

I'd been doing that kind of thing for most of the morning, working my way slowly up the little creek. I had with me my favorite small-stream rod: that tiny little 5-foot 2 weight that I'd built a couple of summers before. It was made to order for these little streams, being short enough to cast in the tight confines that make a blueliner's life so interesting.

On the end of my leader was a size 14 barbless Elk Hair Caddis. I'd ease up on a pool, Ninja-style, staying low, and make a short cast. Sometimes – *splash!* – a brook trout would materialize and hammer the fly.

Sometimes the fish would flip off before I got it to me, but other times I'd bring it to hand. Such beautiful fish! It's been said that God was having a really good day on the day that brook trout were made, and you can see why. Spots of vivid red and electric blue...bright orange fins edged in the brightest white and most intense black you've ever seen...a rich olive back decorated with what the biologists call "wormlike" black markings. They are creatures of beauty, fish to be admired and then ever so gently released.

I was now a couple of hours into the serious fishing part of my adventure. I'd had a pretty good run through a series of riffles, but now the fly was getting a bit waterlogged. I stopped to freshen it up with a shake of floatant.

As I did so, I started to get a funny kind of feeling.

You know what I mean. One moment everything seems fine. Then you get a sense that there's something significant about to happen. Maybe it's a shift in light or sound. Maybe it's the sudden feeling that you're not alone.

That was it – I had the overwhelming sense that all at once I had some company somewhere out there in the middle of the deep, dark woods.

I was sure there were no other anglers on the stream, but the feeling persisted. What could it be?

I slowly looked around, and there was my answer: a black bear that weighed 300 or 800 or maybe 10,000 pounds standing broadside to me in the middle of the creek about 10 yards away.

I must have been downwind of the bear, for it didn't seem alarmed. But I could tell that the bear too had sensed something out of the ordinary. It just stood there and looked at me,

I saw the hair on its back rustle as a whisper of wind blew up the creek.

This, I said to myself, *is getting interesting.*

Bear and I continued to stand there looking at each other. Perhaps 20 seconds ticked away.

What, I asked myself, *do I do now?*

Still the bear stood motionless.

Slowly, very slowly, I turned my head right and then left to see what my options might be. I figured I needed to be prepared, just in case, for I doubted that there was much defensive power in a 5-foot fly rod.

Trying to move no more than necessary, I scanned the hillside on both sides of the creek. There didn't seem to be much in the way of escape routes. My options were pretty limited.

So I turned my gaze back to the bear –

But the bear was gone. As in *gone.* Vanished, Disappeared. Like it had never been there at all.

Had it really been there? Yep.

Was it there now? Nope.

But it was *somewhere.* Yes, somewhere in the woods around me was a 25,000 lb. black bear in stealth mode, and I had no idea where it had gone.

Snap decision: songs! I'd sing a song, and surely that would scare the bear away. Actually, if you've ever heard me sing, you know that's not as farfetched as it sounds.

So sing I did, and loud too.

Just in case the singing wasn't working, I decided I really didn't need to fish that area any more on that particular day. I decided it would be a good time to head back, which I did with no attention at all to moving quietly through water or woods. Picture it: singing, crashing through the creek and underbrush, waving that fly rod like a crazed swordsman, all the while knowing that the bear was still there...somewhere...

I'm writing this now, so you know I made it out alive. By the time I'd thrashed my way a hundred yards downstream, I'd even gotten a grip on reality again. Finally, slowing down in my headlong rush back to the relative safety of the campground, I inevitably went back to fishing.

I'd have a lot to tell Ann that night. I'd found fish in the upper-upper Hooch...and I had *not* been eaten by the bear.   □

Upper Chattahoochee River Campground is a great base camp from which to explore the upper-upper Hooch. You'll find detailed info on the campground in the section on "Campground Trout."

Access and fishing tips:

Bluelining adventure on the upper-upper Hooch

Beautiful surroundings and the peace and quiet of the mountains (plus, if you're lucky, wild trout) are what await you on the upper-upper Hooch.

The art of finding and fishing stretches of small streams such as the upper-upper Chattahoochee is called "bluelining." It's a nod to the fact that such streams may only be known only by the blue lines which represent them on maps.

Bluelining is a fascinating subject. To learn more about it, I encourage you to check out the book BLUELINING 101, which shows you how to find, evaluate and fish these little creeks. It's available from the webstore at chattahoocheemedia.com.

One thing to know about bluelines that in most cases folks don't talk much about them. The simple fact is that a lot of blueline streams wouldn't be able to handle much pressure, and publicizing

From Helen via GA 75: Take GA 75 toward Hiawassee for about 8 miles. Just past mile marker 15, turn left onto FS-44/Wilks Road (if you reach Unicoi Gap, you've gone too far). Continue on FS-44 for about 4.8 miles to Upper Chattahoochee River Campground.

From ALT 75: From ALT 75 going north, look for Chattahoochee United Methodist Church on your left, just before the river. Turn left at the church onto Poplar Stump Rd., which becomes FS-44 when it enters the national forest. Continue for several miles (passing the WMA check station and Low Gap Campground, and crossing Low Gap and Jasus Creek) to Upper Chattahoochee River Campground.

Once at the campground: Continue to the back of the campground to the day-use parking area. Your upriver journey begins at the footbridge crossing the Hooch just a few yards from the parking area.

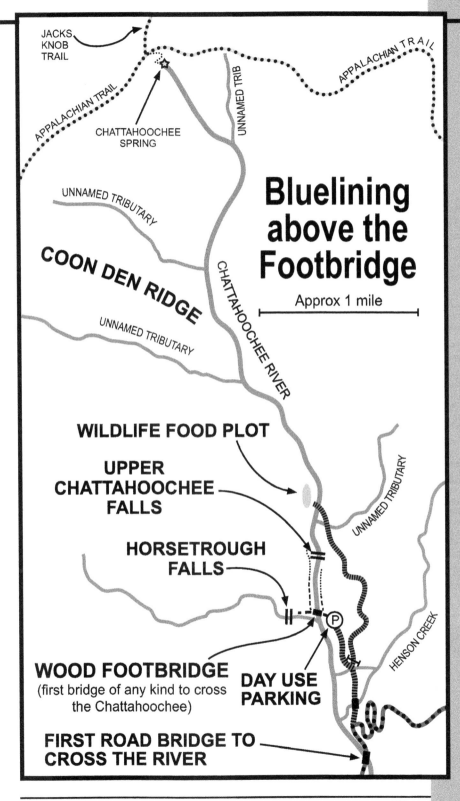

JACKS KNOB TRAIL

APPALACHIAN TRAIL

APPALACHIAN TRAIL

CHATTAHOOCHEE SPRING

UNNAMED TRIB

UNNAMED TRIBUTARY

Bluelining above the Footbridge

Approx 1 mile

COON DEN RIDGE

UNNAMED TRIBUTARY

CHATTAHOOCHEE RIVER

WILDLIFE FOOD PLOT

UPPER CHATTAHOOCHEE FALLS

HORSETROUGH FALLS

UNNAMED TRIBUTARY

HENSON CREEK

P

WOOD FOOTBRIDGE
(first bridge of any kind to cross the Chattahoochee)

DAY USE PARKING

FIRST ROAD BRIDGE TO CROSS THE RIVER

them far and wide could easily mess up the remoteness and unpressured isolation that makes them so much fun to fish.

So what can we say about the blueline parts of the Hooch?.

Blueline streams tend to fall into one of two categories. One is the truly "secret" streams that you simply don't hear about. Yes, I know that there are no truly secret streams. But those particular bluelines are ones that some determined angler may have spent hours of map time and days in the field trying to locate and figure out. That's hard-won knowledge, and those who go to the trouble to gain it often zealously guard the results of their efforts. If a blueliner shares such a stream with you, feel extremely honored and keep it to yourself (if you ever want to get invited again) – and be sure that you pick up the check for lunch. Having someone show you one of their personal favorite bluelines is a very high honor and not something to be taken lightly.

The other category of bluelines includes water that's relatively well known and that's located in fairly easy-to-access places. Such streams are closer to the "open records" end of the secrecy spectrum. They're often the site of habitat enhancement projects, and they provide a great introduction to tiny-stream fishing. They're the

ones that experienced blueliners recommend when someone asks, "Where can I go to try this bluelining thing?"

The upper-upper Hooch is that kind of stream, and so I'm

The day-use parking area at Upper Chattahoochee River Campground will be the starting point for your upper-upper Hooch adventures. Inset: The trailhead at the day-use parking area provides easy access to the headwaters as well as to Horsetrough Falls.

comfortable talking about it here.

By the way, you just might discover some other good bluelines in this same general area...but I'll let you find those on your own!

The key to bluelining happiness: The upper-upper Hooch, as we've said, is relatively easy to access as bluelines go. Yes, it requires some hiking to do so. But once you're there you'll find that the fish are not too difficult to tempt with a fly – if (and it's a big "if") you're careful in your approach.

Here, as on just about any blueline, a stealthy approach is the key to happiness. More than fly selection or length of rod – in fact, more than anything else – approach is the thing.

Why is approach so important? When fishing for wild trout in water like this, you're going after fish that are the "big dogs" in their little corner of the world. The only thing those fish really have to worry about is the arrival of a predator from outside their watery world. These fish are thus acutely aware of anything that seems out of place and will disappear in a heartbeat if something like (say) overhead motion signals possible danger. Things like sudden movement or even the flash of sunlight off a rod's glossy finish can be all it takes to alarm those trout, and an alarmed wild trout is one that won't rise to a fly.

Dedicated wild-trout enthusiasts are serious about this "approach" thing. They'll wear camo shirts and camo hats. One I know insists on rods with matte (as opposed to glossy) finishes. Another blueliner that I know and respect even goes so far as to dab military-style camo makeup on his face and hands. Yes, he looks a little scary as he moves through the woods, and I suspect he's startled more than one unsuspecting hiker. But if you see him, don't worry. He's basically harmless. He's just really, really serious about catching tiny wild trout from little mountain streams.

From the footbridge to the falls: Everything has to start somewhere, so let's decree that the upper-upper Hooch begins at the footbridge over the river near the day use parking area at Upper Chattahoochee River Campground. That 34-site developed Forest Service campground is open seasonally and is a popular destination, especially in fall.

That footbridge, by the way, is the first bridge of any kind to cross the Chattahoochee River. It's part of the trail to Horsetrough Falls, a beautiful waterfall on a tributary maybe 100 yards from the campground. The trail to Horsetrough Falls continues beyond the bridge and ends at a viewing platform near the base of the falls, and it's definitely worth seeing when you're in this neck of the woods.

After checking out Horsetrough Falls, return to the bridge. Then look for trails going upstream along each side of the creek. Facing upstream, the sometimes vague path on your right (that is, on river left) provides best access from the bridge upstream as far as another waterfall, this one known as Upper Chattahoochee Falls.

As you move upstream, you'll spot lots of potential holding water. Try a size 14 or 16 Adams or Stimulator or (a perpetual favorite) a size 14 or 16 Royal Wulff. A simple Elk Hair or Foamback Caddis will also work – and don't forget ants. Remember to pick a fly you can see as it floats on the broken surface of the water.

Dry/dropper rigs can be effective. Try pairing that dry with a small (size 14 or 16) Pheasant Tail or Gold Ribbed Hare's Ear about 16 inches below the dry fly. You'll catch fish on both flies, and once in a while you might even get a double.

Dual-nymph rigs also work well. Use the afore-mentioned nymphs alone or with a soft-hackled emerger pattern. In addition, you might try a bigger (size 8 or 10) stonefly nymph

The author crosses the footbridge at Upper Chattahoochee River Campground, bound for bluelining water upstream. This is the first bridge of any kind to cross the Chattahoochee. Inset: the view looking upstream.

imitation such as Pat's Rubberlegs or some similar pattern. They can tempt some of the bigger rainbows to come and take a look.

Serious blueliners, looking at this stretch, would point out that it's not very "remote" and might even call it "civilized." They'd be right, too, but the fish don't mind. Neither will you, and fishing it will earn you your first bluelining star. And then...

Above Upper Chattahoochee Falls: As you work your way up the creek, the trail you're on will eventually end near Upper Chattahoochee Falls. While not as dramatic as nearby Horsetrough Falls, Upper Chattahoochee Falls is nonetheless popular with waterfall enthusiasts. The flow drops through a tight gap in the rock before splashing through a couple of pools and then regaining its composure as the relatively gentle stream you fished between the bridge and the falls. The best view of the falls, from creek level near its base, is most easily reached by following the creek upstream on that right-side (river left) trail.

In addition to being a neat waterfall, Upper Chattahoochee Falls is the dividing line between the *lower* upper-upper Hooch and the *upper* upper-upper Hooch. Below the falls it's relatively civilized bluelining. But above it, things get wilder in a hurry.

The waterfall is important for another reason too: it forms a barrier that separates the rainbows and browns in the downstream water from the brook trout which live upstream. It's known as a "barrier falls" because it forms a barrier that keeps the rainbows and browns in the lower part of the creek where they won't bother the brookies which live up above.

To get around that barrier, *do not* try to climb the waterfall. Don't do it! Instead, backtrack to the footbridge and cross the creek. Then pick up the trail on the other side of the creek.

That trail soon begins to climb uphill as it parallels the water. It ascends steadily for quite a while. Expect parts of it to be rough, wet or slick. Blowdowns will block your progress at times, requiring you to fight your way through. Exposed roots may try to trip you, and there will be places on the trail where a significant (and often wet) cross-slope can cause trouble if you're not extremely careful. And do be careful, because you don't want to fall. The mountain drops off steeply below the trail, and it would be a bad thing to go down.

If you stick with it, you'll eventually spot the falls again, this time through the trees below you and to your right. Soon thereafter, you'll have to climb up a large rock "step" of sorts. Beyond that step the increasingly faint trail continues on into the backcountry, more or less paralleling the creek. At that point, if you work your way down to the water, you'll be in the land of brook trout.

Another way in, albeit one that bypasses a good chunk of this water, is via a dirt road which swings off the right (just after you cross Henson Creek) as you enter the Upper Chattahoochee River Campground area. This road is gated and closed to vehicles, so you'll have to hoof it. Your route will go up and over a ridge, finally descending to a point where it crosses the creek near a large Wildlife Management Area feed plot. You can hike in this way and start fishing the creek from that point, though be aware that this section of the creek can be very tightly overgrown in places. You can bypass some of the tighter stretches by walking through the relatively wide-open food plot on the far side of the flow, but during warmer weather also be aware of occasional wasp nests in the vegetation. It's not fun if you stumble across one.

As you explore, notice that the creek flattens out a bit. That's often the case with the higher-elevation portion of these small mountain streams, and it's welcome news. A flatter gradient means pools and other holding water – a good sign if you're looking for trout.

Another good sign that this is water worth investigating is the presence of a number of habitat structures built over the last few years by the Forest Service and Georgia DNR's fisheries folks in conjunction with members of the angling community. Designed to create additional holding water for brook trout, these structures take several forms. All are designed to provide deeper areas where trout can hang out and be relatively safe from predators. That's good news for the stream's future brook trout prospects.

What flies work best here? Any of the patterns described earlier for rainbows below the falls, including dry-dropper rigs, will be effective above the falls too. But many dedicated blueliners simplify things and just fish with a single dry fly. Casting small dries will often bring strikes from enthusiastic brook trout, and using the single dry eliminates some of the problems with tangling multi-fly or nymph rigs – particularly as the stream gets tighter. I've introduced a number of anglers to Georgia brook trout fishing using dry flies in this part of the stream, and the experience can be rewarding.

If you're spin fishing (and sometimes it's the best way to fish the really tight spots) use very small inline spinners. Don't go too large, or they'll sink too fast to be effective.

At this point, you've definitely left the world of "civilized" blue-lining and have earned your second bluelining star.

More bluelining stars: I should have warned you earlier. Bluelining can be addictive, and no matter what your wristwatch is telling you it's hard to stop at the end of the day. You always want to see what's around the next bend.

Of course, as a blueline moves closer to its headwaters, "around the next bend" means "smaller and smaller." That's certainly the case here on the infant Chattahoochee.

How far up can you go? The answer to that one varies with each individual angler. Some may consider pushing far up toward the source at Chattahoochee Spring, though the terrain will become very challenging. Others will be content fishing the area we've just described.

When bluelining here, as when bluelining anywhere, it's

Every headwaters fly box should hold a selection of buggy nymphs and high-floating dries.

important to find your personal comfort zone here. Some anglers are at home fishing in true wilderness conditions, while others prefer their off-the-beaten-track adventures to be a little bit closer to civilization. Both approaches are rewarding, but always remember that the further you go from civilization the further you'll have to travel if you need to get back. It's a balancing act where you put fishing on one side of the scale and what you, personally, are comfortable with on the other.

I will suggest this, however. If you decide to go further into the backcountry, do so in the company of another angler. Two really are better than one in the backcountry, Grizzly Adams stereotypes notwithstanding. It's comforting to know that you've got a buddy there with you – and sharing backcountry fishing adventures with a fellow angler is a whole lot more fun that going it alone. ☐

First fish

Where is the very first trout in the Chattahoochee?

"**I** wonder where the first one is?" I had asked my wife over breakfast. "I wonder where they start?"

The "they" in my question is trout – specifically, the first wild trout in the Chattahoochee below the spring where the river is born.

I've always enjoyed bluelining on the upper-upper Chattahoochee. It's a neat place, and for a long time I was happy with that. But then it dawned on me that somewhere up there is the "first fish" – the river's very first trout – and I've decided I want to see if I can find it.

I want to find the first trout in the Chattahoochee.

Just how far up a creek can you go and still find trout? To answer that one, I turn to Leon Brotherton, a fisheries technician with the Georgia Department of Natural Resources. Leon does field work in the north Georgia mountains. He knows what it takes to make a home for trout, and he explains that at some point as you move toward the source a stream simply becomes too small and too steep to provide a place for trout to live.

"Talk to me before you go," he said when I called him and told him what I wanted to do. "I may be able to save you some steps." That works for me.

Leon explains that trout require certain things to become established. Clearly, they need enough to eat. Equally obvious is the need for places to hide. Less obvious, but no less important, is access to other trout, for only then can they make new trout to continue the population into the future.

Those who study such things put this in terms of "first-order" and "second-order" streams. The smallest tributaries are considered "first-order" streams, while the flows formed when two first-order streams come together are said to be "second-order." The creek may remain "second order" for a while, too, even though additional "first order" streams join in.

On high-elevation "first order" streams like the upper-upper Hooch, Leon says, there may be so much drop that holding water is scarce or non-existent. And even if a tiny pool does form, Leon adds, it's likely to be isolated from the rest of the creek by sharp drops. Such drops could keep a trout from moving up and down the creek to find others of its kind.

And then there's the matter of how much food the stream can carry. If trout are going be present, there has to be enough edible stuff flowing by to keep them fed.

I learn that a lot of first-order water may not be up to that task.

"Up near the source, the stream may just be too small," Leon says.

It appears, then, that I can take the very uppermost part of the Chattahoochee (the part directly below the spring) off the table. My knees are happy to hear that.

But what happens a little further downstream?

As a creek flows on down a mountain, the rugged landscape will eventually moderate. The gradient will decrease, and you'll start to see pools connected by runs. Additional tributaries will add their contribution, too, not only in terms of water volume but also in terms of food.

When those little tributaries come together, Leon says, they eventually form a "second-order stream" that may well have everything trout need.

That, I learn, is the key to finding trout in the upper reaches. You look for them somewhere on the "second-order" parts of the stream.

I drive north on ALT 75 to Chattahoochee United Methodist Church and turn onto Poplar Stump Road for the long drive to Upper Chattahoochee River Campground. Across the valley, the mountainsides are living loud. Reds! Oranges! Yellows! Everywhere there's fall color, bold enough to take my breath away. Words don't do it justice. So I put away the notepad and just look out the window at it as I bump along, trying to take it all in.

Let me tell you about Poplar Stump Road. Known as FS 44 once it enters the national forest, it's smooth in places and rough and bumpy in others. If something on your car isn't fastened down tight, Poplar Stump Road might shake it loose. The twists and turns are tricky too if you aren't paying attention – and those who don't stay on top of things can end up down the mountainside in a heartbeat. That is not a good thing.

For a while, road and river parallel one another. Sometimes they are close, like friends or lovers. Then they swing apart for a while like those same friends or lovers a little later in time. But the river always returns.

After a while I pass the Chattahoochee Wildlife Management Area check station on my right. Further on I cross Low Gap Creek, a Chattahoochee tributary. There's a small Forest Service campground there, a nice place if you can get a spot. A little later I cross Jasus Creek, a smaller tributary.

Finally, about 10 miles or so from the little white church, I reach the last place (or is it the first place?) that road and river meet: the concrete bridge just before the Upper Chattahoochee River Campground entrance.

At that point, FS-44 turns right and begins a meandering journey of not quite five miles across the mountains to Unicoi Gap and GA 75. Maybe I'll go that way coming out. But for now I follow the graveled turnoff into the campground. I cross Henson Creek, which I know holds tiny wild rainbows. If I have time when I'm done...

I continue beyond the creek, passing one end of the old logging road (closed to vehicles but open to feet) which climbs over a ridge and then descends to ford a very tiny Chattahoochee near the wildlife food plot. I might make my return hike along the old roadbed, for the going there is easier. But for now the day is young and I'm still fresh. A bit of rough-trail bushwacking doesn't seem nearly as tough now as it will later on.

I drive all the way to the back of the campground, to the day use parking area. There I park the car, get out, check my daypack, and rig up my rod.

I put on my boots and make sure I have the GPS and a printed map, too, just in case. I shoulder the daypack and lock the car.

Then I set out to see what I can find.

My plan is to head up the river as far as I can, working my way upstream to see how far I can go and still catch fish. I know that the creek will get smaller and conditions will get tight. Casting will become difficult, even with the little rod. Meanwhile, the creek will get steeper and the drops between pools will get bigger until, at some point, I'll stop catching fish – because there will be no further fish to catch.

I don't know how much science there is in that approach, but it's loaded with the prospect of adventure. For when I find what I'm looking for, I'll have found that first fish – the first fish in the Chattahoochee.

On the creek now, I follow the trail up and around Upper Chattahoochee Falls. Now comes the big question: when to start fishing?

In the interest of science, I tell myself, *I might as well start now.*

So I do. Carefully working my way down to the creek a few dozen yards above the top of the falls, I thread the rod through the tangle of streamside vegetation and flip the little dry fly onto the glassy surface of a pool the size of a door mat. There's a flash, a splash, and an electric tug as a small wild brookie nails the fly. I bring the fish to me, admire it for an instant, and then put it back in the stream.

I've fished here before, and I know that fish will be present for a ways upstream. So I climb out of the creek and leapfrog ahead, casting now and then but mostly walking. Approaching Coon Den Ridge, I come to the first feeder stream, an unnamed creek that enters from the left. I'm still getting interest in the little dry fly.

Beyond the creek, now, and on upstream. The Chattahoochee, growing smaller now and tighter too, pulls me on. Ahead the flow bends to the left, and I follow. Things get tighter. The river continues to shrink.

I approach another unnamed creek, this one on the north side of Coon Den Ridge, and I realize that I'm not getting as many strikes. Just a few... then only one now and then...

Somewhere in there the strikes stop altogether. That's fine with me because it gives me an excuse to call it a day. I am getting tired. Besides, looking at the map, I see I've come a long way. Progress is getting a lot harder. I decide it's time to stop.

Is this little guy the first trout in the Chattahoochee?

Did I find the first trout in the Chattahoochee? Maybe. Perhaps it was that vibrant little brookie that reeled me in a few yards back. If that's the case, if that was the first trout, then I feel good about the future of this place. The fish was exquisite and indescribable.

Or maybe...

Maybe I should go just a little farther. It looks like there might be another pool up there. Maybe I should push it just a little more. It won't hurt a thing to do so. Who knows? It might pay off. I might get lucky.

Or maybe...

Stop. It occurs to me then that I will never be totally sure whether I have found the first fish or not. And I think I like it that way, for it leaves the door of possibility cracked open just a tiny little bit.

Sometimes, I say to myself, *what you think to be true is truth enough. Sometimes you don't have to know for sure.* □

Access and fishing tips:

Exploring far upstream in the "first fish" headwaters

The fishing can be pretty tough, but the real challenge is just getting there.

From Chattahoochee Spring, the fledgling river begins a headlong rush down the mountain. At first it's too steep for trout to gain a toehold. But somewhere, some distance downstream, it becomes more fish-friendly and trout begin to appear – and somewhere between the spring up at the top and the water down below is the first trout in the Chattahoochee.

If you want to look for that first trout, the map at right shows you the area in which to search. Based on considerations of what trout look for in a stream, somewhere in there is where that first fish is likely to be.

But there's one big challenge awaiting you, and that's the matter of accessing the water.

It's possible, at least in theory, to come in from the top (that is, from near Chattahoochee Spring) and fish downstream, then climb back up when you're done. However, the terrain is *really* steep. The *average* gradient below Chattahoochee Spring is almost 30 percent – bad going downhill and a killer going uphill. Thus, unless you're a mountain goat, it's probably not the best idea to try it.

A better alternative is to do what I did and come in from below (from Chattahoochee Campground). That lets you fish upstream. It will still get steeper as you move up the river, but you can simply turn around when it gets too bad and start working your way back – and the return trip will be downhill.

What about the fishing? It's blessedly uncomplicated but very, very, very tight. Most anglers prefer short rods (5- to 6-foot fly rods or tiny ultralight spinning rods). For flies, it's hard to beat a single high-floating attractor dry such as a Simulator or a Royal Wulff; for spinners, a *very* small in-line spinner with silver in it somewhere is a good call. If you're working water that holds fish, they'll almost certainly be cooperative. Just be careful with your approach. These fish spook easily, and stealth is often the key. □

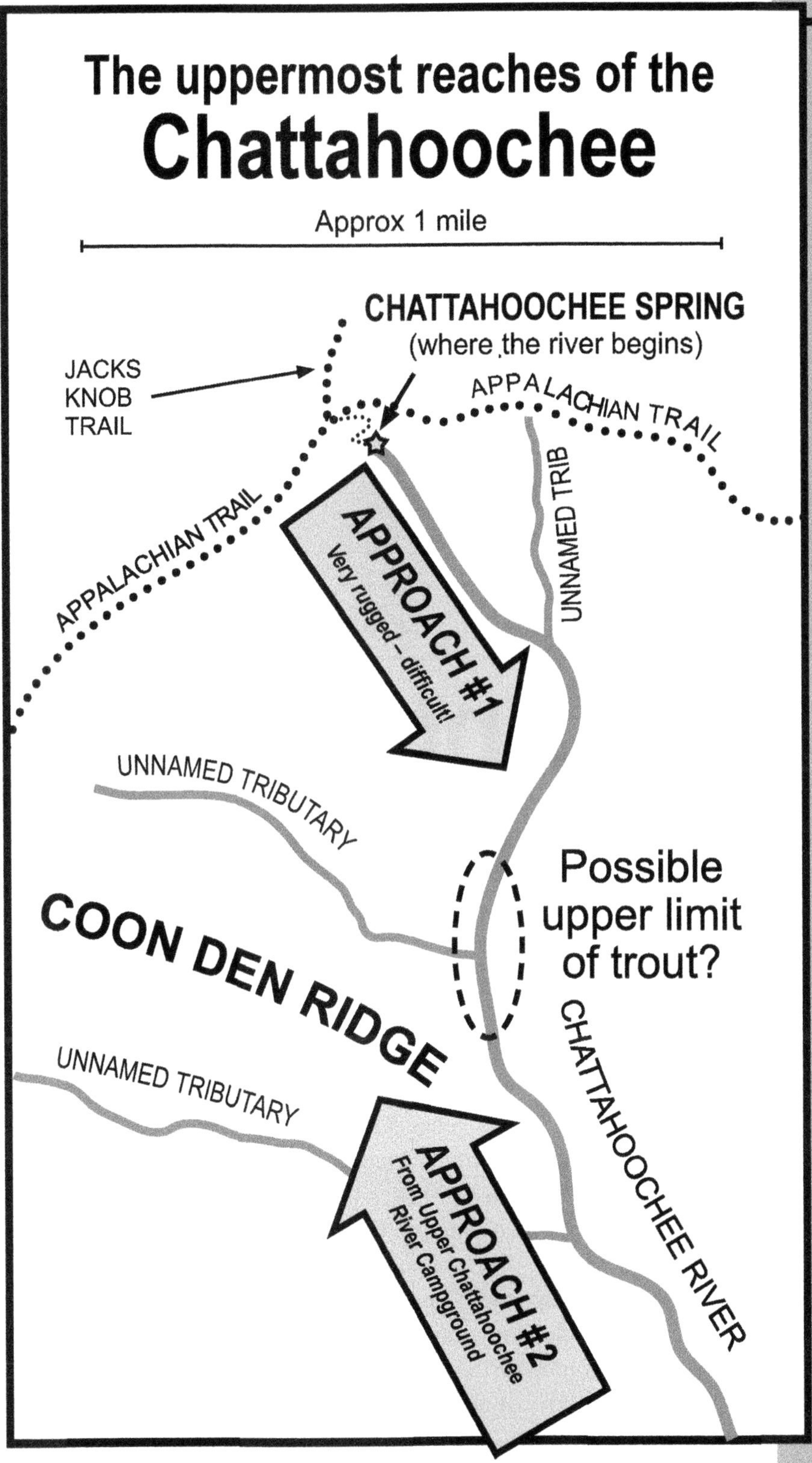

The uppermost reaches of the
Chattahoochee

Approx 1 mile

CHATTAHOOCHEE SPRING
(where the river begins)

JACKS
KNOB
TRAIL

APPALACHIAN TRAIL

UNNAMED TRIB

APPALACHIAN TRAIL

APPROACH #1
Very rugged – difficult!

UNNAMED TRIBUTARY

COON DEN RIDGE

Possible
upper limit
of trout?

UNNAMED TRIBUTARY

CHATTAHOOCHEE RIVER

APPROACH #2
From Upper Chattahoochee
River Campground

Campground Trout

Camping, trout fishing and almost all the comforts of home

"A campground?" says my buddy Max as we turn off FS-44 at the entry to Upper Chattahoochee River Campground. A self-described "friendly curmudgeon of indeterminate age," Max has been fly fishing for a very long time. He knows what he likes in the way of fishing environments, and apparently the middle of a campground is not high on his list.

"Really?" he asks again. "We're gonna fish in a *campground?*"

It's a fair question, I suppose. After all, serious fisherfolk don't drive for hours (including that miles-long run up the mountain on a winding dirt road that'll put a crick in your neck in a heartbeat) to fish among kids and tents and pop-up campers. "It's just not what I expected. Not at *all*. Are you *sure* we want to fish in a *campground?*"

"Yep. Right through it, in fact," I reply.

"Well, okay, I guess," Max says. "But let's don't spend too long here. I want to move on to some real trout water as quick as we can."

"OK," I say. "But give this water a little time before you write it off. Make a few casts first, and then decide."

Upper Chattahoochee River Campground is a 34-site Forest Service campground located far back in the Chattahoochee National Forest on the headwaters of the Chattahoochee River. In fact, the river flows right through it. Many of the fishermen you encounter there are campers who have come for a few days to get away from their individual versions of "the city." But we aren't camping, so we drive straight to the day-use parking area at the very back of the campground and begin to gear up there.

Last time I was here, I was bluelining. The day-use parking area is a great jumping-off point for backcountry small-stream trout fishing. But this time, the plan is not bluelining. Instead, we plan to walk downstream to the FS-44 bridge and then fish our way back upstream for about three-tenths of a mile right through the campground. I've done it before, and I've caught enough fish there to keep things interesting. I hope we'll catch fish on this day too.

Several in-stream habitat enhancement structures have been built in the river through the campground stretch.

I'd mentioned to Max that this water was stocked several times during the stocking season, but I'd also mentioned that small wild fish show up in this section too. With that in mind, he decides to go with a two-fly nymph set-up and has chosen his flies accordingly. For the top fly, Max ties on a gaudy yellow and orange size 14 Y2K, The fly is tied with a tungsten beadhead to help it sink quickly. For his bottom fly, he adds a size 16 brown-bodied soft-hackle emerger.

I decide to go with a two-fly rig, too, but instead of two nymphs I elect to

A stocked brown from the Upper Chattahoochee River Campground section. This one hit a size 14 yellow-bodied Stimulator.

use a dry-and-dropper combo. The dry is one of my all-time favorite topwater flies for mountain streams – a high floating Royal Wulff, easy to see on the water's broken surface. For the dropper, I choose a classic – a Beadhead Pheasant Tail Nymph, size 16.

Following the same graveled road that brought us into the campground, we hike down to the FS-44 bridge. The water there looks good. I make the first cast, targeting one of the runs near the bridge, and a 9-inch stocker quickly grabs the little nymph. A moment later, a 6-inch wild rainbow nails the Royal Wulff. That fish has much more fight than its size would suggest. It appears the day is off to a good start.

I see that Max, suddenly more interested, is getting ready to cast too. Stooping low so he won't spook any fish, he inches his way toward a deeper run near the bridge. Once in position, he flips his two-nymph rig upstream into a shady spot near the upper end of the little pool. I watch as the indicator floats along, ticking and bobbing as the flies drift near along the bottom.

And then the indicator disappears.

Max lifts the rod tip, setting the hook, and a moment later nets a nice rainbow about 11 inches long.

"Hey, that's all right!" he says.

He drifts the nymph rig through the run several more times, but apparently the battle with the first fish had sent out the alert. There are no more takers from that particular spot.

But there is a lot more water to explore between the bridge and the end of the campground where we'd left the car. We take turns fishing the runs and pools, leap-frogging one another as we work our way upstream. One thing I have learned over the years is that it's as much fun to watch others catch fish as it is to fish myself, and I enjoy seeing my friend catch trout every bit as much as I enjoy catching a few more of my own.

So how did we do?

Although it gets a good bit of pressure from campers, there are definitely fish in the campground stretch. It's stocked regularly into mid-summer, and fishing can sometimes be easy. Through the fall and winter, though, the fish you find are holdovers that escaped the summertime crowds. Those fish have grown much more streamwise and can be surprisingly difficult to fool.

We found fish in a variety of settings. Drifting dry flies through riffles proved productive, drawing several lightning-fast strikes. So did running nymphs through deeper runs and pools, especially along the edges of cover.

Most of the fish we caught were SNITs – the "standard nine-inch trout" that the stocking truck usually leaves behind –and most were rainbows. But Max brought a brown to net too; that fish took a Y2K.

Interestingly, among those stocked fish we also encountered several more small wild rainbows. The wild fish seemed to prefer the Royal Wullf dry, though emergers and nymphs also accounted for some wild-fish takes – particularly in riffles between the deeper places.

As we worked our way upstream, we also fished the water around several in-stream structures which had been constructed to enhance the habitat. The deeper water that typically accompanied those structures proved productive, and my largest fish of the day (a rainbow of about 14 inches) came when I drifted the Royal Wulff along a current seam near one of them. The strike was solid, and the fish was electric in its colors – a nice fish for that portion of the river.

I might have had a shot at an even bigger one a few minutes later, though I'll never know for sure. It too hit the Royal Wulff, but I missed it clean. I got just a glimpse of it, but it sure did look big.

Truth be told, I can't blame anyone but me for missing that fish. My excuse? I was watching a squirrel instead of tracking the fly. Duh! I felt the strike before I saw it, and by the time I set the hook the fish was long gone. All I had to show for it was a glimpse of a huge dark shape which rolled as it hit – that and a bunch of "what-ifs" about the fish that might have been...if I'd be paying attention. □

Access and fishing tips:

Fishing Upper Chattahoochee River Campground

Open seasonally, this U.S. Forest Service campground on the upper-upper Hooch offers a great angler's getaway.

Hot chocolate around a campfire is hard to beat, especially if you're a trout fisherman and that campfire is at your site in the Upper Chattahoochee River Campground. This U.S. Forest Service campground, located on the upper Chattahoochee in the Chattahoochee National Forest off FS-44, offers a quiet place to camp with plenty of trout nearby.

The campground section of the Chattahoochee receives regular stockings of trout (mostly rainbows but some browns as well) starting in March. Here, as elsewhere, stocking is done with water temperature in mind, though this far upriver the water temps are usually good.

Most of the fish stocked will be in the 9-inch range, though larger fish are added to the mix on occasion.

Upper Chattahoochee River Campground makes a nice base from which to explore this and other trout fishing in the area. The campground has 34 sites (10 tent-only sites and 24 tent/RV sites) on a first-come, first-served basis. Camping currently costs $12 per night. The campground may be full on weekends, especially during the peak vacation and leaf seasons, but at other times you may have it almost to yourself.

Hand pumps provide drinking water, and there are primitive but functional toilet facilities. There are no showers. RV users should note that no hookups are available.

Flies and lures: Along this section of river, your fly or lure choice may depend on whether or not it's "stocking season." During the spring and summer, when this area is stocked regularly, fly fishers often choose egg imitations such as Y2Ks and Sucker Spawns (12-14) or pink or chartreuse San Juan Worms (size 14). Woolly Buggers (6-10) and buggy nymphs such as Gold Ribbed Hare's Ears or Pheasant Tails (12-16) work well too. So do bright

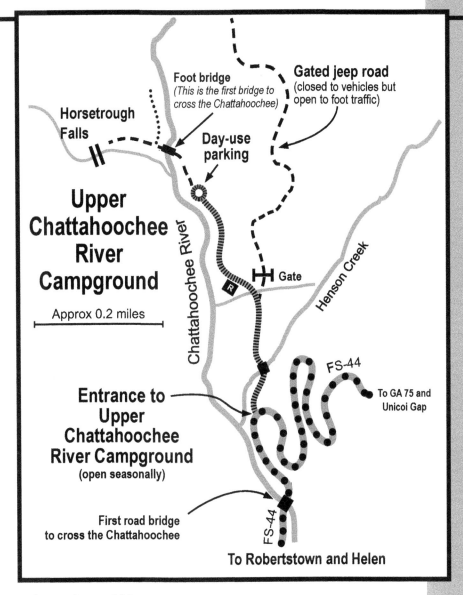

Horsetrough Falls

Upper Chattahoochee River Campground

Approx 0.2 miles

Chattahoochee River

Foot bridge
(This is the first bridge to cross the Chattahoochee)

Gated jeep road
(closed to vehicles but open to foot traffic)

Day-use parking

Gate

R

Henson Creek

FS-44

To GA 75 and Unicoi Gap

Entrance to Upper Chattahoochee River Campground
(open seasonally)

First road bridge to cross the Chattahoochee

FS-44

To Robertstown and Helen

and attention-grabbing streamers.

Once stocking season is over, however, things start to change. Remember that *all* of the stocked fish don't get caught. Some remain, and they quickly become more streamwise. While Y2Ks, worm imitations and so on may still work, more traditional patterns such as the Adams, Elk Hair or Foamback Caddis, or Royal Wulff or Royal Trude also become effective. I've also had good success with Stimulators. On my last visit to this area, a nice rainbow went for a size 14 yellow-bodied Stimulator drifted along a current seam near the FS-44 bridge. Adding a Pheasant Tail Nymph dropper didn't hurt, either, and coaxed several more fish out of hiding.

If you're using spinning gear, year-round favorites include small inline spinners. Here, as elsewhere, bright colors and flashy blades are usually a plus. Bait enthusiasts can do well with salmon eggs, worms, and (on newly stocked fish) corn.

After Labor Day, most of the anglers you see here seem to be fly fishing. Since there's no stocking at that time, wild-trout fishing styles may be more effective as the holdover fish go native. Buggy nymphs or seasonal dries are often the key. You'll may want to go with smaller sizes (as small as 18 or even smaller) during the colder months. But don't hesitate to try something different now and then. For example, big stonefly nymph imitations such as Pat's Rubber-

While visiting this area, be sure to make the short walk from the upper day use parking area to see Horsetrough Falls.

Left: The Upper Chattahoochee River Campground provides a great base of operations with many riverside sites. Below: Water is available, but you'll have to pump it.

legs can sometimes work well.

A note to users of RVs and trailers: If you plan to take your RV or trailer camper to this campground, use caution as you negotiate the twisting gravel road that takes you there. It only takes a moment of inattention to run off the side of the road, and that can be disastrous. Those mountains are steep!

I recently got a look at just how scary this can be. A visitor from out-of-state was hauling a large (and brand new) camper trailer behind his SUV and misjudged one of the switchback turns.

He told me later that he had become distracted while appreciating a scenic view. Forgetting that he was towing a camper, he cut the corner too much and the camper's left wheels went off the road.

The result? His camper hung there for hours at a terrifying 45-degree angle (still attached to the SUV!) as wrecker crews worked feverishly to get it back on the road before it lost its precarious hold and went crashing down the mountainside.

The good news is that no one was hurt and the camper trailer was put back onto the road with only minor damage. Be careful anytime you're driving these roads, and be especially careful if you're hauling a trailer. ☐

NOTE: Even during the off season when the campground is closed, you can still park outside the gate off FS-44 and walk in to access the river and fish.

The Gorge

Exploring the upper Chattahoochee as it goes off the beaten track

As it flows below Upper Chattahoochee River Campground, the river moves away from the road and into a remote part of the national forest, flowing through a steep-walled valley ("The Gorge") for about 4.5 miles before rejoining the road just below the WMA check station on Poplar Stump Road.

Because it's so remote, the gorge (like the upper headwaters section) tends to be the realm of the serious fisherman. Casual anglers rarely go to the trouble to fish it, particularly in its more remote reaches, and *that* means solitude – especially as you move away from the few access points.

Why is it called the gorge? A topo map gives you the answer. For about 4.5 miles, the river flows through a gorge-like valley with valley-wall gradients averaging 30 to 40 percent. That's steep!

Though the valley walls are steep in the area of the gorge, the river itself is relatively level and offers surprisingly easy going.

But the good news is that the gradient of the river itself is not very steep at all. Its elevation changes about 530 feet over a river distance of about four and a half miles, yielding an average *river* gradient of less than 0.02, or 2 percent.

What does that mean for fishing? Bluelining enthusiasts know that mountain streams are fishable up to a stream gradient of about 15 percent. This 2 percent figure tells you that, on average, the river through here is surprisingly flat.

Does that mean there will be no steep spots? No.

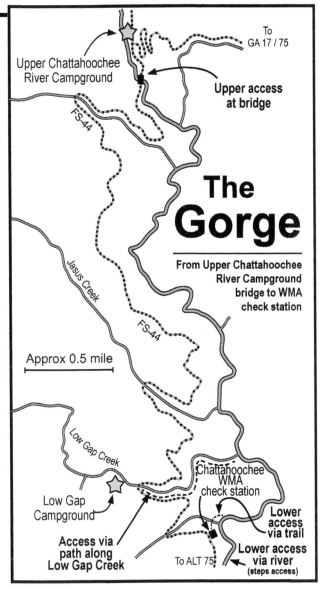

Calculating stream gradients from topo map data only reveals an average gradient for the section in question. However, in this case, the average looks really good. In fact, you'll find that once you get to the water, the going is not too difficult in most places. You'll have to go around some drops and deep spots, of course, but in the backcountry such things are just part of the experience.

But first you've got to get to the river.

If you simply look at a regular map, it appears that accessing the gorge will not be difficult. Through much of the gorge, in fact, the river is only a few hundred yards (airline) from FS-44.

If you lived in Kansas (where things are flat) a few hundred yards would be a walk in the park. But you're not in Kansas, and even a quick look at a topo map reveals that the hillsides are *extremely* steep from the road down to the river – so steep as to be virtually impassable. That means that you've got to consider alternatives.

One is to walk down one of the two major feeder creeks (Low Gap Creek or Jasus Creek) which flow into the Hooch between the check station and Upper Chattahoochee River Campground. Low Gap is easiest since there's a path of sorts (with a length of about eight-tenths of a mile) which follows the creek most of the way to the river. It might also be possible to follow Jasus Creek, though the going is tougher as you near the river.

The other options are to enter the gorge from its upper end (near Upper Chattahoochee River Campground) or lower end (near the WMA check station). It's then possible to move up or down the river either by walking and fishing your way along the river itself or by walking along sections of an old 100-year-old railroad bed.

The rail bed in question was part of the Byrd-Matthews Lumber Company's narrow-gauge railway, which was built to haul logs. The company constructed a sawmill in nearby Helen about 1913 and then set about harvesting timber from the nearby mountains. To transport the logs (some said to have been as much as eight feet in diameter) to the mill, the company constructed rail lines leading along the river and back into the hills. Much of the old rail bed remains, and parts of it are surprisingly easy to follow even after all those years. As an added plus, the rail bed's gradient is gentle enough for easy hiking.

"That old rail bed is not a bad way to get around along the river," one oldtimer told me. "But you'll have to cross the river a few times."

Cross the river, eh? How bad could that be?

"Well," my informant offered, "not really bad so much as interesting. Yeah. Interesting is how I'd put it."

Accessing the gorge from the upper end means working your way down-stream from the FS-44 bridge over the river near Upper Chattahoochee River Campground. Simply walk downstream, following the railbed (it's surprisingly obvious) or pick your way along the creek.

From the lower end, you'll find two ways to access the river near the WMA check station. One is to enter the river below the check station, using one of the sets of wood steps to get from the road to the water. Then, once in the river, work your way upstream. That's fairly easy, but easy access means more fishing pressure.

Is it possible to enter the gorge from farther upstream and avoid the pressured water? Yes, and the key is a small and (at first) very challenging trail tucked away behind the WMA check station. To find this trail, look along the edge of the grass to the left of the check station for a narrow pathway dropping steeply down the hillside.

"Here it is," said my fishing buddy Marty as we set out to fish the gorge one late-summer day. "Think I'll need the hiking stick?"

Maybe. At first, the trail is steep and narrow and twists and turns. There's a little creek to cross (watch out for some potentially tricky footing there), and there are also slick spots to send you sliding (especially if it's been wet) plus of course roots to trip you up (always).

There are also occasional fallen trees blocking the trail, sometimes singles and sometimes in groups of two or three. These deadfalls always seem to be too high to climb over and too low to go under. Working your way through them can be an adventure in itself.

"I guess they're here to weed out the weak," I muttered, huffing and puff-ing as I bent low to crab-walk under yet another downed tree.

This goes on for, oh, what seems like forever. But then you realize that it's been a while since a tree has blocked your path. You'll also realize that you've been hearing flowing water. The sound grows more distinct, and the trail seems better too.

One key to success is to keep a low profile by staying out of the water and using streamside cover (like the log at left) to mask your approach.

And then there it is.

Your first encounter with the river comes at a primitive campsite, where an inviting pool beckons you to stop and make a few casts. We spent a few minutes there (you will, too, I'm sure) and missed one good strike. Then we headed off upstream along the course of those long-gone tracks.

Following the railbed, with the river flowing nearby, is a neat experience. It's not hard to imagine an old steam engine pulling cars laden with logs along the very route you are walking. I found it fascinating to paint that mental picture. Somewhat more uncomfortable to paint, however, was what this landscape must have looked like then, with trees clearcut and hillsides bare. That part of the picture was not nearly as appealing.

As you move up the gorge, the railbed crosses the river several times. In the old days there would have been timber trestles carrying the tracks over the river; today, those trestles are long gone.

At some of the old crossing points, the trail simply fords the river. But at others...

We were walking along the old railbed beyond the first ford upstream from the primitive campsite. The walking was easy despite trees growing in our path. Now and then we'd stop and fish some good-looking water, and since there was a lot of it our upriver progress was not particularly fast. We'd hike a bit, see a good spot, figure out how to get to the water, and then fish a bit. Then we'd make our way back to the railbed and hike some more. Hike...fish...hike...fish...it fell into a kind of rhythm, and it was good.

It was during one of those "hiking" phases that suddenly and unexpectedly the railbed simply stopped. It literally disappeared into thin air. One minute we were walking on a not-so-bad trail. The next we were standing at the edge of the world, looking out into space, like someone had chopped off the trail with a huge carving knife.

It turns out that we were at the site of one of the trestles which used to cross the river. Down below us, the river flowed merrily along. Across it, we could see where the railbed continued on the other side of the gorge. But between where we stood and where the track's route went on there was only a lot of empty air.

"This must be one of those 'interesting' crossings," I thought, for the only way to continue along the railbed was to drop back down to river level and then climb back up to the railbed on the far side.

Or we could simply stay right there and fish – and that's exactly what we did. The fish were cooperative, with the largest – a wild rainbow of perhaps 11 inches – falling for Marty's carefully presented Shelf Liner Ant.

Not surprisingly, few anglers fish all the way through the gorge. The through-trip is long and is more than most want to tackle. Many who have tried it say that as the day wears on they begin worrying more about running out of daylight than about looking for trout.

Still, you have to wonder what's there. You sense the urge, feel the tug, and hear that voice that asks, "What's around the next bend?"

Sooner or later you will have to go and find out.

Welcome to the world of fishing for backcountry trout. ☐

A wild rainbow from "the gorge" section of the upper Chattahoochee near FS-44.

Access and fishing tips:

Fishing off the beaten track in the gorge

It's remote and hard to get to, but it sure is a good place for solitude and wild trout.

The gorge, as many like to call it, offers some of the more intriguing fishing on the upper Chattahoochee. Remote through much of its length, it requires some effort to access and fish. That keeps the pressure down and offers the opportunity for a degree of solitude that is hard to find these days.

The gorge is not stocked. The nearest stocking points are at its upper end where FS-44 crosses the river and at its lower end below the WMA check station. Near them, you may find a mix of stocked and wild fish. But away from the stocking points, the fish you catch will probably be wild.

What kind of fish can you expect? Rainbows will predominate. Marty's 11-inch wild fish was a nice one for this area, though even larger ones turn up from time to time. Wes McElroy, who works at Unicoi Outfitters in Helen, fishes this area a good bit and reports that he's caught wild rainbows up to 12 inches as well as wild browns in the 16- to 17-inch range.

Getting into the gorge: As already noted, there are several ways to access the gorge – from either end, from the trail behind the WMA check station, or from the trail along Low Gap Creek. It's also possible (at least in theory) to access the river by walking in along Jasus Creek, though the terrain becomes difficult as you approach the river.

"The most wilderness and the most remote area is upstream from Jasus Creek," Wes notes.

Flies and lures: Wes does a lot of dry/dropper fishing in this area, especially in the spring and fall. A high-floating fly like a Chubby Chernobyl or a Stimulator, paired with a dropper such as a Golden Stonefly Nymph, works well. A small Pheasant Tail (say, size 16) works well as a dropper too; try it under a Parachute Adams.

During the warmer months, be sure to try ants. Sinking ants can be particularly effective.

Other flies to consider, Wes adds, include crawfish-brown Woolly Buggers. "And in areas where stocked fish are likely, I'll use a Rainbow Warrior," he adds.

If you're spin fishing, it's hard to beat an in-line spinner. Silver/white versions do a good job of imitating creek chubs, and models in various trout color schemes are good choices too.

Other considerations: Remember that fish in the gorge are wild fish. Careless wading and sloppy presentations will quickly alert the fish that something isn't right. Wade carefully and quietly, staying out of the water as much as possible and avoiding sudden overhead motions. You'll also want to be careful not to "line" fish by sending your fly line flying soaring over potential holding areas.

Many anglers fishing here take a page from the blueliner's book and wear camo or, at the very least, drab colors. That applies to your hat too. Sunlight glinting off a bright hat is like a beacon that shouts "RUN, FISH, RUN!"

If you fish here during hunting season, remember that this is a Wildlife Management Area. Check to see what hunts may be going on. During hunting seasons, wear red or orange. I'd suggest avoiding this area during big-game hunts.

Here's one more thing you should keep in mind. Since this section of the river flows through a gorge-like valley, the river's level can come up very quickly with even a little bit of rain in the watershed above where you're fishing. Remember that. You don't want to be caught on the wrong side if an unexpected storm causes the water to rise. That happened to me one summer afternoon a few years back, and I had no choice but to sit and wait for the water to drop enough for me to cross safely and return to where I began.

Let me tell you. That was one long afternoon. ☐

Roadside trout along FS-44

In which I (yes, me!) help stock trout in the Chattahoochee WMA

The coming of spring means the beginning of "stocking season" on many Georgia trout streams. Each year, starting in March, the Department of Natural Resources stocks around a million trout in Georgia's waters. The result is an incredible public trout fishery.

To get a sense of the magnitude of Georgia's trout stocking program, take a look at georgiawildlife.com/trout. There, you'll find a program overview

Georgia DNR trout stocking coordinator John Lee Thompson scoops up trout for stocking into the upper Chattahoochee.

plus a list of stocked streams and insights into how frequently each is stocked. There's also info on which were stocked during the previous week.

From this site, I learned that the Hooch through the WMA is stocked weekly during stocking season. Note that "stocking" season is not to be confused with "fishing" season – in fact, in Georgia, trout fishing season is now a year-round thing.

Of the million trout stocked in Georgia each year, about 24,000 end up in the Chattahoochee WMA. Some are stocked at Upper Chattahoochee River Campground. Others go into Low Gap and Jasus Creeks, major Hooch tributaries within the WMA. But most end up in the heavily fished water between the lower boundary of the WMA and the check station upstream – and I am about to get a firsthand look at how that stocking is done.

It's a warm Wednesday in the middle of July, and I'm riding along with Georgia DNR's trout stocking coordinator John Lee Thompson. He's making the weekly run through the Chattahoochee WMA, hauling a truckful of trout from the Lake Burton Hatchery on Moccasin Creek.

"Where will these fish go?" I ask.

"We'll have to see," he says. "It's all about water temperature."

Finding the right water temperature is like hitting a moving target, and I quickly realize that step one is to figure out where that target happens to be.

We look for it first at the "tubing turnaround," a popular fishing spot on a bend in the river just outside the WMA. John Lee pulls the truck to the side of the road and then retrieves a digital stream thermometer from the center console. Then he hops down from the truck, walks to the river, and gently swings the sensing element out into the flow. A second later it tells us that the water is a balmy 73 degrees.

"Too hot for trout," he says.

What temperature is he looking for? John Lee explains that there's no hard and fast rule. Studies suggest that undisturbed trout begin to feel the effect once water gets above about 68 degrees, though that varies with species and even with individual fish. Other factors have an impact, too, among them the amount of dissolved oxygen and also whether the fish are stressed.

Things are further complicated by the fact that water temperatures change through the course of a typical day – "sometimes by as much as 5 to 7 degrees," John Lee says. The stream is coolest early in the morning or at dusk, but it warms through the afternoon as the sun beats down.

Though it's already warm shortly after noon, when John Lee made that measurement, the water at the turnaround will be even warmer in a few hours.

"The fish wouldn't make it," he says. "We'll have to look upstream."

And so we climb back into the truck and drive on.

Next stop – the bridge over the river at Martin Branch Road. Martin Branch is one of several feeder streams in the area. Its upper reaches hold brook trout. But on this day we're thinking stocked rainbows, not wild brookies, so out comes the thermometer once again.

John Lee stands on the bridge and lowers the probe into the sparkling water. The digits flicker and settle on 71.4.

"That's better," John Lee says. "We'll put some in here."

He climbs up onto the truck, opens one of the tanks, and with a long-handled net flips several dozen fish into the pool. They land with a splash.

When the ripples settle down, I can see the trout milling about in the crystal-clear water as they settle into in the deeper, cooler places. One of the bigger ones noses into the shadow of a rock, chasing away a smaller one who briefly tries to edge in.

John Lee closes the tank and stows the net. Then we get back into the truck and drive on, passing lots of great looking water. Deep pools beckon fish and fishers alike. In several places steps lead from road to river to provide easy access. Now and then we spot a fisherman (sometimes with a fly rod, sometimes with a spinning rod, sometimes alone and sometimes with family or kids). It's like scenes from a fishing magazine.

"We'll hit those spots on the way back," John Lee says. "They'll be cool enough in the afternoon."

Beyond the last set of steps is the check station. Above it, the road swings away from the river. River and road won't come together again Upper Chattahoochee River Campground.

We drive on and soon cross Low Gap Creek, one of two major tributaries to this upper section of the Chattahoochee. We stop at the bridge and check the temperature. It's around 71 degrees, and John Lee puts several scoops of fish into the bridge pool. He puts a few more in the creek farther up Low Gap Campground Road inside the campground too.

At that point, and since I'm a hands-on kind of guy, I ask John Lee if I can give the stocking thing a try. "Sure!" he says. He shows me how to flip the net to launch the fish into the water. I practice, pantomiming the motion. Then he scoops up a few trout and hands the laden net to me. It's surprisingly heavy. I give it a flip, and to my faint surprise the fish arc through the air and land with soft splashes more or less where I was aiming. Who knows? If you catch a trout there, you may have me to thank for it.

Then it's back to the truck and onward to Jasus Creek. Smaller than Low Gap, it's also cooler – about 70 degrees. It too gets some fish.

And then we turn around and head back downstream. We bump down the mountainside, around the switchbacks, past the WMA check station, and at last come again to the section with the stream-access stairs.

John Lee pulls the truck to the side of the road.

"Most of the fish will go into this stretch," he says, scooping up a net filled with trout and launching them expertly through the air. Their flight path is perfect, and they splash like red-striped meteors into the pool below. Several scoops of fish go into that pool before we move on.

Next up is a second stop at the Martin Branch Road bridge.

When we stopped there before, there was no one on the creek. Now there are three kids and two dads, all with big grins on their faces. We speak to them (my notes tell me it was the Cagles and the Hendrixes) and admire the kids' stringers. More grins. More good times.

It occurs to me that even though John Lee works in fisheries, he's not really in the fisheries business at all. Instead, he's in the business of making memories and creating smiles.

While John Lee tosses in a few more fish, I ask the dads if I can take a picture of them all to maybe use in this book. The dads say "sure." "You're gonna be stars!" one of them says as the kids lift their stringers for a picture. After setting the camera back in the truck, I turn to wish them good luck. But the kids are already back to fishing.

We drive on, stopping and stocking at several other points along the way. Those scoops of fish are heavy, and it's got to be a workout. After throwing fish all day, John Lee will not need to go to the gym.

Finally, well down the road, John Lee says, "This should be the last stop." He climbs up onto the truck one more time, scoops up the last of the fish, and sends them flying into the river.

"That's it," he says. "We're finished."

"It was fun!" I say, and it was.

But for those who'll fish here tomorrow, the real fun is yet to come. ☐

Trout fishing brings smiles to the faces of anglers young and old and makes memories that will never be forgotten. Here, members of the Cagle and Hendrix families enjoy fishing for trout on the upper Hooch.

Finding Chattahoochee WMA's roadside trout

Stocked trout plus easy access define this popular section of the river

For quite a few trout anglers, that first exquisite taste of trout fishing came in the Chattahoochee WMA. It's easy to see why too. Within the WMA, the river closely parallels Poplar Stump Road (FS-44) for a bit more than one mile, providing easy access to water that during the stocking season (sometime in March through Labor Day) usually holds plenty of trout.

Chattahoochee First United Methodist Church marks the turn from Alternate 75 onto Poplar Stump Road.

But there will be trout there after Labor Day too. As on other stocked water, all the stocked fish don't get caught. There are always holdovers in the river through fall and winter and even into the next spring. Those holdover fish soon pick up the habits of wild fish, providing challenging cool-weather fishing too.

All in all, it's a great place to be if you like to trout fish.

Accessing the roadside section: Access to this water is easy. From Helen, take GA 17/75 toward Hiawassee. Turn left onto Alternate 75 at Robertstown. You'll almost immediately cross the Chattahoochee. Just beyond the bridge, look for a large tubing operation and a white church (Chattahoochee United Methodist Church) on your right. Poplar Stump Road turns right, running between the tubing site and the church. That's the road that eventually takes you into the Chattahoochee WMA.

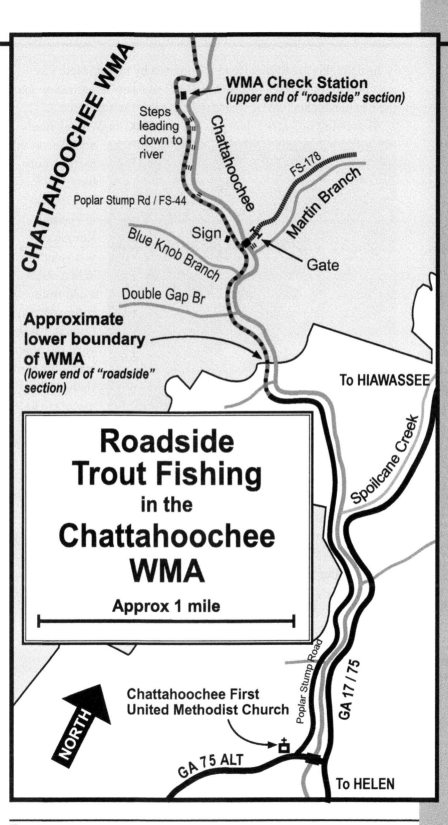

CHATTAHOOCHEE WMA

WMA Check Station
(upper end of "roadside" section)

Steps leading down to river

Chattahoochee

FS-178

Martin Branch

Poplar Stump Rd / FS-44

Blue Knob Branch

Sign

Gate

Double Gap Br

Approximate lower boundary of WMA
(lower end of "roadside" section)

To HIAWASSEE

Spoilcane Creek

Roadside Trout Fishing
in the
Chattahoochee WMA

Approx 1 mile

NORTH

Chattahoochee First United Methodist Church

Poplar Stump Road

GA 17 / 75

GA 75 ALT

To HELEN

Initially, Poplar Stump Road is bordered by private land. Pay attention to those "NO TRESPASSING" signs and continue on into the Chattahoochee WMA where river access is not an issue.

How will you know when you have reached the WMA boundary? According to maps published by the Department of Natural Resources, you enter the WMA about a half mile before Martin Branch. Go beyond the point where the road changes from pavement to gravel. Then, about two-tenths of a mile beyond

You'll find promising water (and plenty of room for spin as well as fly casting) along the roadside section of the river in the Chattahoochee WMA.

that point, look for WMA boundary markers on both sides of the road at a point where what appears to be an overgrown jeep trail takes off down the hill to the river. Beyond that point you're solidly within the WMA.

Exploring the roadside trout water: Once in the Chattahoochee WMA, you'll have no trouble locating promising water. In fact, the challenge is going to be deciding where *not* to fish. The road closely parallels the river, and you'll find yourself constantly spotting good places to stop and try your luck.

Of course, later in summer, this part of the river will be warmer than the water further upstream. Thus, during summer, the lowermost sections may not be the best places to fish. But in spring and early summer (and again in the fall) it's good water to check out.

Continuing upstream, you'll soon come to the turnoff and bridge at Martin Branch Road. Across that bridge is a small parking area (with room for just a few cars) on the right. Nearby, wood steps lead down the sloping bank, ending near a pool with intriguing runs and usually receives fish every week during stocking season.

Continuing upriver, you'll see a large Chattahoochee WMA sign on your left about 200 feet beyond the Martin Branch turn-off. About 1500 feet beyond the sign, look for the first of several sets of steps leading down the steep slope between the road and the river. These steps provide access to some great-looking water.

About 350 feet beyond the first set of steps is a wide parking area on the left side of the road (as you're driving upstream). Beyond it, over the next thousand feet or so, you'll find several other sets of steps. They greatly simplify access to this section of water.

Not far beyond the last set of steps is another wide parking area (on the left of road as you head upriver). Some anglers will leave a car here, hike down the road a ways, and then fish back upstream to where they left the car. Of course, if you prefer downstream fishing, you can do the same thing by parking at a lower parking spot, hiking upstream, and then fishing your way downstream. The possibilities are almost endless.

About 1000 feet beyond that last parking area is the Chattahoochee WMA check station. Above the check station, the river flows away from the road and through the gorge area where more effort is required to reach it. But the roadside stretch below the check station provides plenty of good water to explore.

What to put on the end of the line: When fishing this roadside water, choose your fly or lure based on the kind of fish you're after. By that I mean either "recently stocked" or "more experienced" fish Sometimes (but not always) you'll need different types of flies to interest those different classes of fish.

Here's an example. At the height of stocking season (say, in the spring and early summer) you can just about bet that stocked fish will be present and that you'll be fishing over very recently stocked fish. Those trout are operating mostly on instinct, and instinct tells them to eat things that look eggy or buggy or that try to swim away. But once those fish have been in the river a while (and certainly if they manage to hold over until fall or winter) they will have become much more streamwise and will act much more like wild fish. Thus, you'll want to choose flies or lures accordingly.

Flies: The fly of choice through spring and summer will probably be something from the "egg" or "worm" category. Egg imitations such as Y2Ks or Sucker Spawn can be effective on recently stocked fish. So can San Juan Worms. Pink, red or chartreuse Mop

Several sets of steps lead from FS-44 (Poplar Stump Road) down to the river, making it easier to navigate the steep slope and greatly simplifying the matter of river access.

Flies can be effective too.

With any of those flies, be sure to use enough weight. You want the flies to drift along close to the bottom. Use a strike indicator to alert you to takes, and set the hook whenever the indicator does anything out of the ordinary.

Buggy nymphs often work well on newly stocked fish too. A shaggy (read "buggy") Gold Ribbed Hares Ear in size 12 or 14 can sometimes be the perfect fly for recently stocked fish. Another pattern to try here, especially in the deeper holes, is a Woolly Bugger or a Rubberlegs. Again, a deep drift with no drag is important.

What about minnow imitations? They often work well on stocked fish and can trigger fast strikes. Woolly Buggers can be fished as streamers – that is, by stripping them toward you with foot-long tugs – or you can use a flashy streamer pattern such as the Rolex. The Hudson Streamer, described in the Appendix, is also very effective. Many other streamers will work too.

Are dry flies good for stocked trout in water such as this? At times, yes, especially with buggy dries. Sometimes all it takes to draw a strike is to cast an attractor such as a Stimulator so that it drifts freely in an eddy or down a run. Large attractors float well enough to support a dropper, too, making it easy to combine the attractor dry with a subsurface fly.

Once stocking ends around Labor Day, the holdover fish soon begin to behave more and more like wild fish. You'll need to adjust your fly selection accordingly. As fall moves toward winter, for example, you may see smaller insects active on the stream. If you do, the holdover fish may be feeding on subsurface forms of those insects. That's the time to try a nymph pattern (such as a Pheasant Tail), choosing one that's just a little larger than the adult insects you are seeing. Of course, dries are a possibility too. At such times a Blue Winged Olive or Adams of approximately the same size as the naturals you're seeing will sometimes work, though the subsurface offerings usually work better. To cover all the bases, the best bet may be a dry-dropper set-up.

Spinners: If you're spin fishing, you'll be glad to know that the roadside stretch of the Chattahoochee is great spinning water all year long. Minnows of some sort are always present. Outfitted with light line, a spinning rod lets you cast minnow imitations even in tight quarters. That makes it easy to explore the deeper reaches of some of this section's pools.

For most spin fishers, in-line spinners seem to be the preferred lures to use on this water. As elsewhere, those with white or silver bodies and gold or silver blades are popular. Darker bodies are the choice on a cloudy day or if the water is a little off-color.

Spinning is certainly effective during "stocking season" and works the rest of the year too. As the weather (and water) cool in late fall and winter, remember that you will want to use slower presentations. Thus, choose lures that work well with slower retrieves. Some like to go with a spoon such as the Little Cleo, working it slowly through deeper pools.

For bait fishers: Since this stretch of the river is easily accessible and usually holds fish during the traditional trout fishing months between March and September, it's a good destination for families with kids. It's ideal for introducing kids to mountain trout fishing, and when that's the goal then it's hard to beat fishing with some sort of bait.

Salmon eggs usually work well, as do worms, crickets and Powerbait. One young angler I visited with on a sunny May afternoon last season even had a nice rainbow that he'd caught using nothing more elaborate than a small ball of bread squeezed onto a hook. □

The
Helen
Stretch

3

The Helen stretch

The Alpine way

In which my old buddy Max learns to love the tubes and gets to know some Alpine-village rainbows.

So it's a pleasant weekend near the end of May, and I'm once again fishing with my ol' buddy Max. He's come to north Georgia again for a few days on business...with a little spring trout fishing thrown in.

You remember Max. He's the one who didn't like the idea of fishing in campgrounds until he learned that campground fishing can be pretty good.

I'd picked him up a couple of hours earlier at the Atlanta airport, and now we're bound for the Chattahoochee yet again.

By special request, we're headed for the Georgia mountain town of Helen – and I mean the part where the river flows right through town.

"Ever heard of a place called Helen?" Max had asked me when we talked on the phone earlier in the week. "A buddy of mine visited there last March and said there are a lot of trout in that part of the river. It sounds like it would be fun to check it out. You've caught fish there, haven't you?"

Helen, eh? For years Helen was just a small mountain town. But in 1968, in an effort to revitalize the town as a tourist destination, plans were made to recreate it as an alpine village. Work began the following year, and today it attracts vast numbers of tourists.

Helen offers what you'd expect to find in an alpine-flavored destination, including themed restaurants and myriad gift shops and even its very own Oktoberfest. The Alpine Helen/White County Convention & Visitors

Bureau says it has "the charm of Bavaria in the heart of the Blue Ridge Mountains," and while I've never been to Bavaria I suppose that's a pretty accurate description.

"Helen?" I said, answering his question at last. "Well, yes, I've caught trout there over the years."

"Good," Max said. "Let's check it out."

"Okay," I said. "But remember that March was a while ago, before school let out. Now it's the end of May, and it might not be quite what

During summer, the "tube hatch" can blanket the river with floaters riding multicolored plastic tubes. But once school begins, that same water (below) is once more quiet and peaceful and may offer potentially rewarding fishing.

you're expecting."

Why not? Well, once the weather warms up, throngs of visitors start making their way to Helen. Many of them want to cool off by floating down the river on brightly-colored tubes. This usually starts in May – around Memorial Day if not sooner. Anglers call this the "tube hatch." When it starts, many trout fishers give up on the in-town river and fish elsewhere.

During the tube hatch, there are a *lot* of tubes on the river – especially on weekends. Don't misunderstand; it's great fun to go tubing on a hot summer day. I've done it myself. But for anglers, the fishing is certainly easier during fall, winter and spring when the tubes are not in play.

As summer gets going, one more factor comes into play here too. The river through the town warms significantly and once the water gets too warm for trout then stocking there is discontinued. That usually happens by early July.

As we rode north toward the mountains, I told Max more about the town's history, about the river flowing through it, and about some of the fish I've caught there over the years.

If you can work around the float tubers, there is some good-looking water on the Chattahoochee right in downtown Helen.

Now that I think about it, though, I don't believe I ever got around to mentioning the tube hatch.

But that's okay, I told myself. *He'll find out about it soon enough.*

"You have got to be kidding me."

It was by that time almost 3 p.m., and we were standing on one of the bridges over the Hooch in Helen. Below us the river flowed cold and clear. Or at least we guessed it did. It was kind of hard to say for certain because we couldn't really make out the water for all the tubes that covered it – tens and dozens and hundreds of tubes, each carrying a reclining rider on a gently bobbing float down the river.

Max stood there for a full minute and then said with a faint note of disappointment, "Yeah, maybe it was different in March."

"Uh-huh," I allowed. "But the trout are still there."

"But don't all those tubes mess up the fishing?" he asked.

"Not really," I said, explaining to my friend that if you're in the right place, you can actually catch fish as the tubes are going by. But fishermen tend not to do that. There's too much risk of snagging a tube or a tuber.

"So that's the end of it here?"

"No," I said, and then I let him in on the secret. Once the tubers finish up and go eat supper, the river quickly returns to the way it was before. The fish become active again too and the fishing can sometimes be good.

"That's the trick," I told my friend. "You've got to time it right and fish early before the tubers arrive or late after they've all gone home."

Things were quiet there on the bridge for another minute or so.

"You know what?" I finally said. "Let's get a bite to eat and come back in a couple of hours. The tube hatch will be pretty much over then, and we'll see if we can find some fish."

"Okay," Max said. "We'll see what's happening toward sunset. Now about that supper," he added. "My same buddy who caught all those fish here was telling me about this barbecue place..."

Located right through the middle of an Alpine-themed tourist destination, the Helen stretch really is an intriguing piece of water. To be sure, mid-summer is not the time to fish here. There are simply too many tubers – and besides that, by the time summer arrives in full force, the water through town is much too warm for trout.

But in the winter and spring, and again in the fall, it's cool enough to make trout happy. At those times of year it's really not a bad place to fish.

One nice thing about fishing through Helen is that you don't have to

Gearing up for Helen

Gearing up for the Helen stretch is easy – just use the same gear that you fished with on the lower reaches of the Chattahoochee Wildlife Management Area. For fly fishing, an 8- to 9-foot, 4- to 6-weight rod will be great. If you're spin fishing, a 5.5- to 6-foot rod with 4- or 6-lb. line will work fine.

During spring and early summer, before the water gets too warm and stocking comes to an end, this can be good water to introduce kids to trout fishing. Set 'em up with worms, crickets, or Powerbait, and drift the bait through deeper runs and holes. Your kids will have a blast!

worry about hiking in or about what to do for lunch. There's plenty of pay parking (and a little bit of free parking) close to the water, and the list of possible lunch places (also close to the water) is a long one that offers something for just about every taste.

Though fishing in downtown Helen is definitely not a wilderness experience, it certainly wins top marks in the category of "family friendly." It's a good place to bring kids (at least during times of year when trout are present). And non-anglers in your group can explore Helen while you fish. That can be more than enough to keep everybody happy. In fact, if you stay off private property as you enter and leave the water (definitely be aware of that) and don't mind being the subject of a hundred tourists' photographic memories, it's really not a bad place to be once the tubers all go home.

A little later, refreshed by a barbecue sandwich and a side of banana pudding from North Georgia Barbecue, we were back at the river and rigging up the rods. Tubing was done for the day, and the throngs of visitors were gone. It was like a completely different river.

Trout tournament!

In March of each year, Helen hosts its annual Trout Tournament on the river through town. It's fun for anglers of all ages. The river through town is heavily stocked, and your catch just might win you a prize. Visit helenchamber.com for info on this year's tournament.

We parked at one of the pay lots on Chattahoochee Street near the bridge where Edelweissstrasse crossed the river. That put us about midway through the in-town section and would give us easy access to some promising water.

We started fishing just downstream from that bridge, focusing on a bend where the river curves to the right behind the Festhalle before dropping over some gentle shoals. Sure enough, that late in the day the tubers were all gone. We pretty much had the whole river to ourselves.

"This is more like it," Max said. "This is what I was thinking about when –"

At that very instant his bright orange strike indicator suddenly disappeared. He set the hook and soon had a 9-inch rainbow in his net.

For the next hour or so, as afternoon turned to evening and evening moved toward dark, we slowly fished our way downstream toward our get-out point at the city's Riverside Park. We each caught fish – a number of them, in fact. None of them were huge, but all were trout.

That was good enough. ☐

And spinners?

Choosing spinning lures for the Helen stretch is easy. Use bright and flashy in-line spinners (Roostertails, Mepps), small crankbaits in "firetiger" or "trout," or deeper-running spoons such as the Little Cleo.

Choosing flies for the Helen stretch

The fish you catch in the Helen stretch will be stocked fish. From March through about July 4, they may be very recently stocked fish. That means that "junque flies" such as Y2Ks, 3-D Sucker Spawns, San Juan Worms, and the like should be especially effective. Mop Flies in chartreuse, pink, or orange also do a good job here. Remember to use enough weight to get 'em down deep.

Bright, eye-catching streamers such as the Rolex or Hudson Streamer also work well.

Yes, you'll catch fish on traditional flies too. But you'll probably catch more fish on the patterns just named.

When the tubers go away at the end of summer, any fish that remain (and there will be some) will have wised up a bit. At that time it can pay off to add seasonally appropriate nymphs to the mix.

If you are lucky enough to enjoy fishing after a "bonus stocking" around one of the major winter holidays, remember that you'll again be fishing for recent stockers. Go back to the junque food flies and those streamers.

Access and fishing tips:

Finding Chattahoochee trout in downtown Helen

Is it possible to catch trout right there in the middle of tourist heaven?

For a river that flows through the middle of a tourist town, the Hooch through Helen offers fairly easy access and, at times, some decent fishing. Most of the trout here will be typical 9-inch stockers. But from time to time a few bigger fish may find their way into the river here, too, and an even larger fish occasionally migrates into the public water from the private trophy water downstream at Nacoochee Bend. It's definitely news if one of those big boys is landed in town.

As we have seen, because of the tube hatch challenge and water temperature issues, summer may not be the best time to fish here. Early spring can be good, since stocking typically starts in March and tubing doesn't really get going until things warm up a bit.

And what about fall and winter? While there's no regular stocking during fall and winter, there are no tubers either – and there *are* some holdover fish. The river here may also receive so-called "bonus" stockings (typically around major holidays) if the hatcher-

An easy place to access the river in downtown Helen is at the city's Riverside Park. There's limited free parking there with plenty of paid parking nearby if the park's spaces are full.

ies have extra fish or need to make room for new arrivals.

Gearing up for downtown: The Hooch is a medium-sized stream through Helen, offering plenty of room for fly casting as well as spin fishing. Fly rodders should try egg imitations (Y2Ks and such), Woolly Buggers, and streamers. Large stonefly nymphs can also be effective. In every case, use enough weight to get them deep. With the arrival of spring, fly fishers will continue to have success with those patterns but might want to add some topwater attractor-style dries too.

Spinning enthusiasts may have luck year-round with slowly retrieved spinners, spoons, or jig/grubtail combinations worked through the deeper holes and runs. Of course, bait such as salmon eggs or worms work too.

If you have kids, consider taking them to Helen's annual fishing rodeo in March. There will be lots of fish in the river, and you might even want to stick around once the rodeo is done to see what happens if you throw a weighted Y2K or a flashy streamer.

The matter of access: In Helen, private land and posted property are the norm. Numerous signs make that clear.

In practice, however, if you access the river at a public access

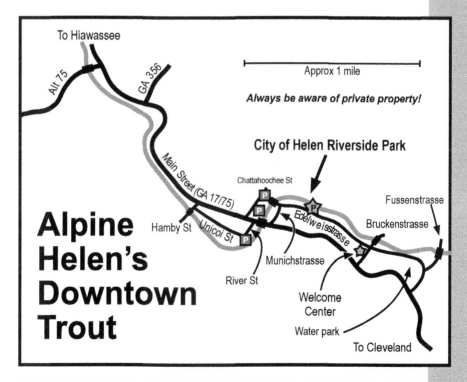

Alpine Helen's Downtown Trout

To Hiawassee

Alt 75

GA 356

Approx 1 mile

Always be aware of private property!

Main Street (GA 17/75)

City of Helen Riverside Park

Chattahoochee St

Fussenstrasse

Hamby St   Unicoi St

Edelweisstrasse

Bruckenstrasse

Munichstrasse

River St

Welcome Center

Water park

To Cleveland

points (which is to say if you pay attention to the "POSTED" signs, staying in the river and off of private land) landowners have tended to be okay with anglers using the river. In fact, as Helen Welcome Center manager Connie Disher recently pointed out to me, you'll see anglers fishing the Chattahoochee River all the way through town. Just respect private property and stay in the water except at public access points.

Finding those access points: There are several potential access spots to consider as you plan your trout fishing adventures in Helen.

Some take advantage of access offered at bridge rights-of-way where roads cross the river. The trick is to park close enough to make this feasible (more on parking in a minute). You also want to be sure there are no "KEEP OUT" or "NO TRESPASS-ING" between you and the water. Private property is taken seriously in this neck of the woods, and land status can change unexpectedly. If you're unsure, the best advice is to err on the side of caution and look for access elsewhere.

Good downtown flies include (clockwise from top left) Mop Flies, 3-D Sucker Spawn, Rolex streamers, and a Beadhead Y2K (not to scale).

One of the most popular public access points is the city's Riverside Park on Edelweisstrasse, between the Festhalle (on the upstream end) and tubing operation on the downstream end. This city park features restroom facilities, a playground, and a covered pavilion. There are also a number of streamside swings – great places to sit and enjoy the river without getting wet.

For fishermen, Riverside Park offers a number of places where you can literally walk right into the water. Once on the water, it's then possible to fish up or down the river, returning to where you started when the fishing is done.

Here's another possibility. If you're staying in riverside lodging, you may be able to access the water right from your motel. That's worth checking on when you make reservations.

When fishing the Hooch through Helen, note that there is posted private water down-river from Helen. *Don't trespass.* Stay upstream of the bridge on Fussen-strasse behind the water park to be safe.

Parking: If you're like most trout anglers visiting Helen, you will arrive by automobile. That means that you will need to find a place to park before taking to the water. Fortunately, finding parking is fairly straightforward.

There is a limited amount of free parking at Riverside Park, but it tends to fill quickly.

There are also a number of pay lots around Helen. The accompanying map shows the general locations of some lots which are closest to the river; other lots a bit farther from the water are not shown. Bring cash to pay for parking, which at the time of this writing ranges up to about $5 per car. □

The traffic challenge

When planning to do some fishing in downtown Helen, be aware that traffic can be a nightmare at certain times of the year. During fall leaf season, for example, it can take an hour or more (sometimes a *lot* more) just to drive from one side of Helen to the other. Traffic can literally back up for miles.

The problem is not only the number of cars but also the huge number of tourists crossing the highway in downtown Helen more or less at will. Be careful to watch for them as you drive through town. Some may not be quite as attentive as they should be.

Traffic in Helen becomes a factor if you're fishing other nearby water, too, if you have to drive through the town to get to your destination. During busy times of year, anglers in the know plan alternate routes to bypass the town. One approach is to use Alternate 75 (which also happens to take you right by Smithgall Woods and legendary Dukes Creek).

Check the Alpine Helen/White County Convention & Visitors Bureau website (helenga.org/events) for a calendar of events, and during the big ones plan for a slow trip through the heart of town.

Nacoochee Bend

No discussion of trout fishing near Helen would be complete without a look at the private trophy trout water of Nacoochee Bend.

Much of the upper Chattahoochee is public water. However, a 1.5-mile section located a short distance downriver from Helen – the water known as "Nacoochee Bend" – offers private trophy trout fishing and the chance to catch the trout of a lifetime.

Nacoochee Bend is operated by Unicoi Outfitters, which also has a fly shop on Georgia 17/15 southeast of Helen. The shop sits near the river about midway through the Nacoochee Bend water.

Remember that this is private water, and all fishing on this stretch must be booked through Unicoi Outfitters. It's catch and release only with barbless hooks.

Jake Darling, manager of Unicoi Outfitters, explains that the Nacoochee Bend water is divided into three sections of about a half mile each, and each section has its own unique personality.

Upper section: Located behind the Unicoi Outfitters shop and stretching upstream from Nora Mill Dam to the upper boundary of the water, this section offers some good dry fly fishing. It tends to be a little flatter than the water

---

further downstream, though it also has some faster water that's excellent for fishing with streamers.

"During March and April, March Browns and Hendricksons often work well," Jake says. There may be "tons of little dark mayflies" present as well.

As summer approaches, terrestrials such as Chernobyl ants, foam ants, and hoppers can be effective in the upper section.

Jake adds that there are some big hellgrammites and big golden stoneflies present in this water too.

"They hatch at night," he says, "but the nymphs are active in the water during the daytime."

Wading the upper section is fairly easy with only a few deeper spots.

"There's not a lot of current except near the area that we call the Rock Wall," he says.

Jake notes that the upper section is good for new anglers ("It holds lots of fish," he says) and also for anglers who want to hone their skills with a bit of sometimes challenging dry-fly fishing.

"There are some big fish in the flat water," he says, "but they can be a tough to fool on a dry."

Middle section: The middle section of the Nacoochee Bend water begins at Nora Mill Dam and extends

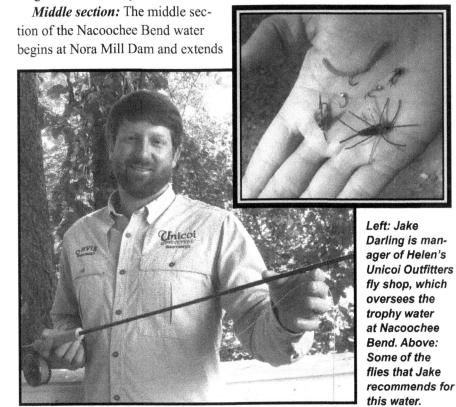

Left: Jake Darling is manager of Helen's Unicoi Outfitters fly shop, which oversees the trophy water at Nacoochee Bend. Above: Some of the flies that Jake recommends for this water.

downstream to the first highway bridge.

"For many of our anglers, it is the favorite section of the stream," Jake says, adding that most of the fish you'll find there are more than 18 inches long. The biggest ones are typically found from the middle portion downstream.

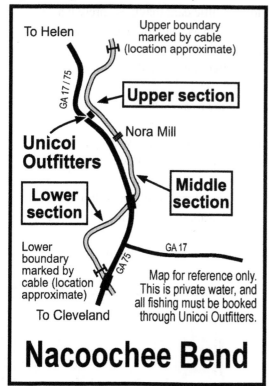

To Helen

Upper boundary marked by cable (location approximate)

GA 17/75

Upper section

Nora Mill

Unicoi Outfitters

Middle section

Lower section

Lower boundary marked by cable (location approximate)

GA 17

GA 75

To Cleveland

Map for reference only. This is private water, and all fishing must be booked through Unicoi Outfitters.

Nacoochee Bend

This stretch is characterized by moving water with plenty of shoals and riffles. There are also several deeper runs. Throughout this section, nymphs are usually the flies of choice. But streamers work well, too, and small midges can be effective down toward the bridge at the lower end. In late spring and summer, wet ants can work well too.

Even though the river here flows close to the road, you may feel like you're out in the woods – everywhere except at the upper end of this section at what's known as the Stadium Pool near Nora Mill. This pool, directly below Nora Mill Dam, is overlooked by a platform where tourists frequently stop to watch you fish. Fishing there really is like fishing in a stadium.

The lower section: The bottom section, which starts at the GA 17/75 bridge where the middle section ends, is where you'll find the actual "Nacoochee Bend," a sharp right-angle bend to the left.

"The lower section's got it all," Jake says – everything from riffles and pocket water to deep holes and flat water too.

"The lower section is a little tougher to fish," Jake notes, adding that it's ideal water for the angler who's looking to learn more about reading a stream and figuring out how to fish it. If you can work out the puzzle, though, the reward may be a truly big trout.

One particularly appealing feature of this section is the presence of long stretches of riffle water. These riffles, which are typically 1.5 to 2 feet deep, are perfectly suited for fishing with a dry fly.

Another nice thing about this section is that it flows away from the road and feels much more like a wilderness stream.

"There's no traffic noise," Jake says. That, combined with the fact that it offers such a diverse line-up of angling challenges, makes the bottom section a favorite of a number of Nacoochee Bend regulars.

Planning a trip: Nacoochee Bend is private water, and you must book a time to fish it by contacting Unicoi Outfitters. The shop offers a variety of different trip options ranging from half- and full-day guided trips to do-it-yourself fishing for anglers with some experience. One of the shop's most popular offerings, Jake says, is the "Gilligan Special," which starts with an hour of on-the-water instruction and then continues with two hours of guided fishing.

It's particularly popular with folks who have not done any fly fishing and want to test the waters, so to speak, before jumping into the sport with both feet.

What's the best time to fish at Nacoochee Bend? The peak season runs from October through the end of May, Jake says, with the best dry fly fishing from mid March into May.

Depending on water temperatures, the fishing at Nacoochee Bend may continue into June. Fishing stops during the summer because the water is too warm.

Angler Marty Lock with a nice rainbow from the Nacoochee Bend section of the Chattahoochee.

Jake adds that winter fishing at Nacoochee Bend can be outstanding.

"You have to downsize tippet and fly size," he says, "but fishing with streamers or with indicator nymph set-ups can be phenomenal."

For information on booking a trip at Nacoochee Bend, contact Unicoi Outfitters at (706) 878-3083 or visit unicoioutfitters.com. ☐

Upper
Tailwater

4

Meet the Upper Tailwater

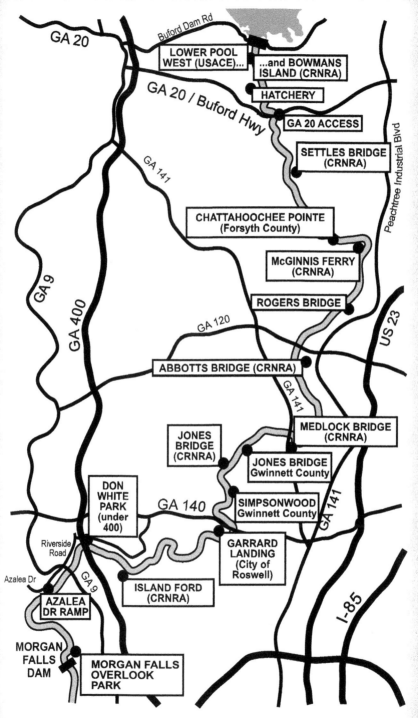

Upper Tailwater (Buford Dam to Morgan Falls)

A solitary fly fisher wades in at Lower Pool West in search of browns and rainbows.

Thank you, Buford Dam

Cold water from the depths of Lake Lanier is good news for trout all the way to Atlanta

The private water at Nacoochee Bend is pretty much the end of the upper Chattahoochee trout water. Downriver from there the water warms to the point that it is no longer good trout habitat and becomes, instead, the realm of bass and other warmwater species. It continues to be so as it flows downstream to eventually form Lake Lanier.

Is that the end of the trout fishery on the Chattahoochee? Not by a long shot. You've just got to get through the lake and below Buford Dam.

The coming of Buford Dam

The date was March 1, 1950. Along with a crowd of about 3,500 interested citizens, a group of Georgia's leaders – including such notables as Herman Talmadge, Walter F. George, Richard B. Russell, and William B. Hartsfield – gathered near the town of Buford, Ga., for the ceremonial groundbreaking of what would ultimately become known as Buford Dam.

Folks had been discussing the project since shortly after the end of World War II. Congressional authorization came as part of the River and Harbor Act, approved on July 25, 1946; that act authorized "a multiple purpose dam on the Chattahoochee River at Buford in the interest of navigation, flood control and power and water supply."

What eventually developed was a big project by any measure. The main dam (what's known as a "roll-filled earth" structure) is 192 feet high and 2,360 feet long. Three adjacent "saddle dikes," also earthen structures, have a total additional length of about 6,600 feet. The main spillway is carved out of rock, and the powerhouse is constructed in a site carved into the rock too. Inside that powerhouse, at maximum flow, turbine-driven generators can produce about 130 megawatts of electrical power.

The dam's gates were closed on Feb. 1, 1956, and the completed dam was dedicated on Oct. 9, 1957. Then, on May 25, 1959 – about nine years after that star-studded groundbreaking – the lake was officially declared "full" with a full summer pool level of 1071 feet above sea level. The lake covers about 38,000 acres (roughly 59 square miles) and has 692 miles of shoreline at normal pool.

Total cost of the project, from planning to completion, was around $44 million – and that was a lot of money at the time.

Was it worth it? Ask a trout fisherman that question, and the answer will be a resounding "YES!" Indeed, the river below Buford Dam holds good numbers of rainbow and brown trout, drawing anglers from throughout the southeast to try their luck in the river's ice cold waters.

What makes the tailwater such great habitat for trout? Temperature, for one thing. At Buford Dam, released water is drawn from the bottom of the lake...and the bottom of Lake Lanier is *cold.* Even during summer, the water coming through the dam is in the high 40s or low 50s. That's more than cold enough to take your breath away if you are a trout angler. But if you're a trout, it's the stuff that of which dreams are made.

Before the dam, this part of the Hooch was a warmwater stream. Longtime residents remember fishing this stretch of river for bass and bream in the years before the lake. But with the completion of the lake and those first releases of cold, cold water from the lake's depths, the stage was set for a world-class trout fishery.

And yet, at first, there were no trout in the river.

Where did the first Hooch tailwater trout come from? The story you hear is that by the early 1960s it was dawning on area fishermen that this reframed river, which had once been the home of warmwater fish, was now

About parking fees

Today, many anglers access the Chattahoochee tailwater either through one of the units of the Chattahoochee River National Recreation Area (CRNRA) or (when fishing near the dam) through the Corps of Engineers property at the Lower Pool West recreation area near the foot of Buford Dam.

Use of any of these requires a parking fee.

Day and annual CRNRA parking passes are available. Daily parking fees can be paid at individual CRNRA units, while annual passes are available from kiosks at some CRNRA units, from CRNRA headquarters at Island Ford, or online (via pay.gov). To avoid the risk of getting a ticket, your CRNRA parking pass or fee receipt must be clearly displayed in your vehicle.

As of this writing, a CRNRA parking pass is also valid at the Corps of Engineers' Lower Pool West recreation area near the foot of Buford Dam. If the fee booth on Lower Pool West Road is not manned, use one of the self-service pay envelopes and be sure to display the receipt portion in your car.

Note that a CRNRA pass will also cover admission at the Corps' Lower Pool West recreation area.

Be aware that state park passes do *not* cover parking at CRNRA or at the Corps of Engineers' Lower Pool West recreation area near the dam.

cold enough for trout. Local trout enthusiasts approached the state with the idea of beginning a trout stocking program below Buford Dam, but there does not seem to have been much interest.

So those anglers took another approach.

Somewhere in there (you'll hear the year 1962 mentioned fairly often) those determined trout fishers pooled their money and acquired upwards of 12,000 rainbow trout in the 2- to 4-inch range from a trout hatchery in North Carolina. Some say that the hatchery's owner was so impressed by the project that he upped the order by about 2,500 fish at no charge.

With no time to waste, the trout commandos quickly transported their finned cargo back to Georgia.

Then, under cover of darkness, they eased up to the river one night and dumped all of those rainbow trout into the Chattahoochee in a shoally section of river about a mile south of

Old Jones Bridge.

How did the trout fare? Well, the transplanted fish apparently found their new digs to be just about perfect. They settled right in and started to grow – by about one inch every month!

The trout continued to thrive, and a year later that section of river held a sizeable population of 12- to 14-inch fish.

For a while, it's said, the midnight stockers quietly enjoyed this secret trout fishery, keeping it pretty much to themselves. But that kind of secret can't be kept for long. Eventually, faced with incontrovertible evidence that the "trout in the tailwater" idea was working, the state's fisheries folks bought into it too.

The Department of Natural Resources has been stocking trout in the Chattahoochee tailwater since the early 1960s. Currently, about 180,000 "catchable-sized" rainbows (that is, fish 9 to 12 inches in length) are stocked into the tailwater between Buford Dam and Roswell Road (near Bull Sluice Lake above Morgan Falls Dam) each year. However, some larger rainbows are also stocked on occasion. Additionally, it's almost certain that at least a few rainbows carry over from season to season; those carryover fish can reach impressive sizes.

What about browns? What was once a stocking-based brown trout fishery has morphed into a naturally reproducing brown trout population in the tailwater below Buford Dam. In other words, the browns have gone wild. Natural reproduction now takes care of the population, and browns have not been stocked between Buford Dam and Roswell Road since 2004.

What kind of size can you expect from wild browns in the upper tailwater? Most of the browns you catch between Buford Dam and Morgan Falls will be in the 8- to 12-inch range.

However, browns of more than 20 inches are now caught in the tailwater every year. The state record brown (with a weight of 20 lb. 14 ounces) was caught here in 2014, superseding the previous record (also caught in this section) of 18 pounds 6 ounces. The big browns continue to turn up, too, and according to Georgia DNR several fish of more than 30 inches in length were caught in this stretch during 2016.

Upper tailwater considerations

When you fish the upper Chattahoochee tailwater, you'll be joining thousands of anglers who have discovered one of the Southeast's fishing treasures. It's a great fishery! On water like this, however, you have to remember several things:

- Because it's a tailwater, flows and water levels on this section of the river are determined by what's happening at Buford Dam. We'll look at that in great detail in a moment. Additionally...

- ...remember that water released through the dam will be very, very cold. Released water is drawn from the depths of the lake, and it will typically have a temperature of around 50 degrees when it re-enters the river below the dam. That's cold enough to present a real risk of hypothermia, and you'll want to dress accordingly. Wearing warm layers under waders is strongly recommended during the cooler months and is not out of the question even in the summertime.

- This is big water – a lot bigger than you think. It can take you longer to move around the river than you might expect, too, particularly if you're moving upstream against the current. Factor that into your planning, particularly as it relates to letting you be sure you're off the water before a release begins.

- Even though it's near Atlanta, parts of the upper tailwater are fairly remote and are some distance from the nearest road. If you're floating the river, you will at times be some distance from civilization (and the nearest bathroom).

- Except at developed ramps and access points, getting into and out of the river can be difficult. In many areas, the banks are high, steep and slippery. Be sure that you know the conditions where you're planning to exit the water *before* you enter the river.

Each of those factors can have a significant impact on your trip, and you need to understand how they interact and how they affect your fishing and your planning.

Bottom line: Never forget that it's a tailwater!

When you're fishing on the Chattahoochee below Buford Dam, it is critically important that you remember that this is a *tailwater* – and you *must* understand what that means.

By definition, a "tailwater" is a section of river located below a dam. Flow rates and river levels are determined primarily by the amount of water being released from the dam. More water being released means high flows and high levels, while less water being released means lower flows and lower levels.

That, more than anything, affects when and where you fish.

Now let's look at some specifics of where and how to fish for trout below Buford Dam.

But first let's check on the goats. □

Goats
(with a mission!)

Fishing at the dam? Be on your best behavior because the goats may be watching...

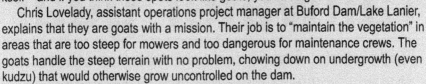

When fishing near Buford Dam you may notice some unusual spots moving around on the dam itself – and if you think those spots look like goats, you'll be right.

Chris Lovelady, assistant operations project manager at Buford Dam/Lake Lanier, explains that they are goats with a mission. Their job is to "maintain the vegetation" in areas that are too steep for mowers and too dangerous for maintenance crews. The goats handle the steep terrain with no problem, chowing down on undergrowth (even kudzu) that would otherwise grow uncontrolled on the dam.

As Chris says, "They'll eat anything."

The Buford Dam goats made their debut in the late 1970s when a site supervisor had the idea of using them to control vegetation around the spillway. It worked, and since then the goats have become a permanent fixture.

They're a unique visitor attraction too. People love to see them, and they even have their own public Facebook group, "Buford Dam Goats."

How many goats are there? "Fifteen or 20," Chris says, and sometimes there are baby goats too. One was born on a rocky ledge but couldn't get off it to join the others.

"So we called the fire department," Chris says. Rescue crews used it as a training exercise, retrieving the baby goat by using ropes to access the ledge from above.

You may also see the goats' guardian angel – a mule – which protects the goats from coyotes.

Where's the best place to see the goats? You might spot them from Buford Dam Road. But if the goats are feeling cooperative, the very best goat watching may be at the far end of the Lower Pool East Park parking area (accessible from Buford Dam Road) or along the road leading from Buford Dam Road down to Lower Pool West.

Here's the Buford Dam mule, guardian of the goats.

Are the goats shy? Sometimes. But other times they'll come right up to the fence. You'll even see folks feeding them through the fence, and a treat of some sort seems to bring the goats closer.

"We don't encourage it," Chris says, "but I've seen people come up with a bag of Cheetos...and here come the goats!" ☐

Tailwater gear

Rods, reels, flies, lures, and various other things you'll need for great tailwater trips

Before we jump into the tailwater, let's take a look at what you'll need in terms of gear.

By the way, there are actually *two* tailwater trout fisheries on the Chattahoochee. The one we'll look at first extends from below Buford Dam to Bull Sluice Lake and Morgan Falls Dam; the second (which we'll explore in a later section of this book) begins at Morgan Falls Dam and extends down to about the US 41 bridge. Though they are very different fisheries, you'll want pretty much the same gear (with a few adjustments to the contents of your fly box) to fish either one.

Fly gear for the tailwater

When choosing fly gear for the tailwater, remember that you'll be fishing *big* water with plenty of room to cast (and the potential for big fish too). Those factors help drive your choices.

Fly rod: One thing you'll want in a tailwater fly rod is versatility. One minute it may be throwing a heavy nymph rig with split shot and a strike indicator, but an hour later it may be called on to throw tiny dries – or even streamers. That's a lot to ask from a single rod.

Some tailwater fly fishers solve the problem by using multiple rods. If you're fishing from a boat or a canoe, that's not hard to do. You might have one rod set up for nymphing and another rigged for dry-and-dropper fishing.

Maybe there's even a third rod set up just for streamers.

But you may not have the luxury of boats and multiple rods. If that's the case, it's hard to beat a 9-foot 6-weight for tailwater fishing. In fact, if there's a "most-popular" tailwater fly rod, that one is probably it. Since the river is wide open, there's plenty of room to cast it. Additionally, the 6-weight will usually have the backbone to cover distance and deal with wind. Both can be important when fishing the tailwater.

So there's a specific recommendation – go with a 9-foot 6-weight for the tailwater. That's what I use, and I think it'll work well for you too.

There is, however, one special tailwater situation where that is *not* the rod I'd choose. If I'm specifically targeting one of those meat-eating monster browns (a situation in which I know I'll be throwing a sink-tip line and big streamers) then I'll go with a heavier rod and pick up my 8-weight. Think "saltwater" with a fighting butt, and you've got the right idea.

Reel: It's easy to pick reels these days thanks to useful reel designations from manufacturers. Simply pick one designed for the line weight you're using.

What about drag? For smaller 9-inch "SNITs" the type of drag (click or disk) doesn't matter too much. Either is fine. But a disk drag system can help you if you hook one of the larger fish.

One thing I do like to have on all of my tailwater reels is a "palming rim." The term refers to an exposed rim on the reel's spool. The idea here is that you can feather the amount of drag simply by applying light pressure to the palming rim with the palm of your non-grip hand. It gives you a remarkable degree of control and can be quite useful when fighting larger fish.

Fly line and backing: For most tailwater situations you want a weight-forward floating line. It's ideal for dries, effective with subsurface flies such as nymphs, and even works with streamers if you don't need to go too deep.

Later on, if you begin to emphasize streamer fishing, add a sink-tip line to help your streamers drop deeper into the water column.

What about backing, the braided line that goes between your fly line and your reel? It builds up spool diameter and also gives you a safety margin in case you encounter a fish that wants to make a very long run. The fact is that you'll never see your backing with most of the fish on the Hooch tailwater. But note that word "most." I've actually gone into the backing several times, and without it I would have lost some big fish.

Sometimes, on the upper tailwater, backing comes into play when you hook a big holdover rainbow or a large brown. On the lower tailwater (below Morgan Falls Dam) it can happen if you hook one of the really big Delayed Harvest trout – or if you end up unexpectedly tangling with something other than a trout. Among the surprises I've encountered on the lower

Leaders for streamers

Streamers fished deep can be effective on the tailwater, and some assume that the way to go deep is to use a long leader. However, that may actually be counterproductive and can keep your streamer in the *upper* part of the water column. The reason? A long leader tends to plane upwards in the current, pulling the streamer along with it.

That's why streamer enthusiasts often use a sink-tip line and a fairly short (say, 5 ft.) and heavy (10 or 12 lb. tippet) leader between fly line and fly. The short leader doesn't seem to bother the fish. Think "short and stout," like the nursery rhyme teapot.

Another useful leader is something like Rio's "VersiLeader," which essentially lets you convert a floating line to a sinking-tip line using interchangeable weighted sections with different sink rates. These can be very effective for fishing not just streamers but nymphs and other subsurface flies too.

tailwater are stripers of 10 to 15 pounds and also an enormous carp. In each case, backing literally saved the day.

Leaders: An informal survey on the Chattahoochee tailwater revealed that most fly fishers seem to gravitate toward a 9-foot leader, choosing tippet size according to fly size. That's usually a good call when fishing dries or (in some cases) weighted streamers if you don't need to go too deep.

For nymphing, choose a leader with a length that lets you position your split shot below your strike indicator by a distance equal to about 1.5 to 2 times the average water depth. Adjust for changing depth by repositioning the strike indicator.

Tippet: The leader's tippet size should be chosen based on the size of the fly or flies. The accompanying table will give you an idea of how the two relate to one another.

Fly size	Tippet
16-18-20-22	6X
14-16-18	5X
12-14-16	4X
6-8-10-12	3X
4-6-8	2X
But there's plenty of wiggle room!	

But if you're fishing those tiny midge emergers that are so effective below Buford Dam, it can pay to throw the chart out the window and go as small as you can with tippet size.

As a case in point, my friend John Cherry, an accomplished Chattahoochee tailwater angler, fishes extensively near the dam with tiny (size 18-ish) midges as droppers under dries, and he swears by quality 7X fluorocarbon tippet. He catches a *lot* of fish; in fact, when we fish together using identical flies, his 7X fluoro set-up usually (okay, almost always) outfishes my 6X mono rig.

Just saying...

Flies for the upper tailwater

Choosing flies for use on the tailwater is simultaneously simple and complex. One one hand, it's simple because these fish are, after all, just trout. They like to eat the things that trout like to eat. On the other hand, you've got to figure out exactly what they happen to be eating on the day you happen to be fishing – and that can vary based on all sorts of factors.

One major factor influencing fly choice is *time of year.* During the summer, for example, the river presents fish with a buffet line-up that's completely different from what it offers during the middle of winter.

At any season, trout get used to seeing certain things. If you can more or less match what they expect to see then your odds of success will go up.

Another factor affecting fly choice is *where* on the upper tailwater you're fishing. Close to the dam, for example, strong flows during releases tend to scour the bottom, creating a habitat that's good for midges but tough for some other aquatic food forms. That's one reason midge emergers are so popular near the dam. But if you go several miles downriver, the force of the water

What are upper tailwater trout actually eating?

According to a study published in 2012 entitled "Growth and Movement of Wild Brown Trout in the Chattahoochee River below Buford Dam," they're chowing down on midges – "by far the most prevalent item," present in about 69 percent of the browns sampled and also in about 53 percent of the rainbows. Caddisflies were next most common, found in 18.5 percent of browns and 11.2 percent of rainbows, followed by stoneflies (16.4 percent and 11.5 percent) and ants (9.8 percent and 9.3 percent). Worms (9.1 and 5.3 percent) and scuds (7.6 and 3.4 percent) were also present.

Other foods noted were "mayflies, terrestrial insects, fish (including incidents of cannibalism by brown trout), fish eggs, mosquitoes, snails, various (hemipteran) flies, crayfish, and a frog."

That's interesting info for any tailwater trout angler – and it just might help you choose flies next time you're on the water.

CHATTAHOOCHEE TAILWATER HATCH CHART

Hatches	J	F	M	A	M	J	J	A	S	O	N	D	Suggested subsurface	Suggested dries
Caddisflies			✓	✓	✓	✓	✓	✓	✓				Beadhead Soft Hackle Pheasant Tail, LaFontaine's Emergent Pupa, Burrell's Copperhead	Dun or Tan Elk Hair or Foamback Caddis, X-Caddis, Parachute Caddis, Scalley's Crippled Caddis
Blue Winged Olive Mayflies	✓	✓	✓	✓	✓	✓	✓	✓	✓	✓	✓	✓	Beadhead Pheasant Tail, WD40	Blue Winged Olive (BWO), Parachute BWO, Thorax BWO, BWO Emerger
Sulphur Mayflies				✓	✓	✓							Beadhead Pheasant Tail, Hare's Ear Nymph, Copper John	Parachute Sulphur, Sulphur Sparkle Dun, Compara Dun, Light Cahill
Stoneflies	✓	✓	✓	✓	✓	✓							Black Girdle Bug, Prince Nymph, Kaufmann's Stone, Halfback Nymph, Anytime-Anywhere	Stimulator, Elk Hair or Foamback Caddis
Midges	✓	✓	✓	✓	✓	✓	✓	✓	✓	✓	✓	✓	Zebra Midge, Brassie, Rainbow Warrior, Blue Assassin	Griffith's Gnat, Cream Midge Palmer, Black Midge Palmer
Terrestrials			✓	✓	✓	✓	✓	✓	✓	✓			Black Woolly Worm, Tellico Nymph, Hardbody Ant, Island Park Special	Parachute Ant, Foam Ant, Foam Beetle, Flying Ant, Dave's Hopper, Yellow Humpy
Minnows	✓	✓	✓	✓	✓	✓	✓	✓	✓	✓	✓	✓	Muddler Minnow, Zonker, Hudson Streamer, Crystal Bugger	N/A
Scuds	✓	✓	✓	✓	✓	✓	✓	✓	✓	✓	✓	✓	Flashback Scud, Epoxy Scud, Kaufmann's Scud, Lightning Bug	N/A
Crayfish	✓	✓	✓	✓	✓	✓	✓	✓	✓	✓	✓	✓	Brown Woolly Bugger, Dave's Soft-Shell Crawdad	N/A
Other	✓	✓	✓	✓	✓	✓	✓	✓	✓	✓	✓	✓	Y2K, Hot Pink San Juan Worm, 3-D Sucker Spawn	Royal Wulff, Royal Trude, Adams, Woolly Bugger

Based on research by Chris Scalley and Chattahoochee Coldwater Fishery Foundation. Used by permission.

moderates and allows weedbeds to take hold, creating habitat for a much more diverse collection of aquatic insects and other food forms. As a result, you'll have many more fly options when fishing at, say, Jones Bridge than when fishing several miles upriver in the shadow of the dam.

It's also worth noting that fly choice can vary even within a given section of the river. On a fall afternoon at Jones Bridge, for instance, small midge emergers might be the fly of choice if you're fishing midriver. But over near shore by that stretch of brushy and overgrown shoreline, you'll find late-season grasshoppers...big and juicy...and few trout can pass up such a hearty meal if it happens to fall their way.

Because fly choice can be such a multifaceted undertaking, a good fly chart will help when you're trying to figure out where to start. Some of the best tailwater fly choice info you'll find is contained in a hatch

Flies for wild browns

Fly selection on the upper tailwater has been complicated a bit by the wild brown trout population below Buford Dam. Those browns are born and raised in the river and have *never* seen the inside of a hatchery. They can be picky. If browns are the target, consider going as close to the naturals as possible.

Don't misunderstand. Wild browns may take a Y2K as enthusiastically as the next guy. But most agree that wild browns demand a bit more in the way of attention to fly selection, and my experience bears that out. You've got to give them what they're used to eating.

What about the big ones? Some browns develop a taste for meat once they reach a certain length and focus on eating other fish. To tempt those browns, you've got to imitate what they want – other fish – and that means using *big* streamers You wouldn't use such streamers fishing for small stocked rainbows, but for those giant browns they're definitely what you need.

River Through Atlanta's Chris Scalley with a selection of big flies for those big tailwater browns.

chart developed by Chris Scalley of River Through Atlanta Guide Service.

That hatch chart, adapted here with permission, resulted from work done by the Chattahoochee Coldwater Fishery Foundation, a nonprofit organization which Chris (along with Georgia DNR biologist Lisa Klein and U.S. Fish and Wildlife Service biologist and author Don Pfitzer) established in 1998 to study aquatic life in the tailwater. Years of stream sampling data (much of it the result of the work of volunteers from the fishing community) went into the making of this chart, and it is an invaluable resource for any tailwater fly fisher.

Tailwater spinning gear

Though many of the trout anglers that you meet on the Chattahoochee tailwater will be fly fishing, you'll find that spin fishing is also popular. In fact, spinning gear can allow you to fish from places (such as the river's bank) where using a fly rod might not be feasible.

Rods and reels: When choosing a spinning rod for the Chattahoochee tailwater, think about the lures you will be using. Usually that means in-line spinners or small plugs, typically with relatively light 4- or 6-lb. line. To handle that assignment, most tailwater spinning enthusiasts prefer light to ultralight rods in lengths of 5 ft. 6 in. to perhaps 7 ft.

My day-in, day-out spinning rod for trout fishing on the tailwater is a 6 ft. 6 in. medium-light rod. In fact, it's an old Shakespeare Wonderod that my wife gave me shortly after we married. As I recall, I'd been dropping hints about that rod for while, and she picked up on them and surprised me with the rod for a birthday present. That rod is older than my grown children, and it's lost a little bit of its showroom shine. But it has landed a lot of fish over the years, including many trout from the Chattahoochee. It does a great job casting small in-line spinners too. One of these days maybe I'll upgrade...maybe I should start dropping hints now for the next birthday!

The afore-mentioned rod is great for most stocked fish. But there will be days when the river's big browns are the target. Big fish want big meals, and that means large plugs – something like that 6-inch-long "brown trout" pattern crankbait I picked up the other day. I couldn't pass it up. That plug would be too much for the little Wonderod, so when I am ready to use it I'll pick up something a bit beefier. Think "bass rod," and you'll have the idea.

What about the reel? Open-face or closed-face is largely a matter of personal preference, though most serious tailwater trout anglers use open-face reels. You'll find good models to choose from in both styles. In any case, look for one with a drag that works smoothly at low drag settings, and make sure that it balances your rod.

Line: Either nylon or fluorocarbon line will do the job on tailwater spinning rigs. Color-wise, clear seems to be the favorite. As on the headwaters, the high-visibility fluorescent lines are often bypassed in favor of lower-vis versions. A hard-to-see line certainly can't hurt, particularly in the sometimes ultra-clear water near the dam.

What about line strength? In most cases, tailwater anglers use 4- or 6-lb. line. The more durable 6 lb. version does offer a bit extra in the areas of strength and sometimes abrasion resistance, and that can be helpful at times.

But some tailwater trout anglers go the other way and choose to fish with 2-lb. line. Such line is so small as to be essentially invisible, and that can pay off where fish are pressured or skittish. Certainly the very fine diameter of such lines makes them a dream to cast. Just don't forget and accidentally use a 4-lb. hookset while fishing with 2-lb. line!

What about fluorocarbon vs. nylon? Low-visibility nylon lines work well in the tailwater, but when it comes to invisibility in what is sometimes gin-clear water it's impossible to beat fluorocarbon. Modern fluoro lines are durable and have good knot strength, and that combined with the low visibility makes fluoro the material of choice in the minds of many trout anglers. Besides, their lower visibility means that you can go a little heavier in terms of line test without alerting the fish. That makes 6-lb. fluoro line perfectly feasible, even when fishing in clear water.

What's my personal preference? Given the choice, I tend to go with 6-lb. fluorocarbon. The little bit of extra strength provides a nice margin of error, if you will, and it's nice to know it's there when a larger fish hits. If I'm not using fluorocarbon, then I tend to favor one of the current crop of low-diameter, abrasion resistant 4-lb. nylon lines.

If I'm specifically targeting big browns, I may go with heavier line – perhaps 8 lb. or even 10-lb. fluoro. Should I hook into one of the big ones, the higher-test line provides a comforting bit of insurance.

Spinning lures for the upper tailwater

When spin fishing for trout in the Chattahoochee tailwater, you're almost certainly throwing lures designed to imitate minnows. These tailwater fish are looking for a good meal, and when "dinner" is on their minds a high-calorie minnow meal is hard to beat. That will be the case with recently stocked fish as well as with fish that have been in the river for a while, for it seems that these fish just instinctively pounce on anything which resembles a minnow (especially a small brown trout).

In-line spinners: You can easily imitate minnows with in-line spinners, the same lures on which many of us cut our fishing teeth. In-line spinners are among the easiest of all lures to fish, too – at its most simple, just cast them out and reel them in. They're great for beginners (especially kids) since the casting itself is fun and all it takes to animate the lure is to turn the crank on the reel. Favorites for the tailwater include Roostertails, Mepps spinners, and Blue Fox spinners, among others. Preferred colors include silver-and-white and silver-and-gold as well as color schemes that suggest rainbow or (especially) brown trout. But don't overlook other colors – and take a lesson from the bass guys and go bright for bright days but less bright (and maybe a little bigger too) if it's overcast or the water is off-color.

One thing to keep in mind when choosing in-line spinners is that trout tend to hold near the bottom. You want a lure that's heavy enough to get down to the fish. In shallow areas, lures in the 1/8 oz. range usually work. However, in deeper water, you'll be more successful with something heavier – say, a 3/16 or even 1/4-ounce lure. Of course, you can always add additional weight to the line

To fish in-line spinners, cast so that the current will carry the lure where you think the fish may be lurking. For a shallow retrieve, start cranking as soon as the lure hits the water. You may want to give the lure a little jerk just as you start the retrieve to get the spinner blade spinning.

To go deeper, count it down once it hits the water and then start the retrieve (again with a sharp tug to get the spinner going). Then, depending on what the fish seem to be wanting that particular day, vary the retrieve rate to allow the lure to flash and flutter as you bring it in.

When probing the deeper pools, it's hard to beat a fast-sinking lure like a Little Cleo. These spoon-style lures sink quickly and show good action even with a slower retrieve, making them ideal for some of the deeper places on the river. After making the cast, allow the lure to sink to near the bottom and then retrieve it slowly enough to keep it as close to the bottom as you can but still fast enough to make it wiggle and wobble as it should.

Crankbaits: Another favorite for the Chattahoochee tailwater is the crankbait. Like in-line spinners, these lures imitate baitfish (or perhaps crawfish). They're available in a range of sizes, and different versions are designed to float and dive or to sink and run at various depths. Something with a length of two to four inches works well for general trout fishing on the tailwater, while bigger ones will attract bigger fish.

Crankbaits are easy to fish on the tailwater. At its simplest, as with the in-line spinners, just cast them out and reel them in, allowing the lure's design to provide the animation. As with in-line spinners, that makes them good lures to put in the hands of beginning anglers, especially kids.

Veteran crankbait enthusiasts take it one step further, adding additional action by varying the retrieve. For example, add short jerks of the rod tip to give the lure an altogether different sort of action. Once you get the hang of this, you can make the lure dance a zigzag path through the water.

As with the in-line spinners, one very effective crankbait color scheme for the tailwater emphasizes oranges and yellows with a touch of red – the colors of small brown trout, now a significant food for bigger brown trout in many stretches of the upper tailwater. Look for lures sporting "firetiger," "brown trout," or similar color schemes.

Jig-and-grub combinations: One more lure that can sometimes work well on the tailwater is a simple painted jig head with a white, yellow, chartreuse, or black curly-tailed grub attached. Jig heads with painted-on eyes seem to have an edge over those with no eyes. Cast across the current and then retrieve through holding water or near areas of cover. Use a moderately fast retrieve – those jig heads are heavy and sink fast, especially when tied to light line.

Because curly-tailed grubtails are available in so many colors, it's easy to fine-tune jig-and-grub combos to suit the conditions at hand. You'll want to carry the grubtails in several different colors, making your choice based on prevailing river conditions.

How to fish these lures: You have no doubt gotten the sense that there are several ways to fish in-line spinners, small crankbaits, jig/grub combinations and similar lures.

Many simply cast across-and-down and then retrieve upstream, imitating a minnow's behavior as it swims or looks for cover. It's a proven technique that works well.

But that's not the only technique that works. Another method is to cast "up-and-across" the current, then retrieve at a speed that lets you keep contact with the lure (just a hair faster than the current) in order to maintain a tight line between rod tip and lure. When fished this way, the lure imitates a disoriented baitfish that is being swept along by the current – easy pickings for a waiting trout.

If you're in an area suspected to hold big browns, don't hesitate to cast close to cover. Drop your lure as close to that cover as you dare. If you get lucky, the payoff just might be the fish of a lifetime.

Regardless of where you're fishing on the tailwater, always try to think like a trout. If *you* were a trout, where would you hang out? Pay particular attention to potential holding water – pools below rock ledges, the edges of gravel bars, the seams between currents, or anywhere else that you notice any sort of change in the river's flow.

Also remember that the fish may be holding in sheltered or protected

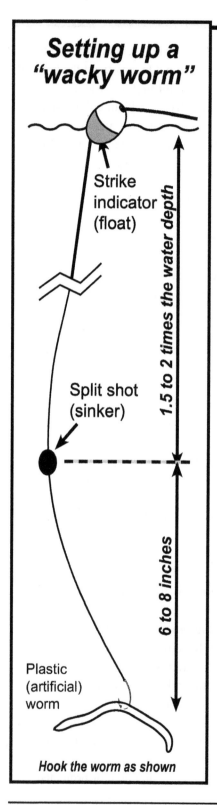

Setting up a "wacky worm"

Strike indicator (float)

1.5 to 2 times the water depth

Split shot (sinker)

6 to 8 inches

Plastic (artificial) worm

Hook the worm as shown

places behind rocks or in blow-downs – places that offer good cover while allowing the current to bring food right to the trout's front door. Such trout are eager to pounce on an unsuspecting baitfish. Once you find such an "ambush" spot, work it carefully. Cast upstream and let the lure drift down to the cover as if it's an unaware baitfish, and let the current swing it into position naturally. Few trout can resist such an offering.

One more possibility: the "wacky worm": Here's another possibility – a 2- or 3-inch-long worm (artificial or natural, depending on what's legal) hooked through the middle and rigged "wacky" style on a size 10 or 12 hook, as shown at left. Add weight to get the worm down deep, and attach a float some distance above the weight, as shown. The float acts as a strike indicator. Cast toward the upper end of a run and let the current carry it through the run. It's the spinning angler's answer to the fly fisher's San Juan Worm, and it's great for young anglers. Strikes can be hard and fast, so be ready!

Remember: In the artificials-only section from GA 20 downstream to the boat ramp at Medlock Bridge Park, the worm must be truly "artificial." Natural (digestible) baits (including Powerbait) are not permitted on artificials-only water.

Bait-fishing set-ups

The portion of the tailwater from the GA 20 bridge downriver to the boat ramp at Medlock Bridge Park has been designated as artificials-only. However, on the rest of the tailwater (except for the Delayed Harvest section of the lower tailwater from Sope Creek to U.S. 41 during the DH season) the regulations currently allow fishing with bait.

Bait fishing, where it's allowed, can be an effective way to introduce young or beginning anglers to the fun of fishing for Chattahoochee trout. Simply set up a float rig with an easy-to-see bobber, a sinker, and a bait hook and let young anglers drift it through pools and runs. This bait set-up can be essentially identical to the "wacky worm" rig as described on the preceding page.

What kind of bait is best? You'll find strong opinions about that one! Many swear by corn, and you'll see it used a lot. It works not because trout like to eat corn but because a kernel of corn bears a striking resemblance to a fish egg.

And yet as effective as corn can sometimes be, the most dedicated bait anglers will tell you in no uncertain terms that it pales in comparison to natural baits such as worms or crickets. A bit of nightcrawler seems to be especially effective.

Powerbait can be effective too and is usually available in a variety of colors and forms. The round versions, which resemble fish eggs, are a trout favorite.

But you don't have to go fancy to have baitfishing success on tailwater trout. As many young anglers will affirm, even a small ball of bread mashed onto the hook will sometimes do the job.

Other gear you'll want to have

I think that covers the "tackle" side of gearing up. But there are a number of other things you'll also want to carry with you to make your tailwater trips as enjoyable as possible.

PFD ("life jacket"): One of the best things you can do to enhance your safety on a tailwater is to wear a PFD, or personal flotation device (a fancy way of saying "life jacket).

This is so important that it's actually addressed by the regulations. They state that any time you are floating the river (in a canoe, kayak, or even a float tube), you are *required by law* to have a Coast Guard approved life jacket with you. Additionally, from the dam down to the GA 20 bridge you are further required to actually *wear* that life jacket on your body. It's not enough just to have it in your possession; from the dam down to GA 20, you must actually be wearing it on your person. That's the law...and yes, they do check. Ignoring this can earn you a citation. I've seen it happen.

Before we go on, let's take a moment and talk about that matter of wearing the life jacket vs. just having it with you. Above GA 20, you *are* required to wear it. That's not negotiable. But come on now. Isn't it a pain to have to wear a life jacket?

And what about on that portion of the river below GA 20, where the law doesn't say that you have to actually have it on? Do you really *have* to wear the darned thing?

I get asked that question at seminars and workshops, and here's my take on it. Trouble on the water happens quickly. If you suddenly find yourself in a bad way, is that the time to worry about finding and putting on a life jacket? Probably not. For that reason, experienced tailwater anglers *wear* that life jacket pretty much all the time when floating. Some (myself included) often wear a low-profile PFD even when wading.

I hope you'll never need your PFD. But if you ever do, you'll need it in a hurry...not two minutes from now. So yes, I say *wear* that PFD.

Waders: One reality of fishing the Chattahoochee tailwater is that the water is going to be chilly. How chilly? Remember that it's drawn from deep in the lake and comes out of the dam at around 50 degrees. That's not chilly. That's *cold!*

I've seen people wet-wading the tailwater, even in the frigid water near the dam. Guide Stephen Tomasovich, whom you'll meet a little later in this book, says that he almost always wades the tailwater "wet" and has, in fact, done so at least one day during every month of the year. He has my respect. Me, I'll be wearing waders...and probably longjohns too!

There are two schools of thought on wader material for the tailwater. One says to go with neoprene, and neoprene is definitely a good insulator. The problem is that it's almost too good an insulator. Specifically, it doesn't breathe and can thus leave you feeling clammy when you sweat inside the waders, which you will do even during cool weather.

The solution is to go with breathable waders worn over long pants with an insulating layer of fleece or long johns underneath. That's what I do.

When thinking about wading attire, don't forget your feet. Some parts of the tailwater (especially near the dam) are known for slick rocks, so be sure that your footwear is up to the challenge. It's hard to beat the grip provided by stud-equipped boots.

Finally, cinch a wading belt around the top of your waders. It will keep cold water from entering in the untimely event of a stumble or fall.

Warm clothes: Many first-time tailwater anglers misjudge just how very cold the river can be. Even on a steamy day in the middle of summer, when it's 97 degrees in the parking lot, the water will still be cold.

I remember one day below Buford Dam. When I pulled into the parking lot, the temperature literally was 97 degrees. Simply putting on waders worked up a sweat. There was no way, I told myself, that I'd need a long-sleeved shirt once I was in the water.

Was I ever wrong. After only 45 minutes of fishing I was so cold that I was shivering. I left the river and returned to the car for warmer clothes. I was sweating by the time I reached the parking lot and sweating even more as I walked back to the river. But later, back in that cold water, I was glad to have made the change.

What sort of clothing is best? Start with your feet. I wear wool or wool-blend socks over thinner polypropylene "wicking" socks to keep my feet from getting cold and feeling damp. Nothing will make you feel cold faster than cold, damp feet. Also make sure that your wading shoes are not so tight that they reduce circulation. That's another sure recipe for cold feet.

Below the waist, and depending on the season, you may want to layer a bit and wear something warm under long pants, as noted earlier. Above the waist, a light long-sleeve shirt over a tee shirt is usually enough. If I'm in the float tube, I'll pack a light rain jacket in one of the cargo pockets in case I get chilly (or it rains). If it's cold, simply add layers as needed.

Finally, carry a change of clothing in the car. Just in case.

Don't forget your gloves...: One item that I've come to appreciate a great deal over the years, especially when fishing during the colder parts of the year, is a set of lightweight wool or fleece fishing gloves. To avoid becoming chilled, it's extremely important to keep your hands warm. Most experienced tailwater anglers prefer the style with no fingertips, since that makes it easy to tie knots.

...or your hat: You don't want to overlook your head. Wear a hat. It protects you from the sun in summer and, during fall and winter, reduces heat loss from your head.

Wading staff: Many wade fishers like to use a wading staff when wading the tailwater, particularly when wading below Buford Dam. It provides an additional point of support (and a great sense of stability) to boost confidence and help you move around the river.

While almost any sort of solid and stable walking stick can be used as a wading staff, the favorite of many tailwater anglers is a collapsible aluminum staff that's easy to open when needed. When not in use, it goes into a holster on your wading belt.

Water and snacks: Whether wading or floating, carry snacks and a bottle of water. You'll be expending a lot of energy moving around the river (and sometimes just trying to stay warm), and a snack can refuel you when you need it. Granola bars or similar packaged snacks are simple and convenient and store easily in your fishing vest or float tube.

Filing a flight plan: Though you may not think about it when fishing on an urban river like the Chattahoochee tailwater (after all, who could get lost on a river that flows through a major city?) it's still important to leave a "flight plan" that tells someone where you plan to be fishing in case you don't get home by the time you're supposed to return.

Will you ever need it? I hope not. But should something go wrong (for example, if an unexpected release leaves you stranded on Bowmans Island) then that itinerary will let others know where to look for you or where to send help.

Upper tailwater access

There's a great deal of public access to the Chattahoochee tailwater.

Starting at the top end, at Buford Dam, access is via the Lower Pool West recreation area, a Corps of Engineers site. A parking fee is required to park in this area.

As you move down the river from the dam, there are numerous access points available to you. For instance, the National Park Service offers great river access through the many Chattahoochee River National Recreation Area "units" that are strung along the river from below Buford Dam to well inside I-285, Atlanta's perimeter highway. Hiking trails within the CRNRA units connect you with numerous put-in or take-out points; you'll find detailed info on these trails in HIKING THE HOOCH, a complete guide to the trails of CRNRA. It's published by Chattahoochee Media and is available from the webstore at chattahoocheemedia.com. Check these CRNRA units, for they really do offer a great way to get to the river and its trout.

Remember that a parking fee or annual pass (or an appropriate federal pass) is required to park at CRNRA sites. Also note that a Georgia state park pass is not valid for parking within CRNRA units.

Additional river access is available through city or county parks along the river, and such parks generally do not charge a parking fee. The list of amenities at such locations can vary, though most of them offer river access.

Before we look at the fishing...

We're almost ready to begin our look at the trout fishing opportunities awaiting you on the upper tailwater. But before we do, there's still one more thing we need to consider. We need to take a look at understanding the all-important matter of water releases from Buford Dam, and that's what we'll focus on next. □

Tubes on the tailwater?

While many tailwater anglers wade, others enjoy the increased mobility provided by a float tube. A tube allows you to move through stretches that are too deep for wading, and it also serves as a wading crutch to help you maintain your footing and balance.

Various parts of the Chattahoochee tailwater (upper as well as lower) lend themselves to float tubing. Later on, we'll mention several areas where using a float tube is feasible.

A complete discussion of float tubing is beyond the scope of this book. However, here are some things to keep in mind:

- It's always SAFETY FIRST in a float tube! If you are at all uncomfortable using one, then simply don't do it. There's no shame in saying that a tube is not for you.

- Float tubes are considered to be watercraft, so you must have a life preserver. But it's important to *wear* it on your body vs. simply *having* it with you somewhere. I *always* wear my PFD when I'm in the float tube, no matter where I'm fishing, and I hope that you will do the same thing.

- Most prefer round tubes to U-shaped tubes for moving water. All things being equal, a round tube tends to be more stable.

- Float tube fins are *not* intended for use on moving water and should *not* be used on any part of the tailwater. There's too much risk of catching a fin tip under a rock. Instead, for maneuvering, carry a set of plastic ping-pong paddles. It won't be pretty, but it works.

- You may get chilly if sitting in a float tube for any length of time. Dress accordingly. Wear warmer clothes (especially below the waist) than you would if wading under the same conditions.

- Remember that your safety on the river is *your responsibility* and yours alone. Always think "safety first" when fishing this or any other water from a float tube. ☐

Dealing with releases

To fish the Chattahoochee below Buford Dam, you must first understand release schedules

Fishing on the Chattahoochee tailwater rises and sets by the water release schedules at Buford Dam and Morgan Falls dams. What happens at Buford Dam directly affects what happens on the upper tailwater. In addition, Buford Dam indirectly affects what happens on the lower tailwater below Morgan Falls Dam (since everything released from Buford Dam must eventually pass through Morgan Falls too).

When water is not being released, the tailwater is a generally peaceful flow that's a great place to fish. But when the turbines get going and the water starts to flow, the character of the river changes dramatically as the peaceful lamb becomes a rampaging lion ready to devour anything that happens to be in its way.

Overly dramatic? Well, okay, I took a little poetic license there. But only a little...for once a release begins, "in the river" is definitely not a place you want to be.

What happens during a release from Buford Dam?

What is it like on the river when water is being released? Anyone who has been caught on any river during a release from an upriver dam will likely describe it as pure terror, and that may be an understatement.

On the upper portion of the Chattahoochee tailwater, for example, the water can come up as much as 11 feet in a relatively short time. It's not like a sudden wall of water; rather, it's an inexorable and unrelenting (and surprising quick) rise in the level of the river.

You don't want to be in the river when all of that's happening.

It is enlightening (and a little bit scary, truth be told) to actually watch a water release take place in real time. On the upper tailwater, just a few hundred yards downriver from Buford Dam, you can do just that without risking life or limb by viewing the release from the safety of the footbridge over the river just below the spillway. That bridge is just a moment's walk from the upper parking area at the Corps of Engineers' Lower Pool recreation area. Show up at the bridge about 15 minutes before the release begins, and you'll be able to see the entire show (the sirens, the rising river, and the disappearing banks and shoals) as it unfolds before your eyes.

The thing that will strike you as you watch a release taking place is just how quickly the water comes up. You'll then understand what the Corps of Engineers announcement means when it says that the waters below Buford Dam are "subject to rapid rises, turbulent flows, and are dangerous."

Following the start of a release, and as the release continues, the water will be high and turbulent. Eventually, however, the release will end and the water will recede. Close to the dam, that return-to-normal doesn't take long. At Bowmans Island (right below Buford Dam) the river will return to non-release levels very quickly. But downstream several miles, at (say) the Jones Bridge access point, the water will recede much more slowly.

Upper tailwater release schedules

Step one when fishing any tailwater is to check the water release schedule and to understand what the release schedule means. The short version is that the closer you are to a dam, the sooner you'll feel the impact of water releases (and the quicker things will return to normal when it's done).

To check the planned water release schedule as it affects the *upper portion* of the Hooch tailwater (from Buford Dam to Bull Sluice Lake and Morgan Falls dam), call the Buford Dam water release info line at (770) 945-1466. A recorded announcement will give you the tentatively scheduled starting and ending times for that day's releases. Additionally, in the area immediately around Buford Dam, you can listen to a low-pow-

High-water mark!

Under extreme conditions, how much can the river come up? Check out these high-water marks at the McGinnis Ferry Boat ramp!

er AM radio station (tune your radio to 1610) that continuously broadcasts information on water releases.

Factoring Buford Dam releases into your fishing

The first thing to keep in mind on any tailwater, including this one, is safety. On the upper Hooch tailwater, that means that you must understand water releases from Buford Dam.

Anglers have died on the Hooch because they forgot (or simply did not know or understand) just how critical it is to be aware of what's happening (and what is about to happen) on the water release front. But experienced Chattahoochee tailwater anglers know the importance of understanding how releases impact the river, and they plan their trips accordingly.

For example, let's say you're fishing near Bowman's Island, which is directly downstream from Buford Dam. You know that a release from Buford Dam is scheduled for 3:30 in the afternoon. Since you know that water will be released at 3:30, you plan your fishing so that you are *out of the river* some time *before* 3:30 – say, by 3:15. You definitely want to err on the cautious side when working around releases.

TIME TO IMPACT OF WATER FROM BUFORD DAM

Estimates only. Actual times depend on many factors including river conditions and the magnitude of the release

Location on the river	Miles from dam	Estimated time to impact (hh:mm)
Buford Dam	0.0	Immediate
GA 20 bridge	2.5	0:30
Settles Bridge	4.7	0:30
McGinnis Ferry	8.5	1:45
Rogers Bridge	11.4	2:30
Abbotts Bridge	13.0	3:00
Medlock Bridge	17.5	3:30
Jones Bridge	19.6	4:00
Island Ford	27.7	6:30

Times are only estimates of approximate time to impact of released water. Actual downriver impact times may vary depending on factors such as precipitation, river level, and quantity of water being released. Be cautious!

Set the alarm on your watch or cellphone, and as release time approaches, don't get distracted.

What do you do when that alarm goes off? Do you have time to make a few more casts? No. The alarm is telling you it's *time to go.* There is no "few-more-minutes-of-fishing" that's worth the risk of getting caught in a rising river below a dam.

When planning your exit strategy, remember that it will take time to move from where you're fishing to where you will exit the river. Don't forget to factor that travel time into your planning, and note that it definitely takes longer to move upriver (against the current) than it does to wade downriver (with the current).

The bottom line is this: No matter where you fish on the tailwater, the best approach by far is to be overly cautious. Understand the release schedules, plan your fishing accordingly, and *stick to that plan no matter what.* When your schedule says it's time to get off the water, then *get off the water.* Doing anything else when a release is coming down the river toward you can get you killed.

How long till a release impacts where you're fishing?

If you think about what happens to the river during a release, you'll realize that a release does not affect the entire river all at once. Clearly, the impact is felt soonest (within minutes) close to the dam (and that includes the river around Bowmans Islans). But the farther downriver you are, the more time you'll have before the water starts to rise.

The chart on the preceding page will give you an idea of how long, on average, it takes for a release from Buford Dam to begin to be felt at various points downriver. The info is based on numbers from the Chattahoochee River National Recreation Area, part of the National Park Service, and from other experienced users of the river.

But if you do much research, you'll discover that various charts may differ greatly in detail, especially as you move further downriver from the dams. Lots of factors can affect the time between a release and when that release begins to impact any given point on the river. Those factors include the magnitude of the release as well as the condition of the river at the time of the release. Always give yourself a good safety margin.

Downriver impacts

Obviously, the most immediate impacts of any release from any dam will be felt on the portion of river closest to that dam. Note that on the upper Chattahoochee tailwater, one of the most popular fishing areas (around Bow-

---

man's Island) is almost in the dam's shadow. Released water impacts the river near Bowman's Island very quickly – within minutes.

But what if you're fishing some distance downstream?

If you look into the question of how long it takes water released from Buford Dam to impact various points on the river below the dam, you'll find a lot of highly variable information. Estimates of time-to-first-impact are often based on the estimator's personal experience, on accepted average water flow rates (in miles per hour) and so on. In truth, the actual time it takes water to reach any given point on the tailwater will depend on a number of factors, including the level of the river at the time of the release, the quantity and duration of any recent precipitation, the size of the release, and possibly even the speed and direction of the wind.

Clearly, predicting when released water will impact any particular point on the river is something of an inexact science. Thus, it seems prudent to go with generally agreed-upon *minimum* times to impact. That's the safest thing to do.

Rise and fall times following a release

We have noted that a water release does not impact the entire river all at once. The released water has to flow downriver, and as it moves along the river's course the pulse of water tends to spread itself out a bit. That means that the rise and fall of the river's level will be sharpest near the dam but more gradual the farther downriver you go.

Here's how that might work in practice. Again, let's say you're interested in fishing at Jones Bridge. You know that a release is scheduled from Buford Dam that afternoon starting at 4 p.m. and ending at 6 p.m.

Near the dam (say, at the upper end of Bowman's Island) the water will rise and recede very quickly. The top graph on page 147 shows how that might look in terms of river level; in fact, the chart shows actual river height data at the dam for a release that took place on June 6 around 4 p.m. The delay between the release of water from the dam and the rise of the river immediately below the dam is essentially zero. In other words, you can figure that for all intents and purposes, what happens at the dam will immediately be felt at Bowman's Island

But what happens some distance downriver? What can you expect if you are fishing at Jones Bridge?

The Jones Bridge area is located about 20 river miles below Buford Dam. The bottom graph shows the river height at the USGS gauge located at the Highway 141 bridge about two river miles above the CRNRA's Jones Bridge Unit. That's the nearest gauge to Jones Bridge. Note that the water began to rise on that gauge about four hours following the start of the release at Buford Dam, and note too that the rise was more gradual than what you saw further upriver.

Since this gauge is two miles upriver from the Jones Bridge Unit, there's going to be a short delay (around a half hour or so) until the rising water is felt at your fishing spot at Jones Bridge.

Equally significant is what the graphs reveal about how the water level in the river drops following the end of the release.

In our example, the release at Buford Dam stopped very suddenly. Once that release ended, the water level in the river directly below the dam dropped very quickly. That means that (for example) the area between the dam and the top of Bowman's Island would be back to normal and wadable again within a fairly short time.

But what if you're interested in wade fishing at Jones Bridge?

At Jones Bridge, the river will drop much more slowly than it did near

A PFD ("Personal Flotation Device") will help keep you safe on the tailwater. In fact, you are required to wear (not just have) one when fishing above the GA 20 bridge. But I'd wear it all the time.

the dam. In fact, the graph tells us that in this case it took the water at the 141 gauge about 15 hours to fall back down to its pre-release level. If you were planning to wade fish at Jones Bridge *following* the release from Buford Dam, that can help you figure out when the river at Jones Bridge might return to a wadable and fishable level.

Figuring all of this out does indeed get a little complex sometimes, but it's something that you absolutely have to do.

Putting gauge data to work

To become comfortable with how all of this impacts the river's level (and thus how it impacts your fishing), you'll want to spend some time looking at the USGS river level data for the area where you want to fish. Check out the gauge locations to see how relevant they are to where you'll be fishing; you can identify the gauge locations on the map that you'll find at **maps. waterdata.usgs.gov/mapper/index.html?state=ga** on the web.

Additionally, compare release times with subsequent water levels downstream. Look at how the level at one point can eventually determine the level at another point further downriver. By doing so, you will get a better idea of what to expect.

Gauge data is certainly useful. But you still can't beat checking out the river with your own eyes. With all the variables that come into play, looking at the water firsthand is the only way to *really* know what the river is doing at any particular point in time. If you look at it and don't like what you see, then don't get into the river – no matter what the online gauge data might be telling you.

Can you trust the release predictions?

Clearly, obtaining and utilizing information on planned water releases is critical when planning a fishing outing on the Chattahoochee tailwater. Fortunately, tentative or "planned" release data is available, as we have seen.

But can you count on that predicted release data? Is release information carved in stone? Not necessarily. As the voice on the recording so succinctly puts it, "these schedules can change with hydropower demands or

USGS gauge data illustrates the lag between a release at Buford Dam and the water impact at a point downstream – here, at the gauge at Medlock Bridge about two river miles above the popular Jones Bridge fishing area. There is about a four hour delay between release and first impact and 15 hours between the end of the release and the time when flows near Jones Bridge drop back to a minimum. For an even more complete picture, the bottom chart shows data for the same time period for Island Ford, a few miles further downriver.

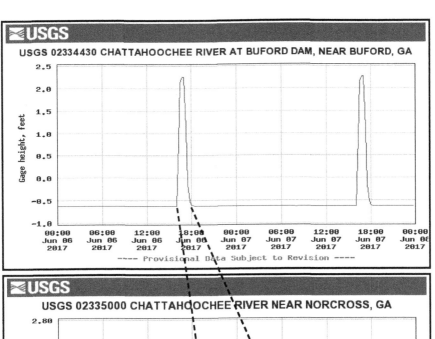

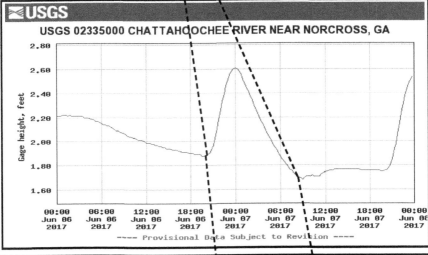

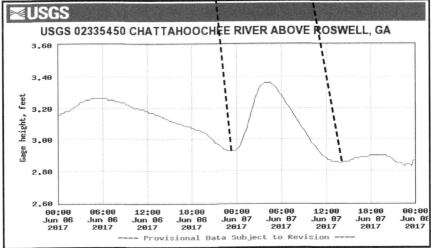

equipment failure." In other words, while the announced schedule is usually accurate, you don't necessarily want to bet your life on it.

Thus, there's one more thing to add to your Chattahoochee tailwater river-awareness package, and that is to stay attuned to what the river itself is telling you when you're actually out there in it.

Can you tell if the water's coming up?

While published release predictions are a good place to start, don't overlook that little footnote which says that they can change. All sorts of things, including equipment failure and changes in power demand, can affect the schedule. Thus, when you're on the tailwater, you should always be attuned to the river and aware of your surroundings.

Near the dam, the first sign that a water release is coming will usually be the sound of a siren. The Corps of Engineers sounds sirens prior to and during the early part of a release, and if you hear the siren you should *immediately* get out of the river.

But sirens are machines, and machines sometimes break down. Generally, the wailing sirens will give you some warning. But just in case it's a bad day for the siren system, you should be aware of other warning signs too.

One early sign may be a change in

Close, but (fortunately) no cigar

It was the first time I'd fished just below Buford Dam. I'd been invited by a seasoned veteran, and since I was the newbie, I was following his lead.

"There's a water release at 5 p.m.," he told me as we started. "We'll fish as long as we can."

Release time neared – and then came the first siren. "Time to go!" my friend said, immediately heading for shore. But being the newbie, I made one more cast and then followed.

The second siren sounded, the release began, and within a minute I felt the difference on my waders. I was only yards from shore, and what had been ankle-deep when I started was knee-deep by the time I covered those last few feet. And by the time I'd gathered my wits on dry land a few minutes later, the river was up a good three feet and still rising.

I realized then that I shouldn't have made that "one more cast." If I'd been much farther from shore, I'd have been in trouble.

These days I'm older and wiser, and I give myself plenty of time to get out before a release begins.

how the river sounds. Particularly near the dam, you may literally hear the change. Trust your ears, and take no chances if things start to sound more "rushy," for lack of a better word, than before.

If you're a little ways downstream from the dam, another sign that the water is coming up may be a slight clouding of the water. As the flow rate begins to pick up, the increasing current will pick up fine sediment and thus "muddy up" the water. Also look for the appearance of leaves, sticks and

Key tailwater gauge locations

Several USGS gauges monitor the level of the Chattahoochee tailwater below Buford Dam and below Morgan Falls Dam. Use the gauge numbers given below to access gauge data at waterdata.usgs.gov.

You can find a map showing the locations of the various USGS gauges on the Chattahoochee tailwater at this site:

https://maps.waterdata.usgs.gov/mapper/index.html?state=ga

GAUGES BELOW BUFORD DAM

Gauge location: At **Buford Dam** (below the dam):
Gauge identifier: USGS 02334430 CHATTAHOOCHEE RIVER AT BUFORD DAM, NEAR BUFORD, GA

Gauge location: At **McGinnis Ferry** (0.5 miles upriver from CRNRA McGinnis Ferry unit)
Gauge identifier: USGS 02334654 CHATTAHOOCHEE R 0.5 MI US MCGINNIS FY

Gauge location: At **GA 141 Bridge** (Medlock Bridge) about two river miles above CRNRA Jones Bridge access
Gauge identifier: USGS 02335000 CHATTAHOOCHEE RIVER NEAR NORCROSS, GA

Gauge location: Near **Island Ford** (just upriver from CRNRA Island Ford Unit)
Gauge identifier: USGS 02335450 CHATTAHOOCHEE RIVER ABOVE ROSWELL, GA

GAUGES BELOW MORGAN FALLS DAM

Gauge location: At (below) **Morgan Falls Dam**
Gauge identifier: USGS 02335815 CHATTAHOOCHEE RIVER BELOW MORGAN FALLS DAM, GA

Gauge location: Near **Cochran Shoals** (at Powers Ferry and I-285)
Gauge identifier: USGS 02335880 CHATT R AT POWERS FY & I-285 NR ATLANTA, GA

Gauge location: US 41 bridge at **lower end of Delayed Harvest water**
Gauge identifier: USGS 02335990 CHATTAHOOCHEE RIVER AT US 41, AT ATLANTA, GA

Dealing with the unthinkable

Caught in a release!

What if the unthinkable happens and you are caught in rising water? It might happen if an unscheduled release takes place...or if you decide to make that fateful "one more cast" (we've all been tempted) and then run out of time to get off the river.

Should that happen on this or any tailwater, experts agree that there are things you can do to increase your odds of survival. Here are some suggestions, including several from the TVA.

First, stay calm. That's easy to say, but it's critical in a situation such as this.

Second, immediately drop everything you're carrying – even your rod. You've got other more important things to worry about (notably your life) and you don't want to be distracted by fishing tackle.

Try to float on your back, feet pointed downstream. That helps you deal with rocks while reducing the risk of getting your feet trapped.

Do not try to swim upstream. You'll exhaust yourself. Instead, try to swim diagonally toward shore.

Do not try to stand up until you reach a shallow area of slow current.

If you crawl from the river only to find yourself on an island or large rock, don't try to swim from there to shore. Stay where you are and signal for help. Many carry a small whistle in a pocket against just such an eventuality, knowing that the shrill blast of the whistle will be easy for rescuers to hear.

other debris in flow lines on the surface. These things show up following a release because rising water picks up debris which was high and dry when the river was low.

The increase in the amount of this floating debris, which may of course include things besides leaves and twigs, is sometimes very obvious and should never be ignored.

"When you see a tennis ball floating by," notes Chattahoochee guide Chris Scalley of River Through Atlanta, "then you know

Anatomy of a release

What actually happens during a water release from Buford Dam? To find out, I went to the footbridge over the spillway the other day, arriving about 4:30 to observe a release set to begin at 4:55.

Here's how it unfolded.

4:55   First siren sounded

4:58   Second siren sounded, and the sound coming from upriver at the dam definitely changed.

5:02   Third siren sounded and the flow picked up noticeably within seconds.

5:07   The water was up significantly and continued to rise.

The siren continued to sound every 4 to 5 minutes for close to a half hour.

that the river is probably coming up."

Any shift the sound of the flowing water may well indicate some change in the rate of flow. Similarly, if you begin to sense an increased tug on your waders, check to be sure that conditions have not changed.

Be aware of how your surroundings look too. For example, pick out a partially submerged rock, noting the water level on it. Glance at that rock periodically. If the water starts to come up on that rock, exit the river.

One long-time tailwater angler says that when wading anywhere on the tailwater, he will take a $50 bill and place it under a rock somewhere near the water's edge.

"I don't want to lose fifty bucks," he says, "so if I think the water's starting to rise then I get out of the river fast to recover the cash."

I've never been completely sure whether that's really what he does, but his point is well taken.

Remember: If you sense that things appear to be changing (even if you have not heard a siren), then the only smart thing to do is to exit the river. You don't want to take chances with rising water.

A final thought on safety

Please don't let this discussion of water releases from Buford Dam keep you from experiencing the great fishing that the upper Chattahoochee tailwater has to offer. But do tell yourself that you'll *always keep safety first,* that you will check the planned release schedule, that you'll always have your PFD, that you'll give yourself plenty of time to get off the river before the water begins to rise, and that you'll stick to your plan no matter what.

That's a lot to remember, but it's all important.

If you do those things, you can reasonably look forward to enjoyable fishing on the Chattahoochee tailwater.

Now: On to the tailwater

The Chattahoochee tailwater is much too big and much too variable to even attempt to look at it in a single section. Thus, the pages that follow break it down into manageable stretches with comments and observations on each to help you with trip planning and fishing.

In the remaining portion of this section, we'll cover the upper tailwater starting at Buford Dam and working downriver to Morgan Falls Dam.

Then, in the section which follows that, we'll take a similar look at the lower tailwater below Morgan Falls Dam and at the river's Delayed Harvest trout fishery, which extends from Sope Creek down to US 41.

First, however, let's answer a question. ☐

"Is the river clean?"

That question comes up frequently when people talk about the Chattahoochee tailwater. You may even have asked it yourself. Here's a look at one part of the answer.

On urban rivers such as the Chattahoochee, there is one inescapable reality that can't be ignored: the more the river flows through urbania, the more urbania will have an impact on the river's water quality.

That means that in addition to understanding how water levels and release schedules impact the river, you must also consider something called "turbidity."

Turbidity (defined as the cloudiness of the water) is important to tailwater anglers for a couple of reasons. For one thing, fish such as trout are primarily sight predators and must be able to see something if they're going to grab and eat it. Obviously, clear water makes it much easier for the fish to see things (including your flies or lures) as they pass within range.

A second (and very important) reason to pay attention to turbidity is that it has a direct correlation with the number of bacteria in the river – that is, the "bacteria count" that you hear about so frequently on the evening news.

There will always be bacteria in any stream, even a wild stream located far back in the mountains and many miles from the nearest town. But following a rain event the number of bacteria in an *urban* river can skyrocket. Factors which drive the increased counts include storm runoff (which may pick up nasty stuff like dog poop from countless urban yards) as well as overflow from leaky sewer systems or defective septic tanks. All of it eventually flows into the river.

When this occurs, the result will be a spike in bacteria counts – and your first clue that it's happening is often cloudy or murky water.

If the water is very "turbid" (that is, if the "turbidity" reading is 10 or greater) experienced Hooch trout fishers know that it's probably best to stay home and tie flies.

As it turns out, there's online data to guide you in the area of turbidity. You can access this data via the Chattahoochee Riverway BacteriALERT site:

http://ga2.er.usgs.gov/bacteria/default.cfm

You can learn a great deal more about turbidity and bacteria counts at the following site:

**http://ga.water.usgs.gov/projects/bacteria/
understanding-data.html**

One of the many things you'll learn from the information on that website is that *E. coli* counts of less than 177 colonies per 100 mL of water are apparently considered a "low risk" to health. Here's what the National Park Service site has to say about the matter:

"[A]s determined by the U.S. Forest Service, a person in direct contact with the river water (i.e. swimming, diving, wading) [when the *E. coli* count is less than 177 colonies per 100 mL of water] has a LOW chance of getting sick. The water is in full compliance with recreation water-quality criteria."

On the other hand, if *E. coli* counts are above 235 colonies per 100 mL of water, the site tells you that "contact with the river is NOT recommended."

Generally speaking, knowledgeable anglers won't wade the Chattahoochee unless they see "turbidity" readings of 9 or less – the lower the better. Remember that lower readings indicate clearer water and also that there appears to be a strong correlation between low turbidity and low *E. coli* counts.

Can you estimate turbidity based on how the water looks? Turbidity readings between 0 and about 2 or 3 suggest that you can easily see the bottom in 3 or 4 feet of water. Such low numbers are good news for anglers because they suggest that it will be relatively easy to see into the water and thus to move around the river. They're good news for fishing too because they tell you that fish will be able to spot the flies or lures that you're tossing their way.

Remember: When the numbers indicate a turbidity of 10 or above, you might not want to be in the river. ☐

Dam and Bowmans Island to Hatchery and GA 20

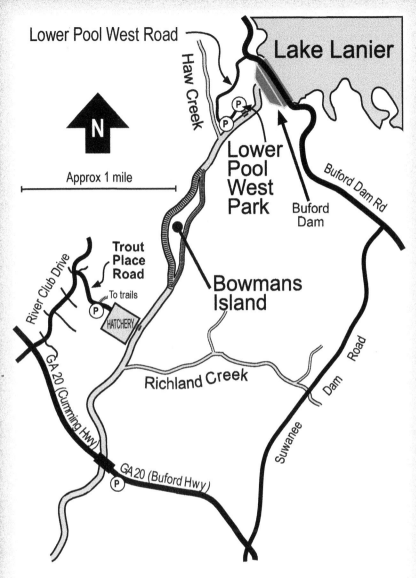

Overview

Dam, Bowmans Island, and Buford hatchery
(GA 20 shown for reference)
For clarity, only major features are shown here

Hot fishing... *cold* water!

Discover good trout fishing (and some truly cold water) in the shadow of Buford dam

It's 95 degrees in the parking lot at Lower Pool Park just below Buford Dam, and I'm sweating before I even unpack my waders. But I'm still wearing longjohns because the Chattahoochee right below the dam is as cold as this June day is hot. I'll just have to endure the heat for a few minutes – long enough to make the short hike from the car to the river. Then I'll be in the river, and the 50-ish-degree water will work its magic and take the edge off this sizzling summertime afternoon.

Long johns in the summertime? I laughed out loud the first time somebody advised that. But then I'd never before fished at "the dam." Now I'm glad I have 'em on. For even though the above-the-waterline part of me is basking in the balmy Georgia heat, the below-the-waterline part is definitely feeling the chill.

I look up to get my bearings, and what do I see but another fly fisher coming down the boat ramp toward the river. It's Chattahoochee trout guide Stephen Tomasovich, known on the river as "Big T."

I like Big T. He's one heck of a fisherman – and it seems like he's always smiling. We need more of that in this troubled world of ours.

Right now I see that he's got a fly rod in hand and a chest pack that's no doubt full of flies. Clearly he's going fishing.

But he's not wearing waders.

Wait. What? No waders? Has the lad lost his mind?

Big T is a relative newcomer to trout fishing and to the world of guiding others. In fact, he only picked up the sport about six years ago.

"I was driving over the river one day," he recalls with a smile, "and I saw somebody in a kayak fishing in the river. I decided I wanted to learn to do that," he adds, and so he did – first with a spinning rod and then with a fly rod. He took to his new passion quickly, and his enthusiasm grew to where he decided to change careers from the mortgage and insurance business to become a fly fishing guide.

These days, Big T is on the river close to 300 days a year and loves every minute of it. He does a little competitive fishing, too, but what he enjoys most is sharing his knowledge with others.

He sees a number of similarities between being a fishing guide and what he did in his previous career.

Stephen Tomasovich, a.k.a. "Big T," in one of his favorite places – knee deep in the Chattahoochee tailwater below Buford Dam.

"In each case, you're educating people," he says. "I was always very consultive in my approach to sales, and I still do that as a guide."

Guiding on the Hooch tailwater, in fact, has proven to be a perfect way for him to help anglers at all levels of their game. He enjoys working with beginners as well as experienced anglers, but he says that his favorite clients are always those who want to learn something new.

Sometimes that "new" something is a specialized technique such as Euro-nymphing, which works well in broken or faster water (of which there is much below the dam). At other times, it may be the use of dry/dropper combinations, which is good for those smoother glide-like stretches which are also very common below the dam. The possibilities are almost endless.

One of Big T's favorite excursions on the Chattahoochee tailwater is what he describes as "fishing Bowman's Island."

"When I say Bowman's Island, I mean the tailwater from the dam down to the bottom end of the island," he says. "I think of it as my home water, and I love it.

"This is not secret water by any means," he adds, looking around at the crowd of anglers (most of them fly fishing) stretched out along the length of this section of the river. Some are wading, many in long sleeves against the chill despite the summer heat. Others are in float tubes. There are even a couple of folks in kayaks. There must be something good going on here for all of these people to be fishing.

That brings us to the big question: Why does Big T like this water so much?

"It's by far the most populated section of river below Buford Dam," he says, and he's referring to the fish. The Georgia Department of Natural Resources stocks it regularly with significant numbers of catchable-sized rainbow trout. Years ago they stocked brown trout, too, but that hasn't been

---

"So where should I fish?"
(Hint: Take the path less traveled)

With so much room on the tailwater below Buford Dam and around Bowmans Island, it's no surprise that Big T gets that question a lot. Everybody wants to know how to find those special spots – and Big T has an answer for them.

"I tell them to notice where everyone else is wading," he says, "and then look for a good spot at least 10 feet away from that track."

If you plotted where people wade on the tailwater, he continues, it would look a lot like a hurricane prediction map.

"Most fly fishers, like most hurricanes, pretty much go along the same routes," Big T says. "But if you can get away from those routes, there's a good chance you'll be on water that most other folks don't bother to fish."

---

done since 2004. Why not? Because browns are now reproducing in the upper tailwater. In fact, all the browns that you catch are wild streamborn fish.

Whether fly fishing or spincasting, there's plenty to like along this section. Access from the bank is good in some areas, particularly near the Lower Pool recreation area or from some spots along the Bowmans Island Trail. And since parts of the river through here are relatively shallow when water is not being released, it's great water for wading anglers. On a sunny weekend day it's not unusual to count dozens of anglers out in the river. The fishing can be great, but it's not the place to go for solitude or to escape from the crowds.

And yet there are ways to avoid the multitudes. One is to fish during the week when pressure is not so high. You may see very few anglers on the water during the week, particularly if you can fish during the hours when others are at work. Once in a while you might even have it all to yourself.

Another strategy is to float this water rather than wade it. Many fly fishers do just that, using float tubes to help them get around the river. More about that in a moment.

Whether bank-sitting, wading, or floating, however, remember that you're fishing very close to a major dam. The impact of water releases will be felt almost the instant that a release begins. *Always check the release schedule before you go!* And remember: just like the recordings say, release schedules "are subject to change." Stay attuned to the feel and the sound of the water, and always have an exit strategy just in case. On this or any other water, remember that *you*, and you alone, are responsible for your own safety.

Once you're on the water, what then? What sort of flies and techniques work best on the part of the river nearest Buford Dam?

That's a key question and one that Big T works to address with many of his clients, teaching them what to use and when to use it under the many and varied conditions you'll encounter in the water below the dam.

Nymphing

Many fly fishers come to the dam with nymphing in mind, and that is indeed an effective way to fish this particular section of the tailwater. But it's nymphing with a difference, and the difference has to do with size. The reason? The strong, take-no-prisoners flows which the river endures during each release tend to scour the bottom, to put it mildly – and that means that you won't find as much subsurface insect habitat as you might see in other places farther downriver.

However, the rocky bottom of this part of the river does provide a lot of real estate for certain aquatic insects, particularly midges. Most every rock you pick up will have dozens upon dozens of tiny midge larvae clinging to its underside, and those larvae are the foundation for a constant supply of tiny but apparently very tasty insects.

To imitate those midges, you'll want something small. How small? Newcomers to Buford Dam are often amazed at the very tiny flies which experienced anglers use there. Size 16 is about as big as you'll see, and size 18s and even 20s are much more common in the fly boxes of those in the know. You'll do well with still smaller flies too – size 22, 24 and even 26 (if you can see them!), and that's all that some Hooch regulars use. But if you go with 18s you should be okay.

What about patterns? Which are best? The trout here seem to be much more concerned with size than with a specific pattern. In other words, if the midges you present are buggy looking and correctly proportioned, you may find that you're successful with a wide range of patterns.

One fly Big T specifically mentions is what he calls the Moonshine Midge, a fly of his own design. It's tied on a size 16 or 18 curved-shank hook with a copper-colored tungsten bead. The abdomen is black thread; it's ribbed with a single strand of copper-colored flash wrapped in an open spiral over the thread abdomen. He varies the spacing of the flash to vary the look of the finished fly, with closer spacing yielding a flashier look.

Big T often leaves a strand of the flash extending beyond the rear of the fly as a sort of tail.

"I find that it tends to fish better with that added," he says.

Sometimes he will tie the fly with no thorax, but "the majority of the time I do like to add a thorax," he says. Sometimes he uses black dubbing, but more often he prefers to go with peacock herl.

"The fuzziness of the herl provides a great gill effect," he says.

Big T has found the Moonshine Midge to be a good pattern in many different settings and in different seasons too.

"This pattern has been extremely effective and consistent regardless of the time of year I fish it. It has a low profile, sinks quickly, and fishes great." He adds, "It flat out spanks fish on the upper part of the Chattahoochee and has consistently caught fish everywhere else I have used it."

The Moonshine Midge is indeed a great pattern. Are there other patterns that you might want to have in your midge box for the dam too? Some that you'll hear anglers talking about a lot are Zebra Midges, Rainbow Warriors, and Blue Assassins (another personal favorite).

And what about the exact colors of those midges?

"Just about any midge color combination can work," Big T says. But he specifically mentions copper and black – several times, in fact – and the midges that he shares with me (and that subsequently account for a number of nice tailwater browns, at least until I lose 'em both to an inaccessible underwater snag) do in fact have copper and black in the mix somewhere.

Hey, I'm a fast learner. If those colors are good enough for Big T, then they are good enough for me. Certainly, the trout approve.

When fishing these tiny nymphs in the tailwater, especially near the dam, many fly fishers like to use some sort of a strike indicator. That can definitely help you pick up on strikes that you might otherwise miss.

One key to suc-

Fly fisher Ben Fairchild with a nice brown trout from the tailwater near Buford Dam.

cess when indicator nymphing is to choose an indicator that floats well and that you can see. Some like a floating plastic indicator, while others go with a yarn indicator of some sort. Either will do the job. As for color, choose the one that you can see best on the water – and the color you choose may be different from the one that's best for me. For instance, I find I can see yellow very easily on the water, but red causes me some problems. One of my regular fishing buddies, however, is the exact opposite.

Even with a high-floating indicator, you may miss strikes until you learn how quickly these trout can hit a midge emerger. The fish are adept at picking up and spitting out flies in a microsecond. Set the hook immediately if you even think you might be getting a take. This is something that many newcomers to the dam may have to think about, at least until it becomes automatic, but if you'll get in the habit of setting the hook quickly then you'll end up catching more trout.

Dry/dropper rigs

The indicator-based approach to fishing midge emergers works very well near the dam. But what would happen if you replaced the strike indicator with a high-floating dry fly?

Ask Big T. He does it all the time.

"It seems that because of the water's extreme clarity, a regular indicator will sometimes bother the fish," Big T says. Besides, he adds, every time a fish hits the indicator (and that happens surprisingly often) you'll wish that your indicator had a hook in it.

The solution to both problems is to replace the strike indicator with some sort of a high-floating dry. The dry thus becomes the indicators. That's a dry/dropper rig, and it works very well indeed.

Just how well it works was brought home to me one afternoon while I was fishing the tailwater with John Cherry, a regular on the Chattahoochee tailwater below the dam. As we geared up, I asked John what he would be using, and – like many knowledgeable near-the-dam fly fishers – he said he was going with a dry-and-dropper combo. For the dry, he chose a small and highly visible parachute-style Blue Winged Olive. Below it, on a piece of

"See all those midges flying?" Big T asks as he looks through his fly box for just the right pattern. "They're everywhere at the dam. That's why I fish such small flies." Popular midge emerger imitations for use near the dam include (left to right, with a dime for scale) the Moonshine Midge, Blue Assassin, Rainbow Warrior, Red Zebra Midge, and Black Zebra Midge.

7X tippet about 4 feet long, he tied on a size 18 midge emerger.

As I watched John fish with that dry/dropper rig, I noticed that he was getting a great many strikes on the dry – in some areas, almost as many as he was getting on the dropper. Even though we saw little in the way of surface activity, it was not at all unusual for him to draw a topwater strike or two in every stretch of water that he fished.

Dry/dropper rigs are also a favorite of Big T, and he enjoys teaching others when and how to use such a set-up.

He finds it especially effective right after a water release has ended.

"Because the water recedes so quickly," Big T says, "it's almost as if it pulls bugs out of the rocks and into the water. It certainly gets the bugs active, and that makes the fish active too."

Big T's setup of choice following a release is a multi-fly rig consisting of a dry and two droppers, each chosen with an eye to what's happening on the water. Usually, he says, that means a top fly such as Stimulator or an Elk Hair or Foamback Caddis, generally somewhere in the size 12 or 14 range. The dry serves as a the strike indicator, showing you what's going on below the water, but it can also draw strikes on its own.

Below that dry fly he attaches two small tungsten-beadhead midges – typically something such as a Moonshine Midge or Zebra Midge. The top emerger is usually at least 18 inches below the topmost dry fly, and the second emerger is another 18 inches or so below that.

What size should those droppers be? As with stand-alone nymphs, they'll occasionally be as large as size 16. But much more often they're size 18 or even smaller – sometimes as small as size 24 or 26.

As you've probably figured out by now, a tungsten bead is an important part of any midge emerger on the tailwater. The bead adds the weight needed to sink those tiny flies and get them down where the fish are.

As for bead color, Big T says that he prefers bright beads on bright days and more subdued colors on cloudy or overcast days. That's the same advice that bass fishermen will give you - bright on bright days and less bright when the light is more subdued. Regardless of the species being sought, that seems to be a universal.

When fishing these dry-and-dropper rigs, Big T suggests casting across and then mending the line as required to maintain a connection with the flies as the whole thing drifts downstream. He favors this approach rather than the more traditional up-and-across presentation because it simplifies the matter of dealing with the many and complex currents, and he uses frequent small mends to maintain as straight a connection between rod tip and flies as possible.

Streamers

While tiny midge emergers appear to be the bread and butter of the trout near the dam, it's important to remember that just about any fish (and that includes Chattahoochee tailwater trout near the dam) will jump on a bigger and meatier meal in a heartbeat. That takes us into the realm of streamers, and as it happens a well-presented streamer can be a very effective fly on this part of the river.

On the same trip where my friend John Cherry demonstrated the effectiveness of the "dry" in a dry/dropper rig, I had a chance to do a little fly evangelizing myself – only I was waving the flag for streamers. Trout (particularly the wild brown trout that now inhabit this part of the river) see a minnow among midges as a chance to get a big meal instead of just another appetizer, and they'll often attack a streamer with gusto.

You'll have good luck with a variety of streamer-type patterns below the dam. A simple Olive or Black Woolly Bugger, actively stripped, works well. So does an Olive Leech, a pattern which has proven to be very effective when stripped through likely-looking areas with slow to moderate flow. I like to tie these with fine silver wire ribbing that is worked down into the body to provide just a little hint of flash.

Other favorite streamers include a small Clouser in chartreuse and white or in brown, orange, yellow and tan (brown trout colors) – and don't forget to bring a few flashy all-gold or gold-and-silver Rolexes. They frequently work well too.

On that particular evening, however, I was fishing with a pattern that folks have taken to calling the Hudson Streamer. It's a flank-wing streamer

Euro-nymphing at the dam

Indicator-free nymphing (including various Euro-nymphing techniques as well as what the old-timers call "tight-lining") can be effective near the dam. A multi-nymph rig with a heavy fly on the bottom and smaller midges tied along the leader at intervals, fished with no strike indicator, allows you to explore many different parts of the water column on any given drift. The heavy anchor fly gets the tiny midge emergers down, and since there's no indicator you can make almost instantaneous adjustments to deal with variations in depth. The details of Euro-nymphing techniques are beyond the scope of this book, but you'll find plenty of how-to info from many other sources.

with guinea fowl or grizzly wings and a weighted body, a red dubbed collar and a large bead head; it can also be tied without flank wings (that is, with only a hackle collar. The fly sinks well, and there seems to be something about it that fish (especially browns) have a hard time resisting.

I'd started the day with a dry/dropper combo. I'd seen some surface activity near an underwater ledge that paralleled the east bank of the river. Working within casting range, I spent 15 minutes floating my dry-and-dropper combo through the run. If I say so myself, I did a pretty good job of it, painting the bottom thoroughly. But there were no takers.

Hmmm. I knew there were active fish in there, but they weren't interested in my midges. What to try instead?

How about a streamer? I tied on a Hudson Streamer in size 8, made a cast and promptly missed a strike.

Encouraged, I picked up the fly and cast again. Again came a strike, but this one held on. A few minutes later I was releasing a beautiful streamborn brown of about 14 inches.

While John continued to slay 'em on the dry/dropper a hundred feet upriver, I man-

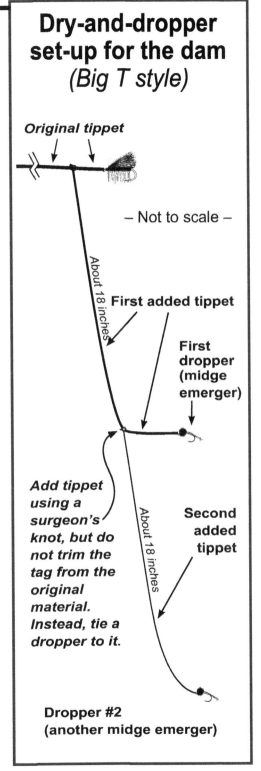

Dry-and-dropper set-up for the dam *(Big T style)*

Original tippet

– Not to scale –

About 18 inches

First added tippet

First dropper (midge emerger)

Add tippet using a surgeon's knot, but do not trim the tag from the original material. Instead, tie a dropper to it.

About 18 inches

Second added tippet

Dropper #2 (another midge emerger)

aged to bring in a couple more browns on the same streamer and might have picked up a few more had I kept fishing. But it was getting dark, and the tailwater isn't a place to be wading in low light. So I turned back toward the boat ramp where we'd started, making a note to bring a few more streamers next time just in case the trout decided to pass on my midges.

Other fly possibilities

Are there other flies that work well in this section? Absolutely. Big T mentions several that he uses with good results; these include an Olive Woolly Bugger (often with a UV ice dubbing body) tied on a size 10 jig hook. He will also use small Gold Ribbed Hare's Ear nymphs.

And if he's fishing just for fun, he may even use a "junk food" fly such as a Mop Fly in chartreuse or even pink.

"Mop Flies are effective," he says, noting that the river's wild browns apparently are not bothered by the sometimes heated discussions among fly fishers regarding whether the Mop Fly is legit or not. He adds, "I figure if the wild browns are eating them, then they must be okay to use!"

How's the wading?

As you'll quickly discover, much of the area from the boat ramp down toward Bowman's Island is wadable. However, you'll want to be careful.

"Stay on the gravel," Big T advises. "Stay off the flat rocks."

The reason, I quickly discover, is that those flat rocks are as slick as that proverbial greased glass.

There I was, walking along in about two feet of water. My attention was focused on an actively rising fish near the tailout of a run about 20 feet in front of me. *Probably taking midge emergers,* I surmised. *Guess that means I should tie on a –*

A truly helpful hint
(already stated but worth repeating)

When wading near the dam, stay on gravel. Those large flat rocks look good, but they are slick as greased glass.

One minute I was on gravel, but then with the very next step my foot came down on a large flat rock. Quicker than I can even think it, that foot slipped and down I went. Only the float tube saved me from a very, very cold baptism.

Slick rocks are a fact of life between the dam and Bowman's Island, but regular tailwater anglers have developed ways to deal with them.

One is to use a wading staff. It's a huge help when wading in this part of the tailwater.

"I have a wading staff with me all the time," Big T says, and it helps him to move around the river with ease.

What about the soles of your wading shoes? Felt, at the very least, is essential. However, studs add even more stability and will yield a much more secure footing. Just don't step on your fly line.

If you know the river, it's possible to wade most of the water between the boat ramp to the lower end of Bowman's Island.

"There's a few hundred yards of non-wadable water on the main river side of the island," he says, adding that parts of the river get too deep to wade toward the island's lower end. But that leaves lots and lots of room for wading anglers to explore – even those like Big T who don't wear waders.

And that thought again brings the big question to mind.

"Aren't you freezing?" I ask him.

"Nah," he says. "You get used to it. In fact, I wade it wet nine months out of the year...and over the past 12 months I have waded wet at least one day every month!"

Now there's a man you've got to respect.

Moving a few yards further across the flow, Big T continues fishing. He is having no trouble coaxing the trout to hit. In fact, he's just brought one to net, a fine wild brown.

He admires the fish and slips it back into the cold, cold flow – and then he goes back to fishing, still wet-wading, always smiling.

That's Big T.   ☐

"Big T" (right), a.k.a. Stephen Tomasovich, helps angler Marty Lock figure out the unique trout fishery that exists below Buford Dam.

Access and fishing tips:

Dam, Bowmans Island, and the Hatchery

This section of the tailwater has plenty to offer wading anglers plus some great tube fishing too. Here are tips to help you get the most out of this water.

The stretch of the tailwater between Buford Dam and Bowmans Island is arguably one of the most heavily fished parts of the river. It's not unusual to see dozens of anglers working this water. Some will be fishing from shore with casting gear or bait, while others will be trying their luck out in the flow with fly rods or spinning gear. Some will be wading; others may be in float tubes, on pontoons, or in kayaks or canoes. It's usually a genial group. Most everybody will be having fun, and many of them will be catching fish. That's one reason this is such a popular area.

Another reason for this area's popularity is that the river here is relatively easy to access. The primary access is via what's known as the Lower Pool West recreation area, a Corps of Engineers-developed park that sits (you guessed it) on the west side of the river.

Float-tube anglers will particularly enjoy this section. In fact, many consider the Dam-to-hatchery (or to Settles Bridge) float to be among the better float tube excursions on the river. Starting at the dam, tubing anglers can enter the river at the Lower Pool West boat ramp and, at the end of the trip, exit the river via a set of steps located behind the hatchery (outside the hatchery fence) and hike back to where they started. The Bowmans Island Trail makes that hike an easy one to do. Another possibility is to take two cars for a shuttle back to the starting point, as we'll see in a moment.

What about accessing the river from along the Bowmans Island Trail? If you hike along that trail, you'll see several places where fisherman's access paths lead down to the river. But except for those paths, river access from much of the Bowmans Island Trail is difficult. The same scouring currents that make this such good midge habitat have also cut into the river's banks over the years, creating steep banks that are very difficult to climb. That tends to

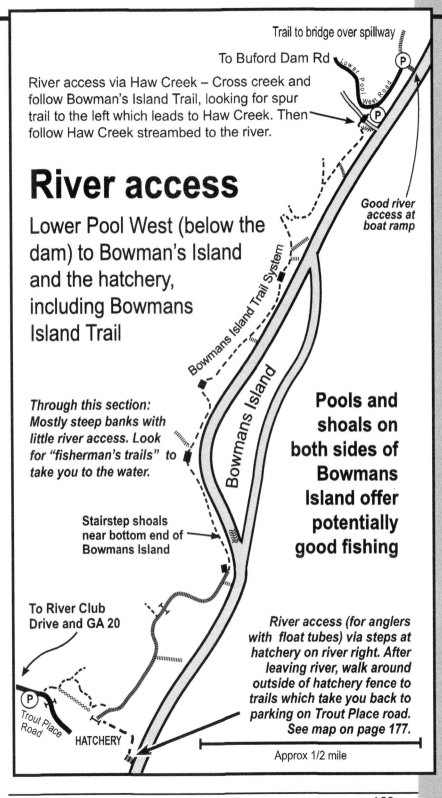

Trail to bridge over spillway

To Buford Dam Rd

P

Lower Pool West Road

River access via Haw Creek – Cross creek and follow Bowman's Island Trail, looking for spur trail to the left which leads to Haw Creek. Then follow Haw Creek streambed to the river.

P

River access

Lower Pool West (below the dam) to Bowman's Island and the hatchery, including Bowmans Island Trail

Bowmans Island Trail System

Good river access at boat ramp

Bowmans Island

Through this section: Mostly steep banks with little river access. Look for "fisherman's trails" to take you to the water.

Pools and shoals on both sides of Bowmans Island offer potentially good fishing

Stairstep shoals near bottom end of Bowmans Island

To River Club Drive and GA 20

P

Trout Place Road

HATCHERY

River access (for anglers with float tubes) via steps at hatchery on river right. After leaving river, walk around outside of hatchery fence to trails which take you back to parking on Trout Place road.
See map on page 177.

Approx 1/2 mile

Trout

limit access to this stretch, though (as noted earlier) there are those fisherman's trails for you to find.

Most anglers begin at the boat ramp at Lower Pool West. It's easy to find; simply follow the road to the far end of the parking area, and the ramp will be on your right. From the ramp, access to the river is a piece of cake.

Finding Lower Pool West

To get to the Lower Pool West park from GA 400, take GA 20 (exit 14) and go east for 0.3 miles to Market Place Blvd. Turn left and go 0.8 miles to Buford Dam Road. Turn right and go 4.3 miles to Lower Pool West Road on your right. Turn right and go down the hill to the parking areas. Note that a parking fee or a CRNRA pass is required to park.

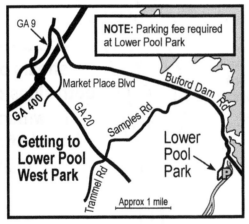

NOTE: Parking fee required at Lower Pool Park

GA 9

Market Place Blvd

Buford Dam Rd

GA 400

GA 20

Samples Rd

Getting to Lower Pool West Park

Trammel Rd

Lower Pool Park

Approx 1 mile

It's also possible to access the river via Haw Creek. To do so, park in the first parking lot that you come to. Then follow the Bowman's Island Trail (which begins at the well-marked trailhead at the back of the lot). The trail immediately crosses Haw Creek and turns left toward the river. Look for a well-used spur trail on your left which leads toward the creek. Work your way down to the creekbed, and follow it to the river.

Entering the river at either point will put the dam to your left and Bowman's Island downriver to your right.

Where are the best places to look for fish? You'll find them scattered throughout this section, and most pieces of promising looking water will hold a fish or two. If you spot a run that's even a little deeper than the surrounding area, make some casts. The fish are adept at finding places to hold in the river, and one key to success near the dam is to look for and thoroughly fish such places.

In fact, you'll be looking at fishable water almost from the moment you enter the river. There are promising runs right in front of the boat ramp and also right in front of the mouth of Haw Creek. But those are just two of dozens.. Potentially good spots are everywhere.

As you explore the area between the boat ramp and Haw Creek, you should find it possible to pick your way across the river (at low water, of course) to fish most of the water you see. The river bottom is a mix of ledges, gravel patches, deeper runs, and those bothersome slippery flat rocks. Wherever you see a change in the

The pedestrian bridge over the spillway is easily accessible from the Lower Pool West parking area and makes a great sidetrip – especially if you time it to watch a release from Buford Dam.

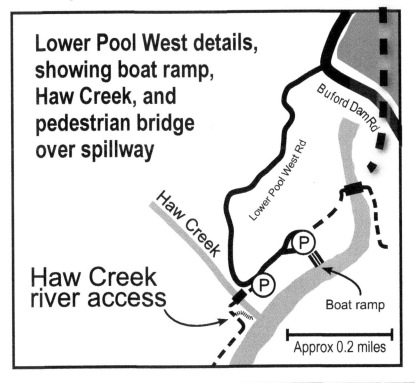

Lower Pool West details, showing boat ramp, Haw Creek, and pedestrian bridge over spillway

Buford Dam Rd

Lower Pool West Rd

Haw Creek

P

P

Haw Creek river access

Boat ramp

Approx 0.2 miles

bottom contours, assume that a fish is present and make some casts. Give some thought to how your flies will drift, and adjust your casts to keep your offerings in the pay zone.

The key, as on any big water, is to think of this as a bunch of small creeks that happen to be flowing side by side. In other words,

instead of worrying about trying to fish the *entire* river, focus only on one particular "creek."

Another way to broaden your options is to remember Big T's "hurricane path" analogy and wade off the beaten track. That'll put you on different "creeks" than others fishing.

The most popular access point for fishing near the dam and Bowmans Island is via the Lower Pool West boat ramp (above). Anglers also enter the river via Haw Creek (below), which is accessed from the Bowmans Island Trail.

There's lots of good water on the west (ramp) side of the river, but don't overlook the opportunities across the river along the far bank. Much of the opposite side is approachable if you are careful with your wading.

You can spend hours exploring and fishing the water in front of the boat ramp, but sooner or later you will probably want to explore downriver toward the island too. The main channel is on the west (boat ramp) side of the river, and as you approach Bowman's Island you'll find some deeper pools and enough splashy riffle water to keep you busy for quite a while.

As you fish your way downriver along the side of Bowman's Island, you may find that the easiest going is on the island side of the main channel. Near the top of the island, notice the large pool-like area on river right, a zone of deeper water with plenty of large submerged rocks. It offers good fishing, but it's not a place that most people care to wade. Similar spots elsewhere in the area are also worth checking out.

While much angling attention is focused on the main river channel on the west side of Bowman's Island, don't overlook the somewhat smaller channel on the island's back (east) side. It too offers that nice mix of riffles and pools, and the fact that it's harder to get to means it receives less pressure than does the main channel.

If you fish around the island or in the back channel, remember that it will take a while to get back to your starting point. Keep that critical fact in mind as you plan the timing of your trip.

There's a good bit of wadable water around the island, but sooner or later you'll encounter deeper spots. That's when floating anglers gain an advantage. Near the lower end of the island, for example, there's a set of shoals ("Stairstep Shoals) in the main channel. But accessing them requires getting through the deeper water upstream. Using a float tube is one way to get to 'em.

Those shoals, by the way, are great dry/dropper water. For the dry, use a big and easy-to-see attractor-style dry such as a Royal Wulff, a Humpy, or a Chubby Chernobyl. For the dropper portion

---

Strategies for the dam: a quick review

Midges: Fish beadhead midges with enough weight to get them down where you want them. Look at the flow, and target areas near edges or along current seams.

Nymphs: Use tungsten beads or added weight to get nymphs deep, with a strike indicator to make you aware of what's happening subsurface. Set the hook at any departure from the regular drift pattern.

Dries and **dry/dropper combos:** Fish 'em dead-drift, with particular attention to avoiding any drag. Edges and seams are good, especially for dry/dropper combos (a high-floating dry and one to three midge emergers or other nymphs). Line mending skills will prove useful.

Streamers: Cast toward cover or holding areas, count down if desired, and strip. Vary the retrieve to find what works. Keep your rod tip low and the rod pointed at the fly. And remember: Bigger streamers may mean bigger fish.

---

of the rig, try something like a Copper John, a Zebra Midge, a Blue Assassin, a Moonshine Midge or a Pheasant Tail.

One popular run for float tubers is from the dam to the Georgia Department of Natural Resources' Buford Trout Hatchery. That float covers a bit less than two river miles. The takeout for this float is on river right at the hatchery, where a set of steps (you'll see them on river right just before the hatchery's water outflow structure) makes it relatively easy to get up the river's steep bank. Those steps were constructed to allow hatchery personnel to access and monitor the river, but hatchery manager Pat Markey notes that they're also popular with floating anglers who use them to exit (or sometimes enter) the river.

Note: While these steps at the hatchery are okay for use by an angler carrying a float tube, they are *not suitable for exiting the river with kayaks or canoes.*

The idea of floating from the dam down to the hatchery is appealing to many tailwater anglers. The float is not too long and not too difficult, and it gives you access to some promising water that you might otherwise never see.

However, there is one question that has to be addressed: How do you get back to your car once the float is done?

One solution is to make the trip with a buddy, taking two cars. Leave one at the downstream end of the float (outside the hatchery gate) and then drive the second car to the put-in at the dam, where you'll start your float adventure. Later, at the end of your float, exit the river at the hatchery steps. Then use that first car to drive back to Lower Pool West to get the second car. Just don't park the first car inside the hatchery gate because it's locked when the hatchery closes – and if you run late you might not be able to get to your car.

How do you get from the steps back to your car? You can't walk through the hatchery. Instead, from the top of the steps, look to the right for a path that follows along the outside of the hatchery fence. That path is the way back to your car (which of course you parked in the designated parking area *outside* the hatchery gates).

Now follow the path around the corner of the hatchery fence, continuing to parallel the fence. It may be wet going if it's rained recently. Eventually, the path intersects a gravel road. Turn right, hike a few dozen yards, and then turn left on the Chattahoochee River National Recreation Area's Bowmans Island Trail, which takes you back to Trout Place Road as shown on the map on page 177. Pick up the first car for the ride back to the Lower Pool West site to complete your trip.

What if you've only brought one car? Then go to alternate plan B, which involves a hike between the hatchery and the dam via the Bowmans Island Trail. Leave your car at one end or the other of the float and use the Bowmans Island Trail to complete the circuit. I recommend parking near the hatchery and doing the hike first (hiking upriver) while you're still fresh. Enter the river at Haw Creek (or farther upriver at the boat ramp, if you want to explore that water too) and then float and fish your way down to the hatchery.

Just don't miss the takeout or you'll have to keep floating to GA 20 or Settles Bridge!

Bringing a nice tailwater brown to net – a common occurrence when you're fishing below the dam. This one took Kevin Griffin's variant on the Moonshine Midge. Photo courtesy Kevin Griffin.

As you fish this section of the tailwater, remember what Big T suggested about fishing a little ways off the main travel routes. Anglers really are creatures of habit, and I'm as guilty as the next guy. In fact, once I find a route across a river, I tend to stick with it no matter what.

One day a couple of months ago, however, I decided to depart from my accustomed path. I suppose Big T had inspired me. There's a place on the far bank that I like to fish, and I'd usually go around the downstream end of a large rock to get there. Others apparently fell into the same pattern, too, for virtually every angler I had ever seen fishing in that area took the same down-and-around route.

But on that particular day I found myself reflecting on Big T's advice about fishing off the beaten track and so decided to check out the possibility of an above-the-rock route instead.

Sure enough, I found that such a route was feasible – and as I made my way along I found that my brand-new perspective revealed a couple of nice runs that I had never noticed before. Suddenly excited at the prospect of "new" water, I flipped the little dry/dropper combo to the top of the nearest run and was rewarded with a brown on the very first cast – and this from water I'd walked past many times but had never really stopped to check out.

Judging from the number of fish that I have caught there since that time, it may be water that few others have ever fished either.

There's one thing to keep in mind when fishing between the dam

Above: Buford Trout Hatchery manager Pat Markey on the steps (behind the hatchery) which float tube anglers sometimes use to exit (or enter) the river. Inset: Here's how the steps look from the river. They are a good take-out or put-in point for float tubing anglers but are not for those using canoes or kayaks.

and Bowmans Island. While solitude is always nice when fishing, and while there will be those days when you seem to be only one on the water, the fact is that this is a very well-known and very popular area. You'll rarely have it to yourself, and you'll often have anglers passing above or below or even in front of you as they too move around the river.

When that happens, what should you do? Pack up and go home in a huff because someone has invaded your water? No, don't do that! Instead, keep fishing! On this portion of the tailwater, the parade of anglers does not seem to bother the fish too much at all. I've caught nice trout here in runs that just moments before were thoroughfares for other anglers who were only passing through.   □

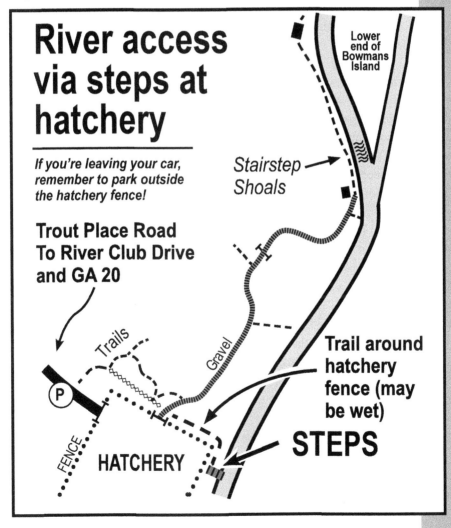

River access via steps at hatchery

If you're leaving your car, remember to park outside the hatchery fence!

Trout Place Road To River Club Drive and GA 20

Lower end of Bowmans Island

Stairstep Shoals

Trails

Gravel

Trail around hatchery fence (may be wet)

STEPS

FENCE

HATCHERY

P

Access and fishing tips:
And on to Highway 20?

Can you continue your float trip beyond the hatchery and on downriver to the Highway 20 bridge? Well...

Wading is the norm from the dam to Bowman's Island, and float tubes are the norm for fishing from the dam down to the hatchery.

But what if you want to float a little farther?

If you've considered that possibility, then you may have looked at the Georgia Highway 20 bridge. Is there river access there? Well...

The Highway 20 bridge, which is the next road crossing below the hatchery, has always had potential as an access point. It's the first possible exit point below the hatchery, making it a logical jumping-out spot for those who would like to make longer floats from the dam.

For years there was no formal river access at the GA 20 bridge. Fishermen would simply park beside the highway or in nearby parking lots and take their chances. Sometimes that worked out okay, though at other times it earned a personalized greeting from local law enforcement.

But now, thanks to a widening project on GA 20, there's a small paved parking lot just east of the river on the south side of the road. A sign as you enter the parking area reads "TRUE FISHERMEN DON'T LITTER" and suggests that it was even constructed with anglers in mind.

Does it provide good fishing access?

It all looks so promising at first glance. From the parking area, a dirt trail leads along the south side of the road toward the river, eventually going down a slope to connect with a narrow sidewalk-like strip of concrete that passes under the dual GA 20 bridges. But that's all the concrete pathway does. In fact, it ends just beyond the outer edges of the set of bridges. It's a straight piece of concrete, and that's it.

This sidewalk to nowhere has caused more than one tailwater angler to scratch his or her head in puzzlement and wonder why

The Highway 20 parking area (above, beyond the speed limit sign) will handle 14 cars. From the parking area, a dirt path leads down to a sidewalk-like concrete path beneath the bridges. Between that path and the river, however, you find large boulders and underbrush (below) – but no easy river access. Maybe in the future?

there's no good access to river. Perhaps it is not really a sidewalk but is instead part of a runoff control system? Could be.

In any case, the fact is that there is presently no convenient way to get all the way to the water – particularly if you're toting a canoe

---

or a kayak. The riverbank between the sidewalk and river's edge is covered with large riprap (massive chunks of stone which cover the ground between the sidewalk and the river, presumably as an erosion control measure). In some areas, undergrowth is taking hold between the boulders, too, complicating things even more. With all of that between you and the water, you'll need a very sure footing (and perhaps a little bit of luck as well) to safely make your way down to the river's edge.

Because of the difficulty of actually getting to the water here, this cannot be considered any kind of reasonable access point for anglers using boats.

However, it might be feasible if you are using a float tube (and if you have the rock-hopping ability of a mountain goat). Just be sure that you know what you're getting into first.

If you're thinking about accessing the river at GA 20, my advice is to visit the site and personally check out the conditions there before committing. Be honest about whether you can make it safely, and then decide.

By the way, no parking fee is required to utilize the 14-space parking lot. But 14 is not a very large number. When the lot is full, it's full.

The rapids above the GA 20 bridge: There's one more thing to be aware of when floating to or beyond GA 20. To this point, the river has been fairly easy, with just a few gentle shoals to liven things up as you've worked your way down the river. But about 300 yards above the GA 20 bridge is a significant Class II rapid.

This rapid is a favorite play spot for whitewater enthusiasts. But if you're more into fishing than whitewater boating, even a relatively straightforward rapid like this one can be a bit intimidating – but that's not necessarily a bad thing. One key to safely enjoying a river like the Chattahoochee is to be aware of the challenges along the way, and this particular rapid is one of them.

Your canoeing buddies will hardly give it a second glance, and depending on the water level it may be an easy and uncomplicated run. But if you're not experienced at running rapids, the prospect of going through it can be a little bit intimidating.

If you're taking out at the hatchery, then the rapid will never come into play. You'll leave the river before you reach it. However, if you're making the longer dam-to-Settles-Bridge float (one of the most popular float trips on the river) then you'll have to either go around it or through it.

We'll talk more about that particular rapid a little later in this guide when we take a detailed look at the dam-to-Settles-Bridge float.

If you do float through this section, no matter what sort of water-craft you're in, remember that you are required to *wear* your PFD (life jacket) above the GA 20 bridge. That includes the entire stretch discussed so far. That is the law, and yes, it is enforced. Just having that PFD in your boat or tube is not enough, and I've seen more than one person get a ticket for wearing a PFD.

Besides, it's just common sense. □

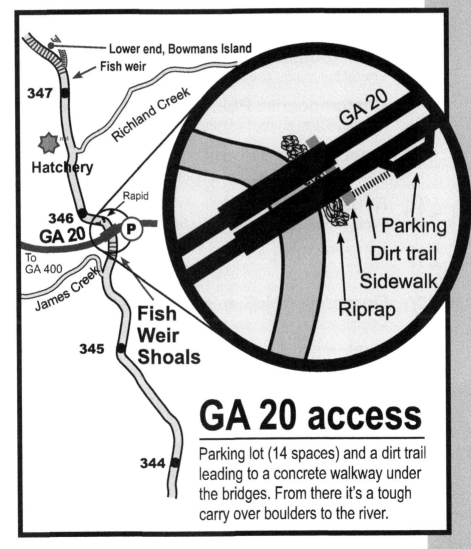

GA 20 access

Parking lot (14 spaces) and a dirt trail leading to a concrete walkway under the bridges. From there it's a tough carry over boulders to the river.

The "bridges" stretch

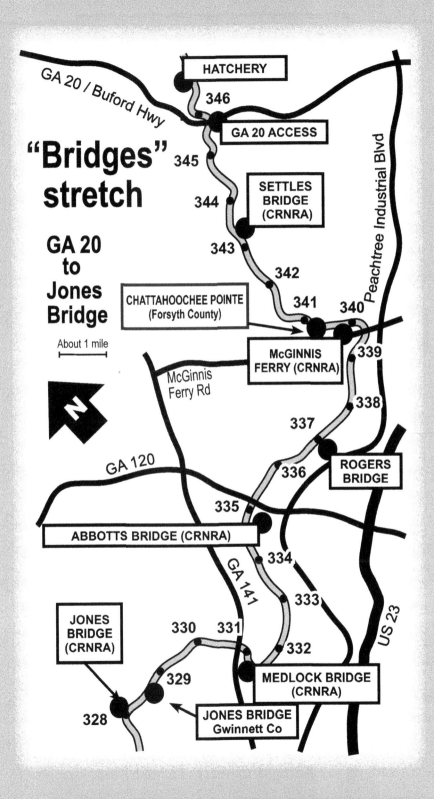

"Holy cow! Did you see that?"

Fishing in the land of the legendary browns.

The place: Somewhere on the Chattahoochee tailwater between Bowmans Island and Jones Bridge several miles downstream.

The time: Noon, more or less, with a little while to go before an earlier release of water from Buford Dam begins to make itself felt.

The boat: Made for river fishing and outfitted with an outboard jet motor.

The captain: Chattahoochee legend Chris Scalley, founder of River Through Atlanta Guide Service (riverthroughatlanta.com) and a great supporter of the river.

Since launching River Through Atlanta in 1994, Chris (along with his brother John and a cadre of other guides) has introduced thousands of fly fishers to Chattahoochee tailwater trout. His enthusiasm for the river and its fish is evident, and most days you'll find him somewhere on the tailwater sharing that passion with others at all levels of the fly fishing game.

Today, however, is a busman's holiday. Chris himself is fishing, and his first order of business is to check out a rumor that there's a big brown hanging out in this one certain place near some blowdowns and submerged logs.

He positions the boat in the gentle current and makes a cast. He's throwing a minnow imitation – a *big* one about six or seven inches long. It lands with a soft *splat* near the tangle. Chris begins to work it back to the boat.

Nothing. Another cast. Another zero. Another cast –

This time a shape appears, a long and trouty shape that materializes from beneath the blowdowns and heads for the enticingly wiggling minnow imitation. It's a brown, a big brown, a *huge* brown, one of those fish of legend that the river might give you if you're really, really lucky.

I see it. Holy cow, it's *huge.*

Chris retrieves faster. The fish accelerates. It rushes, swipes, misses, and then turns and disappears with a swirl that breaks the surface.

There's a moment of stunned silence in the boat.

"Did you *see* that?" Chris says. "Did you see the size of that thing?"

He casts again. So does Gary Zimmerman, one of the River Through Atlanta guides who's also enjoying the day off. Both throw big minnow imitations back toward the hot spot. No takers.

But we know it's still in there – somewhere. Will it hang around?

"It will," Chris says, and I can see him making mental notes.

"Big browns are more common here than we ever dreamed they would be," he says. "That fish was at least 25 inches. At least an 8-pounder."

How old would such a fish be? That's hard to say. In some watersheds, biologists determine age based on layers in one of the fish's ear bones. It becomes a simple matter of counting. But growth patterns in the tailwater

Chris Scalley, founder of River Through Atlanta guide service, has introduced thousands of anglers to the Chattahoochee tailwater.

---

make that hard to do on these wild Chattahoochee browns.

"Still, if I had to guess," he says, "I'd say about 10 years."

We float on, and Chris and Gary are talking about what it takes to fool big fish. The key, Chris says again, is big flies. He mentions patterns with names like Sex Dungeon and Circus Peanut and shows me the flies he likes to use. They're big – bigger than a lot of the fish I catch up in the mountains.

Behind him, Gary opens a bright yellow fly box the size of a small briefcase and says, "Take a look at these." It's filled with giant articulated streamers. There's enough tying material on those flies to stock a small shop, and if "big" is what it takes then these flies should do the job.

"Big flies for big fish," Chris says again.

Clearly, throwing super-sized flies is not a job for your little 4-weight. When pursuing such leviathans, Chris uses an 8-weight rod and a sink-tip line. His leader, about 8 feet long, is made up of sections of 20- and 15-lb. fluorocarbon.

So much timber
(...so little time!)

One thing you'll notice on the tailwater is that there's a lot of timber along the shoreline. Dead trees have tangled together and piled up to create "strainers," which get their name because they can literally strain things (like kayaks, canoes or float tubes) out of the water. You want to make sure that does not happen to you.

For *fishing,* however, strainers can be a *good* thing. Small fish like 'em because they provide protection from predators, while big fish like 'em because they hold small fish.

Which strainers are best? That's hard to say, because (as Chattahoochee guide James Dudley puts it) there are so many logs and trees that fish could be anywhere. Any tree or any log could hold a big fish.

Fish strainers thoroughly. You never know what you might find.

Yeah, it's overkill if an ambitious 14-incher grabs the fly. But if one of the big boys decides to have a go at it, you may find yourself wondering if even the 8-weight and the heavy line are enough.

As you can imagine, simply casting those big flies can be a workout, and as soon as they're in the water then fast and vigorous stripping becomes the order of the day.

"Strip the fly a foot or two at a time," Chris advises.

There's no other way to put it. Fishing for big trout is serious business.

"But that's what it takes," Chris says. "When I'm fishing for the big ones,

I'm working my tail off – a lot of the time for no reward."

But when the payoff comes, and eventually it will, then all the effort is instantaneously worthwhile.

What about smaller streamers? They certainly work, though they won't work as well when you're hunting the giants. Tied on sizes 6-10 hooks, patterns like the Rolex, Muddler Minnow, and Matuka streamers can be effective. Classic patterns such as the Mickey Finn and Black-Nosed Dace can also be good choices, Chris says.

Drifting...casting...talking trout...and the river starts to change as the released water at last comes our way. There's a slight change in the flow, and the look of the water changes too: a subtle shift from crystal clear to slightly murky. Leaves are showing up in the lines along the current seams.

"Yeah, it's coming up," Chris says.

"Downstream?" Gary says. "Stay ahead of it?"

"Yes," says Chris. He starts the boat, and the jet from the outboard pushes us downstream ahead of the rising water.

It was just a little release, only about an hour's worth. "A burp," Chris calls it. It will spread out and dissipate fairly quickly – but not before it changes the character of the river for a while. The water will get faster. It will become cloudier and then murkier and then all but opaque as the increased flow picks up sediment, the unfortunate product of careless development in the watershed.

We'll be in front of all that, however, trying our luck in the clear water downriver – at least until the rising flow catches up with us again. Then Chris will crank up the motor and we'll move downriver some more.

But we'll still be thinking about that enormous brown.

We're well into the "bridges" section now, a long stretch defined by the names of the bridges which span (or once spanned) the river. Their names echo history – Settle's Bridge, McGinnis Ferry (there's a modern bridge there now), Rogers Bridge, Abbotts Bridge, Medlock Bridge, Jones Bridge, and Holcomb Bridge. You'll encounter them as you fish. Some are modern steel and concrete affairs; others are long-abandoned structures now centerpieces of public parks. Each has played a part in the history of this part of the river.

It's fascinating to drift under one of the old bridges and wonder what this area was like in the 1800s – before Atlanta's explosive growth and long before the river's trout. There are three of the old bridges still in existence on the tailwater – Settles Bridge, Rogers Bridge, and Jones Bridge – plus a

In shallow areas, it's necessary to "walk" boats through shoals, as River Through Atlanta's Chris Scalley is doing here.

tantalizing remnant of an old covered bridge at Holcomb Bridge.

Sitting up front and lost in thoughts of history, I haven't been paying attention to the fishing. Only when a flash of motion from Gary's rod catches my eye do I realize that we're now back in clear water. Time to fish again.

Gary is casting toward a good-looking spot off to the right – deep water near a blowdown. He's still using that big minnow imitation, and soon his rod bows to another brown. It's a decent fish by most standards, but everything that day will be measured by the one that almost was.

Though we're taking advantage of those windows of relatively clear water, Chris notes that water that's just a little off-color may actually help fishing. The browns especially seem to feel more secure when the water is less than crystal clear, he notes, and some anglers even prefer such conditions.

But why does the river become murky? It sounds like a simplistic question, yet the answer touches on a number of things that may be going on in the river corridor as well as in the lake.

One is land disturbance, which often leads to muddy runoff when it rains. Runoff enters the river, and eventually the mud settles out and accumulates, especially near creek mouths. There it sits until the next release comes along to stir it up and wash it down and and mess up the river for miles.

The picture is further complicated by the fact that Georgia has been experiencing drought for some time. Drought means more water is held in the lake ...which means less water is released...which means silt isn't flushed out very often but accumulates over time. Then, when there *is* a release and the river does rise, the flow really stirs things up and turns everything into tomato soup. In technical terms, the "turbidity" skyrockets. In practical terms, the water becomes so opaque that the fishing pretty much stops.

At certain times of year, there's yet another factor which messes with the water. It's "turnover," something that originates in the lake itself. As temperatures drop in the fall, released water takes on a greenish-brown color. The chemistry involved is beyond the scope of this book, but the short version is that iron and manganese end up being released from sediment at the bottom of the lake and subsequently cloud the water coming from the dam. For a while every year that messes up the tailwater, sometimes for quite a ways downstream – though it eventually goes away as the iron and manganese compounds precipitate out. First to clear is iron, which settles out as a red precipitant. Most of the iron will have settled out by the GA 120 bridge. The manganese, however, hangs on a while and gives the water a greenish stain even further downriver.

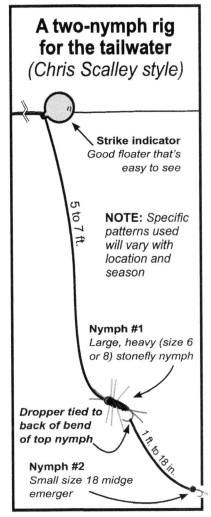

A two-nymph rig for the tailwater
(Chris Scalley style)

Strike indicator
Good floater that's easy to see

5 to 7 ft.

NOTE: *Specific patterns used will vary with location and season*

Nymph #1
Large, heavy (size 6 or 8) stonefly nymph

Dropper tied to back of bend of top nymph

1 ft. to 18 in.

Nymph #2
Small size 18 midge emerger

What does that do to fishing? Fly fishers can find it a real challenge since trout may not be able to see flies in the cloudy water. But the solution, says Chris, may be as simple as upsizing your flies.

"The trick," he says, "is to bump up your fly a size or two. Go with 14s or 16s instead of using 18s or 20s."

Another good turnover trick, he adds, is to use streamers. A streamer, being larger, presents the fish with something that's easier to see.

Spin fishers are less affected by turnover since large crankbaits and similar lures are easier for fish to see. Such lures "push" a lot of water, too, sending out attention-grabbing vibrations that let fish know they're there.

But turnover happens in late fall. During summer, the big challenge is

---

Trout

usually just one of avoiding high-turbidity water.

We've talked and fished so long that the release is catching up with us again. As before, the change is easy to see. One minute we're drifting along in fairly clear water, with the river bottom clearly visible below the boat. Then it's a little murky – and then a lot, just like before. Chris again says, "Let's head on down the river." He starts the jet, and off we go.

We run downriver, heading for water where nymphs have been fishing well. The heavy gear is put away in favor of lighter rods and two-fly nymph rigs. The top fly, about six feet beneath an indicator, is a weighted

The author with a rainbow that took a nymph in the Chattahoochee tailwater.

beadhead stonefly. How big? The ones Chris uses range from small 10s up to big (and sometimes articulated) size 2s. Most will be size 6 or 8, and all are weighted.

About 18 inches below the stonefly nymph is the second fly, which today is a sparkly pink egg.

When setting up a leader for tailwater nymphing, Chris says, he rigs for an average depth of about 5 feet. That means that the leader will be about 8 feet long – and fluorocarbon.

"Fluoro is important," he adds. "It sinks quicker than ordinary mono, and that helps a lot with small flies."

Although we're fishing the stonefly and the egg, other combinations work well too. Good droppers include San Juan Worms, Y2Ks, Shaky Worms, and tiny midge emergers such as the Blue Assassin, Moonshine Midge, or the Fly Formerly Known As Prince. The emergers may be very small (18 or 20), especially when the water is particularly clear.

There are also times when he uses a three-fly dry/dropper rig, fishing two small emergers below a high-floating hopper or caddis. The first dropper goes about 4 feet below the dry, with the second a foot or two below that.

As Chris deftly maneuvers the boat with the oars, Gary drops his nymph rig so it drifts along the edge of a current seam. Seconds later there's a hit, and soon a nice butter-bellied brown of about 15 inches is in the net.

"Nice fish!" I say as he casts into the flow once more, and it isn't long until yet another fish finds the fly. Both have taken the sparkle egg.

Indicator nymphing is an effective way to fish the tailwater, Chris says, especially for less experienced anglers. The visual cues provided by the strike indicator signal takes that might otherwise be missed. It can be a great way to bring significant numbers of fish to the net.

And yet some don't want to fish that way.

"I'll sometimes have a guest and his spouse," Chris notes. "The guest may be an experienced fly fisher who has fished many places, and he wants to fish with something like a dry."

Alas, the dries that worked so well for him out west may not cut it on the tailwater – but the spouse is catching one after another on the nymph rig.

"Eventually," Chris adds, "I may ask the guest if he wants to catch fish or if he just wants to look good. And then the guy will finally say, 'Let me give that a try.' Then he starts catching fish too."

We drift another hundred yards or so. Then –

"Why don't you fish some?" Chris says, offering me the rod. I've been happily doing the writer thing and just generally soaking it all in, but I figure that the world of outdoor journalism won't collapse if I set down the notepad and pick up the fly rod for a little while.

And so I do. Chris offers suggestions on where to drift the fly, and his advice is spot on. I quickly get a strike – so quickly that I miss it completely.

I put the flies out there again, turn to look at a turtle –

"Steve!" Chris says, and I look just in time to see the indicator bob to the surface. Yep, that was another strike, with the key word being *was*.

Okay, Hudson, if you're going to fish, then you need to fish," I say to myself. So I ignore all the distractions and start paying attention.

Pretty soon, it pays off. I'm watching intently when the next strike comes a few minutes later, and I feel the fish for a just an instant before it becomes unbuttoned. Well, at least I'm getting closer.

But then I get another chance, and this time the rod stays bent. The battle is epic. Chris nets the fish for me and we take a picture.

Yes, even writers catch one now and then. □

Get the net!

Those stories of big browns on the Hooch are getting more and more common. Here's how one such fish tale came together.

Sunday, July 17, 2016, was a day that Chattahoochee anglers Ryan Johnson and Michael Mayne will never forget.

It was the day of the really, Really, REALLY big trout.

Ryan and Mike had set out on the Chattahoochee River at daybreak. Their sights were set on big fish – big brown trout, to be specific – but they had no idea just how big a surprise they were about to receive.

Ryan, a fly fisherman, had the gear he'd need – a heavy 8-weight flyrod, a full-sink line, a 20-lb.-test leader, and a huge 7.5-inch-long articulated streamer fly. The fly was designed to imitate a big fish, for Ryan knew that big browns like big meals.

Not long after the boat was in the water, Ryan started casting the fly near some structure along the bank.

"I was just blind casting," he recalls, "and it was literally the tenth cast of the day." He stripped the fly toward the boat…three strips…four strips…and then came that strike that he will never forget.

"It just about took the rod out of my hands," he says.

Ryan instantly realized that he was into a truly big fish.

"I started hollering 'Get the net, Mike! Get the net!' "

Thanks to the big-fish gear, the battle was intense but brief. Within just a few minutes Ryan had the fish to the boat.

"I had no words when I saw the fish," he says, and Mike echoes that sentiment.

"I thought it was going to be 'big' like in the 20s [inches]," Mike recalls, "but that fish was insane. It was the biggest fish I'd ever seen from the Chattahoochee."

Now it was Mike's turn to do his part and get the fish into the net – and the process of netting the fish, Mike adds, "was "one of the most nerve-wracking moments I've ever had."

How big did the trout turn out to be?

"It measured 30 inches on the nose," Ryan says, "and had a girth of 18.5 inches." Based on those measurements, he estimates that it weighed about 15 pounds.

What do you do with a gargantuan trout like that? They took some photos and then set the fish back in the water. Fully revived, it swam back into the depths.

"Now he's back out there in river." Ryan says, "waiting to be caught again."

And where, exactly, is that particular spot? Ryan doesn't say much about that except to note that it's somewhere between Buford Dam and Morgan Falls.

But he does comment on the conditions that seem to favor such catches, and as an experienced trophy trout angler his observations are definitely worth noting

"I'm always the crazy guy out there when the water is muddy," he says, adding that relatively high turbidity readings are what he looks for. He also prefers overcast days.

"Bright bluebird days with clear water are my enemy," he says.

What's next? Are there bigger trout yet to be caught in the Chattahoochee? Maybe so, Ryan says.

"It may be time to start throwing 10-inch flies," he says.

And time, he adds, to get a bigger net.

Ryan Johnson with his monster brown. The fish measured 30 inches long and had a girth of 18.5 inches. Its weight? An estimated 15 pounds.

Access and fishing tips:

The "bridges" stretch

This 20-mile section of the upper tailwater has multiple personalities. But if you take the time to figure them out, the fishing can be unforgettable.

The "bridges" stretch, which covers just over 20 miles of the upper tailwater, extends from near Settles Bridge and GA 20 down to Garrard Landing and Holcomb Bridge Road. It's so named because of the many bridges (modern as well as historic) and ferry locations that are found along its length – an impressive list that starts with Settles Bridge and continues with McGinnis Ferry, Rogers Bridge, Abbotts Bridge, Medlock Bridge, Jones Bridge, and Garrard Landing.

The good news for anglers is that most of those afore-mentioned sites provide public access to the river and open the door to some memorable fishing adventures. Additionally, the fact that they are scattered throughout this section makes it possible to plan a variety of different types of outings.

At some of these sites, you'll find paved ramps suitable for use by those with boats on trailers. Sites within this stretch which offer trailer accessibility include the Chattahoochee River National Recreation Area ramps at McGinnis Ferry, Abbotts Bridge, Medlock Bridge, and Jones Bridge.

WORD TO THE WISE

When floating anywhere on the upper tailwater, be careful if you find yourself drifting beneath overhanging limbs. Such spots are often good holding water and tempt many to make a cast or two, but it's not unusual for such a cast to miss its mark and become hung up in the trees. If that happens, sometimes there's nothing to do but break off the fly or lure...then there it stays, hanging from the trees waiting to snag (literally) the angler who happens to be floating through. Keep your eyes open, and don't let that angler be you!

The "bridges" stretch up close

In addition to those sites with trailer-friendly ramps, a number of other access points along the "bridges" stretch offer canoe and kayak (and float tube) access only. These include the Chattahoochee River National Recreation Area's Settles Bridge and Jones Bridge Units (note that CRNRA's Jones Bridge Unit includes multiple river access sites); Forsyth County's Chattahoochee Pointe Park; Gwinnett County's Jones Bridge Park; the City of Duluth's Rogers Bridge Park; and the City of Roswell's Garrard Landing Park. Access at any of these sites typically requires a carry of some sort – sometimes short and easy but at other times a bit longer.

Note that there is additional boat access (including a ramp suitable for trailers at the City of Roswell's Azalea Park) downriver from the "bridges" section. We will look at those access points later in this guide.

REMINDER
(Don't forget!)

It's **artificial lures only** from the GA 20 bridge downriver to the Medlock Bridge boat ramp.

What awaits you through the "bridges" stretch? In some areas, you'll find good places for wading or for float tubing. Other stretches are deep and better suited for boats – but even on the deeper sections you will often find shallows where you can anchor, get out and wade. Some of those deeper places can be fished from a float tube, but there may be spots where the current is so slow that tubers may find their down-the-river progress slowing to almost zero. At times, and depending on wind direction, your downstream movement may even go negative as wind literally pushes you upstream.

In areas where it's feasible to do so, it's a good idea to scout the river (especially your takeout) from shore before getting into the water. At the very least, take a close look at maps or at satellite imagery to get an idea of what the river looks like along the section you'll be floating. Be realistic about what you see and about how it meshes with your equipment and your abilities.

The previous section of this guide looked at the upper tailwater from the dam down to the Georgia DNR hatchery (near GA 20). In this section, we'll continue exploring downriver to Garrard Landing (near Holcomb Bridge) and look at how these access points can set the stage for some memorable tailwater trout fishing. ☐

Settles Bridge

Just a little more than two river miles downriver from the puzzling access point at the GA 20 bridge is your next opportunity to get into (or out of) the cold, clear flow of the tailwater – the Settles Bridge Unit of the Chattahoochee River National Recreation Area.

The river access at the Settles Bridge Unit stands in marked contrast to what you find at GA 20. Suitable for canoes, kayaks, and float tubes, the Settles Bridge launching site is the first real access point for boaters floating down from Lower Pool West and the dam. It's popular with recreational kayakers and canoeists who are

drawn to not only by the river and also by the rapid above GA 20 (see page 200 for a look at the float and some comments on the rapid). Because it's so popular, don't be too surprised if you find the parking area packed with cars on weekends and holidays.

This Settles Bridge access point is also very popular with fishermen. Fly rodders and spinning enthusiasts alike use it either as an access point for the shoal areas just upriver from the put-in ... or as a put-in/take-out point for starting or ending various floats. When floating in this area, however, keep in mind that as the river begins to flatten in sections, the current will start to slow and, as a result, floats can take longer than you might think. That's especially true if you take time to fish along the way, which is (after all) the reason you're there in the first place.

And how is the fishing? At Settles Bridge, you don't have to look far to find good water. Right in front of the canoe launch, in fact, is a deep section that often draws

Getting to Settles Bridge

To GA 400 · 346 · GA 20 · Suwanee Dam Rd · James Creek · **Fish Weir Shoals** · 345 · 344 · SETTLES BRIDGE UNIT (CRNRA) · Johnson Rd · Settles Bridge Rd · P · **Historic Settles Bridge (closed)** · **Fish weir**

attention from anglers (and sometimes from swimmers too).

This area of deep water, like similar water elsewhere, is probably best fished from a boat. You'll want to use flies or lures that sink quickly. Try a heavily weighted nymph rig, a heavy streamer and a sink-tip line, or a fast-sinking spinner, spoon or trout-like crankbait.

Upstream from the canoe put-in, you'll find several relatively shallow runs (located close to deep water – always a good con-

figuration!) along with rocky areas on river left (the same side of the river as the canoe launch). These are accessible to wading or rock-hopping anglers when the water is low. This area is easy to access, too, thanks to a foot trail which goes upriver from the canoe launch and follows the river's left bank.

From that foot trail, look for well-used fisherman's pathways lead-

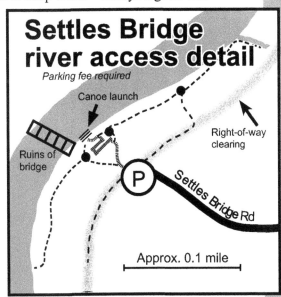

Settles Bridge river access detail

Parking fee required

Canoe launch · Right-of-way clearing · Ruins of bridge · P · Settles Bridge Rd

Approx. 0.1 mile

Popular with canoeists and kayakers, the Settles Bridge parking area may be crowded on weekends.

ing from the main trail down to the river. There are several of these trail-to-river connector paths in the area, and some are not too steep (at least by upper tailwater standards) and can take you to potential fishing spots. But watch your footing, and beware of roots which might cause you to trip.

Looking upriver from the canoe launch, you'll see some inviting wadable water that offers good access to nice runs.

When wading at Settles Bridge, one of the first things you'll notice is that the water here is often very clear – so clear that it can be difficult to accurately judge the water's depth. That's why experienced Settles Bridge anglers use polarized glasses (so they can better see the bottom) as well as a wading staff (used to provide that all-important additional point of balance while wading). Without those aids, it's easy to move into unexpectedly deep water without meaning to do so.

Because of the risk of accidentally stepping into deep water, it's always a smart idea to use a PFD when wading here too. Inflatable suspender-type PFDs are good for anglers and don't get in the way. But remember that even the best PFD will do its job only if you wear it.

At low water, which is when most anglers will be fishing the Settles Bridge area, it is not too difficult to paddle a canoe or kayak for quite a ways upstream from the Settles Bridge canoe launch. Then you can float and fish your

The zigzag ramp at Settles Bridge makes it easy for almost anyone to get down to the river.

way back downriver to your starting point.

Here's another way to fish this area. It's possible to carry a float tube upriver (along the trail which follows the left bank upstream), find a place to enter the river, and then float back to the canoe launch, taking your time and fishing as you go. That can be a very relaxing and effective way to fish this portion of the tailwater.

Floating anglers who are comfortable running the Class II rapid that's located a short distance above the GA 20 bridge frequently use the Settles Bridge canoe launch as an ending point for float trips starting at Lower Pool West (near Buford Dam). We will take a look at that particular float (from the dam to Settles Bridge) on the pages that follow. ☐

Dam to Settles Bridge

Here's a look at one of the most popular float trip routes on the upper tailwater

L et's take a look at one of the most popular floats on the tailwater – the run from the ramp at Lower Pool West near Buford Dam down past the fish hatchery and under the GA 20 bridge to the canoe/kayak/tube takeout at Settles Bridge. This float lets you fish about five miles of water on one of the most scenic sections of the river.

Remember that life jackets are required to be worn by all persons on the river from Buford Dam to the GA 20 bridge. If you're using a tube, you should wear it all the time whenever you're on the tailwater.

With one exception, this is a fairly easy float. Although float times are difficult to estimate because of the number of variables involved (not the least of which is how long you spend fish-

This sign, visible from the river, signals that you're nearing the Settles Bridge canoe and kayak access. However, most floaters just look for the ruins of the old bridge. They're impossible to miss, and the take-out is on river left.

ing!) most say that it usually takes at least six hours to make the run. Be sure that you are comfortable with a float of this duration (and with your ability to handle the Class II rapids above GA 20) while floating in your chosen means of conveyance.

The first notable feature you'll encounter is Bowmans Island. Follow

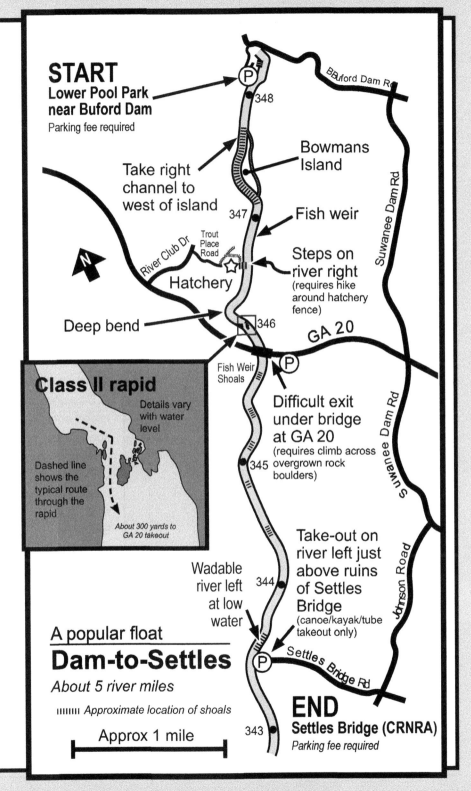

START
Lower Pool Park near Buford Dam
Parking fee required

348

Buford Dam Rd

Take right channel to west of island

Bowmans Island

347

Fish weir

River Club Dr
Trout Place Road
Hatchery

Steps on river right
(requires hike around hatchery fence)

Deep bend

346

GA 20

Suwanee Dam Rd

Fish Weir Shoals

Class II rapid

Details vary with water level

Dashed line shows the typical route through the rapid

About 300 yards to GA 20 takeout

Difficult exit under bridge at GA 20
(requires climb across overgrown rock boulders)

345

S Suwanee Dam Rd

Wadable river left at low water

344

Take-out on river left just above ruins of Settles Bridge
(canoe/kayak/tube takeout only)

Johnson Road

A popular float
Dam-to-Settles
About 5 river miles

ıııııı *Approximate location of shoals*

Approx 1 mile

Settles Bridge Rd

343

END
Settles Bridge (CRNRA)
Parking fee required

the main channel around the right (west) side of the island. Take time to fish the deeper water that you see there, particularly where fallen timber has piled up along the bank. Such places are favorite haunts of brown trout. Most of the usual offerings will work, but remember that advice about big flies for big fish. This is one section of the river where it really might pay off.

Above: Though it's especially popular as a put-in or take-out for kayak and canoe anglers, Settles Bridge holds potential for anglers on foot as well. Below: Entering the Class II rapid above GA 20.

You'll encounter some shoals toward the lower end of Bowmans Island and, soon thereafter, you'll come to the hatchery on river right. Earlier, we mentioned the access steps

at the hatchery. It can be worth making a few casts in that area.

Beyond the hatchery is a stretch of relatively gentle water where you can drift and fish at your leisure. Pay attention to deeper areas and to the outside of the bend on your right. And then (just a little ways beyond that bend) comes the biggest challenge on this float. It's the Class II rapid located about 300 yards upriver from the GA 20 bridge.

As you approach this rapid, there's a rocky area on river right. Just beyond it is a large rock outcrop located mid-channel with a chute between the outcrop and the west (right) bank. Take that right channel, lining up before you enter it. You'll quickly drop over a ledge and through fast water. Be sure you have on a PFD. It's required by law here...and (yep, I'll say it again) by common sense.

If you're not sure about running the rapid, you can portage around the rapid (over the rocks on river left) and re-enter the river below it.

One great way to learn about this rapid without getting wet is to check it out on Google Earth. There, a bird's-eye view shows the rapid and its approach. Search for "Settles Bridge" and look downriver near GA 20, or go straight to it by entering these coordinates:

34 07 49.79 N, 84 05 39.34 W

For further insights into what this rapid is like, put the web to work for you and check out any of a number of videos on Youtube which (thanks to the current crop of on-the-spot action cameras) allow you to run the rapid from the comfort of your own home. They're fun to watch, and they're great confidence builders too. Search for "GA 20 rapids on Chattahoochee" or something similar to find these videos.

Once past that rapid,it's straightforward. A few hundred yards downriver is the GA 20 bridge. It's an easy float from GA 20 down to the take-out at Settles Bridge, which awaits you a bit more than two river miles further downstream. ☐

Settles Bridge to McGinnis Ferry

Fly and lure recommendations

Flies: Near the dam, midges are the thing. Tiny size 18 or smaller midge emergers (fished individually, with one or two additional nymphs, or as a dropper or droppers beneath a dry) are the thing here. Favorite patterns include Blue Assassins, Moonshine Midges, Zebra Midges and a host of other tiny emergers. For the "dry" part of a dry/dropper rig, use a suitably-sized Adams or an Elk Hair or Foamback Caddis – or a Stimulator.

Don't overlook streamers, particularly as you drift into deeper water at the lower end of this run. Something resembling a brown trout (even a relatively big 6- or 7-inch brown trout) can be effective, especially when fished near timber.

Lures: When selecting lures, think "brown trout." Roostertails or Mepps Spinners in gold/black or silver/black are popular. So are crankbaits with a firetiger color scheme.

Bait is permitted in this section of the river down to the GA 20 bridge, and bait enthusiasts do well with worms, crickets and corn. Powerbait works too.

Chattahoochee Pointe / McGinnis Ferry

One of the good things about the metro Atlanta area is that there's widespread awareness of the value of the Chattahoochee. The river corridor is recognized as an exceptional recreational resource that offers a great range of recreation opportunities to folks with a variety of different interests.

In many quarters, there's active and ongoing interest in establishing new public spaces along the river. Thus, it's not surprising that several new park facilities have appeared along the Chattahoochee in recent years.

The Chattahoochee Pointe canoe launch (above) requires a short carry along a graveled road (inset). The launch itself, while not fancy, is perfect for a quick float-and-fish excursion down to the McGinnis Ferry ramp.

This section will focus on two of them – Chattahoochee Pointe (a Forsyth County park) and the McGinnis Ferry boat ramp, administered by the National Park Service.

These two access points are separated by only a little more than a mile of river. Though neither site offers wadable water, there's float access at both – a canoe/kayak/tube launch at Chattahoochee Pointe and a full-fledged trailer-friendly ramp at McGinnis Ferry. Best of all, because they're so close together, a float from one to the other is easy to do.

Chattahoochee Pointe

Located not quite three river miles downstream from CRNRA's Settles Bridge Unit boat ramp, and easily accessible from McGinnis Ferry Road, Chattahoochee Pointe is one of the newest public parks

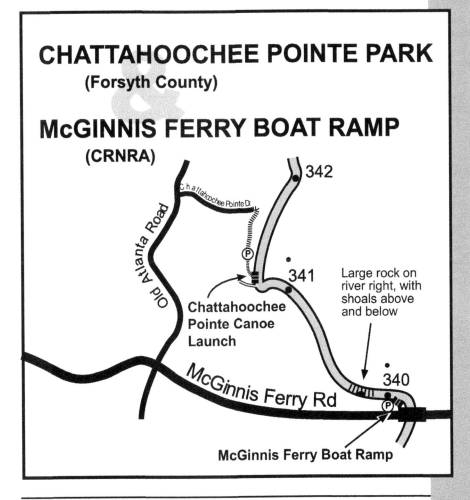

Part of the fun of figuring out new water is discovering what's around the next bend. This particular bend, located just downriver from the Chattahoochee Pointe canoe launch point, offers some intriguing deep-water fishing possibilities on the outside of the bend.

to offer access to the river. This delightful Forsyth County park is located just over a mile upriver from the McGinnis Ferry boat ramp. It provides anglers with an intermediate access point between the ramps at Settles Bridge and McGinnis Ferry, thus allowing even more flexibility when planning excursions on this part of the tailwater.

The canoe launch is located a short distance beyond the parking area at the far end of the park's road. It's a basic gravel launch, and it puts you in the river in an area of deep water just upstream from the mouth of a fairly substantial creek. Like other deep places on the tailwater, this one seems to beg for a deep-running streamer or other subsurface offering.

There are no real wading opportunities right at the Chattahoochee Pointe canoe launch. But what about the water below the put-in? As you face the river from the launching area, look to your right. On the far side of the river you'll see a tantalizing sandbar extending out into the flow.

At first glance it looks like might be the tip end of an island, but that's just a trick of perspective. What you're seeing is actually a sandy point on the inside of a very sharp bend in the river. A sharp bend? Aha! Bends usually mean deep water on the outside, and that's certainly the case here.

You know what deep water might mean. To get to it, you'll have to cross the river; to avoid getting caught in the eddy below the launch, paddle straight out and across.

What lies beyond that sandy point? It's a fairly short float from the Chattahoochee Pointe canoe launch downriver to the McGinnis Ferry ramp. That provides anglers with another short-trip possibility, and the shuttle back to Chattahoochee Pointe park is easy and straightforward.

Note, however, that the current is relatively slow between those two access points. Float tubers will have plenty of time to appreciate the river through this section, particularly if the wind is blowing out of the south. In fact, if the wind is strong enough, float tubers may

Approaching the McGinnis Ferry boat ramp following a float trip on the upper tailwater. Inset: The McGinnis Ferry bridge, as seen from the boat ramp.

The McGinnis Ferry boat launch provides a great starting point for floats on the upper tailwater. The paved McGinnis Ferry ramp is suitable for canoes, kayaks and trailered boats. It's great as a take-out for trips starting at Settles Bridge and also as a put-in for trips to Rogers Bridge or Abbotts Bridge.

find downstream progress to be slow or nonexistent (or even negative if the wind blows you upriver). For that reason, some find a canoe or kayak to be the most effective way to fish this section of the river.

McGinnis Ferry

From a fisherman's point of view, one of the real gems on the upper tailwater is the paved boat ramp on the west side of the river (river right) at the McGinnis Ferry bridge.

This ramp, which will handle trailers with no problem, provides floating anglers (whether using canoes, kayaks, power boats or tubes) with a great way to gain access to the water. It's popular as a take-out for trips which start upriver (at the dam, Settles Bridge, or Chattahoochee Pointe). It's also a popular put-in for excursions heading downriver to Abbotts Bridge or beyond (or upriver, if you have a boat and motor capable of handling the challenges that an upstream trip will present).

As at Chattahoochee Pointe, the wading prospects are pretty much nonexistent at McGinnis Ferry. The water in the area is just too deep. But what about fishing from shore? It's possible to make some casts with a spinning rod from the area right around the boat ramp, where you'll find promising water right in front of you and on either side too. But wade fishing here in its classic sense is just not going to happen.

Upriver from the boat ramp, a fence blocks upstream access to the riverbank. I checked with the county's parks and recreation department and learned that the land above the ramp is owned by Forsyth County's water department, not its parks department, and at the time of this writing that fence does indeed block upstream access above the ramp.

There have been anecdotal reports of land-based anglers being ticketed for walking past the fence. For that reason, you'll want to respect the fence.

Hopefully, at some point in the future, the parks department will be able to acquire some of the upstream property and the opportunity to fish and access the river from the west bank above the ramp will return. If that happens, then there will indeed be additional foot-based fishing opportunities to be enjoyed upriver from the McGinnis Ferry ramp.

But even though there's no foot access above the ramp, you can certainly float this section of river. Many trout anglers love to do just that.

And that brings us to yet another upper tailwater float profile, this one focusing on the float trip which starts upriver at Settles Bridge and takes you down to the ramp at McGinnis Ferry. □

Remember that it's artificials-only from GA 20 downriver to the Medlock Bridge boat ramp. This section is part of the artificials-only water, so don't use bait.

Settles Bridge to McGinnis Ferry

While there may not be a lot to say about the wade fishing possibilities at the Chattahoochee Pointe or McGinnis Ferry river access points, there is a *lot* to talk about if the subject turns to float trips through that same area. In fact, the Settles-to-McGinnis float is one that is particularly popular with many Chattahoochee trout anglers.

From the Settles Bridge canoe launching point, it's not quite four river miles down to McGinnis Ferry. A little over two miles into it is the intermediate access point at the Chattahoochee Pointe Park canoe launch; look for that launch point on river right at the start of a prominent bend and just before a beach-like sandy point (it will be apparent at low water) on the inside of the bend to the left.

There are two ways to approach a Settles-to-McGinnis float.

One is to launch a canoe or kayak at Settles Bridge and float downriver (note that the put-in at Settles Bridge is for kayaks and canoes and is not accessible to trailers). Most anglers allow three or four hours, plus or minus fishing time.

A second approach is to launch a powered boat at McGinnis Ferry, motor upriver, and then drift and fish your way back down to where you started. Just be sure that your boat is suitable for use on the river.

About two-thirds of a mile below Settles Bridge, look for the remains of an historic fish weir. Scholars believe that it was constructed in the early 19th century by Cherokee Indians. To use it, people would get into the river upstream of the weir and splash their way downstream, driving fish in front of them. Others would wait at the weir's outlet and catch the fish as they passed through.

The weir is still a good place to fish, and you'll want to make a few casts above and below it.

Another eight-tenths of a mile puts you near the site of a proposed re-regulation dam which was once planned for the river. Approved by Congress in 1986, the dam was to have been constructed to address concerns over minimum downstream flows while also making sure that the Atlanta area had enough water. Pre-construction studies, however,

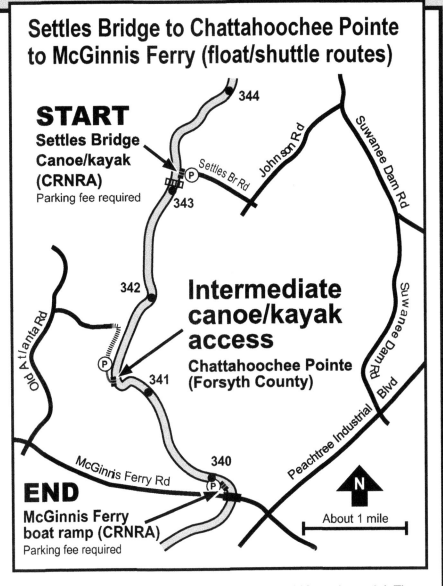

Settles Bridge to Chattahoochee Pointe to McGinnis Ferry (float/shuttle routes)

344

START
Settles Bridge
Canoe/kayak
(CRNRA)
Parking fee required

Settles Br Rd

Johnson Rd

Suwanee Dam Rd

343

342

Intermediate canoe/kayak access

Chattahoochee Pointe
(Forsyth County)

341

Old Atlanta Rd

Suwanee Dam Rd Blvd

Peachtree Industrial

340

McGinnis Ferry Rd

END
McGinnis Ferry
boat ramp (CRNRA)
Parking fee required

N

About 1 mile

made it clear that the environmental impacts would be substantial. They also put the spotlight on project costs, which looked like they would be very high. Faced with those facts, the Corps of Engineers backed away from the project in the late 1980s and went with other alternatives (notably earmarking more of Lake Lanier's water for Atlanta's ever-thirsty pipes). One result of that was the "water wars" involving Alabama, Florida and Georgia. That battle still goes on.

By now you're approaching Chattahoochee Pointe. The flow is fairly gentle with more deep areas. Soon, you'll see that sharp bend to the left

Ready to take out at the McGinnis Ferry boat ramp. This ramp provides great access to this section of the river.

which signals the lower end of the Chattahoochee Pointe Park area and lets you know that you're approaching the unpaved canoe launch on river right just before the bend. That launching point provides an intermediate take-out or put-in for those who want a shorter trip.

The sandbar itself is just beyond the Chattahoochee Pointe launch. If you're in a canoe or kayak, the water through here is slack enough that you should have no trouble fishing a little ways downriver and then paddling back to the canoe ramp.

Once beyond Chattahoochee Pointe, forward progress may slow as the current flows too. That's not a problem if you're in a canoe or kayak, but wind can make it a hassle if you're in a float tube. Here, as elsewhere on the river, wind may actually push a tube back upriver at times.

The mostly gentle water continues to the takeout at the McGinnis Ferry boat ramp (on your right before the bridge). Note the large rock on river right as you approach the bridge; the shoally area around that rock is popular with anglers who throw deep-running flies or lures. The takeout itself is about as easy as they come thanks to that nice concrete boat ramp.

Fly and lure recommendations

Flies: The Settles-to-McGinnis stretch is transitional. It's still close enough to the dam to be impacted by strong flows, but as you move downriver the flows moderate and deeper water becomes more common. Because of that mix, try a range of flies including small midge emergers, larger stonefly nymphs, and more traditional nymphs such as Pheasant Tails and Soft Hackle Emergers. As at the dam, a dry/dropper rig consisting of a Blue-Winged Olive and a midge emerger can be effective, especially when drifted along bubble lines which mark the seams between currents. But other types of flies will work too.

Streamers are definitely worth trying. To target the really big fish, go with large (6- or 7-inch-long) streamers tied to resemble brown trout. Work them around the many timber accumulations along the bank.

Lures: Roostertails or Mepps Spinners in gold/black or silver/black, as well as crankbaits with a firetiger color scheme, do a good job of suggesting small brown trout and can be effective.

One more reminder: It's artificials-only from GA Hwy 20 to the boat ramp at CRNRA's Medlock Bridge Unit just upstream of GA 141. This section is part of the artificials-only water.

As you float and fish this section, notice the bankside timber accumulations in many areas. They make good holding water for browns, and it never hurts to cast a streamer or crankbait toward them or to drift a nymph near them as you go.

Here's one more thing to note. As you're getting out of the river, check out the high-water marks on the McGinnis Ferry ramp's concrete walls. Wow! Though it is hard to imagine as you stand at river's edge at low water, the river does indeed get that high at times. Those marks represent a *lot* of water – and I admit it: thinking about all that water roaring down the river's channel is just a little bit scary.

That's all the more reason to treasure those days on the tailwater when the river is low. □

Remember that it's artificials-only from GA 20 downriver to the Medlock Bridge boat ramp. This section is part of the artificials-only water, so don't use bait.

Rogers Bridge Park

The next access point downriver from McGinnis Ferry is Rogers Bridge Park, operated by the City of Duluth. It's about three river miles from McGinnis to Rogers Bridge. In addition to a great deal of meadowlike green space, amenities at Rogers Bridge Park include a picnic pavilion, a playground, a volleyball court, and one of the most architectural canoe launch facilities you'll ever see.

Rogers Bridge Park is also right next to the Chattapoochee Dog Park, a truly neat playground for dogs that you and your pup are sure to enjoy...when you're not exploring the river with a fishing rod, that is. Ellie, my resident mini Schnauzer puppy and a great fishing companion in her own right, insisted that I mention the dog park prominently. After all, as she so gently reminded me, fisherfolk are not the only ones who need some recreational time. Puppies like to play too.

The structure that we call Rogers Bridge was named for John Rogers, one of the area's early settlers. He lived on a farm here

The skeleton of Rogers Bridge still crosses the Chattahoochee. the old bridge is just upriver from the take-out point (on river left) and is an impossible-to-miss landmark.

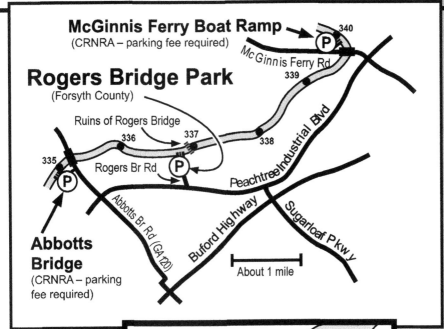

McGinnis Ferry Boat Ramp → 340
(CRNRA – parking fee required)

McGinnis Ferry Rd

Rogers Bridge Park
(Forsyth County)

339

Ruins of Rogers Bridge

336   337   338

Peachtree Industrial Blvd

335

Rogers Br Rd

Abbotts Br Rd (GA 120)

Buford Highway

Sugarloaf Pkwy

Abbotts Bridge
(CRNRA – parking fee required)

About 1 mile

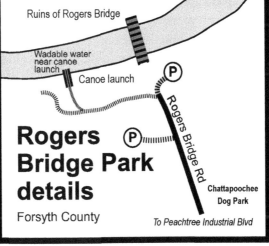

Ruins of Rogers Bridge

Wadable water near canoe launch

Canoe launch

Rogers Bridge Park details

Forsyth County

Rogers Bridge Rd

Chattapoochee Dog Park

To Peachtree Industrial Blvd

with his wife Sarah. John and Sarah raised an even dozen children, and John still somehow found enough time in the day to run the family farm and also to operate a ferry which crossed the river.

Eventually, as so often happened at the old ferry sites, a bridge was built to replace the ferry. That bridge continued to carry traffic across the Chattahoochee until late in the 1970s. Today, Rogers Bridge is pretty much just a steel skeleton spanning the water from bank to bank (though it does carry a pipe across the river).

Interestingly, there has been some talk of possibly restoring the

Remember that it's artificials-only from GA 20 downriver to the Medlock Bridge boat ramp. This section is part of the artificials-only water, so don't use bait.

bridge for use by hikers and bicyclists and even interconnecting the bridge with future multi-use trails. That would truly be a neat thing, and many with a stake in recreation in this area hope that those plans will indeed come to pass.

Here's the canoe launch at Rogers Bridge. From the top, it's a medium-long but easy carry to your car.

What's left of the old bridge can be seen about 100 yards upriver from the Rogers Bridge Park canoe launch. The ruins provide a great landmark if you're floating down the river to let you know that the Rogers Bridge canoe launch is coming up just beyond the bridge on river left.

This particular canoe launch, by the way, is impressive and elaborate by canoe launch standards. It provides a paved entry point (with some steps) for those wishing to enter or exit the river, and the carry to the launch from the park's nearby parking areas is not too long to handle.

There's even more good news, however. You'll find wadable water near the canoe launch, so anglers without boats can enjoy fishing this portion of the river too. ◻

A floating angler gets ready to make a cast near one of several historic Native American fish weirs along this section of the tailwater.

Abbotts Bridge Unit (CRNRA)

About two river miles below Rogers Bridge Park, and just a little ways below the point where Abbotts Bridge Road/GA 120 crosses the river, you'll find the next access point on the tailwater – the boat ramp at the Abbotts Bridge Unit of the Chattahoochee River National Recreation Area.

The Abbotts Bridge Unit features (in addition to an honest-to-goodness boat ramp) picnic facilities and a covered pavilion as well as a restroom facility. There's some limited hiking there too.

Since Abbotts Bridge is a CRNRA unit, a parking fee is required.

The Abbotts Bridge access point marks the beginning of a change in the nature of the river's shoreline. Above Abbotts Bridge, the shoreline is relatively undeveloped and the river often has an almost wilderness feel. As you move below Abbotts, however, development increasingly begins to make itself known (and seen) – often in the form of big houses and sprawling golf courses which sit not far from the river.

However, despite the gradual onslaught of these trappings of

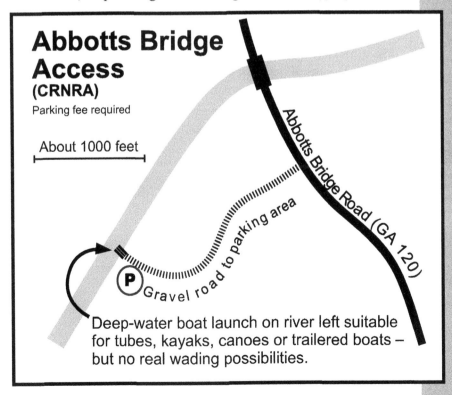

Abbotts Bridge Access
(CRNRA)
Parking fee required

About 1000 feet

Gravel road to parking area

P

Abbotts Bridge Road (GA 120)

Deep-water boat launch on river left suitable for tubes, kayaks, canoes or trailered boats – but no real wading possibilities.

The Abbotts Bridge boat ramp will handle tubes, kayaks and canoes as well as trailered boats.

urban life, the river remains a good place for fishing and a home for brown and rainbow trout. It's just not the more remote-feeling river that you were getting used to upstream.

As you can imagine, the presence of a boat ramp draws many users to Abbotts Bridge. As you'll quickly discover during the warmer months of the year, that ramp is heavily used as a take-out point by non-anglers too who are out to enjoy a lazy day of drifting

Floating and fishing below the Abbotts Bridge boat ramp.

down the Hooch. It's not unusual to encounter shuttle buses pulling into Abbotts Bridge parking area to pick up tubers at the end of their runs.

But anglers also use this site to access the river. The ramp will handle tubes, canoes, kayaks and trailered boats, opening the door to a variety of boat- or tube-based fishing excursions.

Although it pretty much eliminates the possibility of wading, the deep water in this section of the river provides good cover for fish. The abundant timber which you will see all along the shoreline creates great holding water too. Experienced tailwater anglers know that such timber accumulations create great habitat for brown trout. There is always the possibility of encountering a big brown here.

By the way, when visiting the Abbotts Bridge Unit, you'll want to take a little while and see some of the enormous oak trees which stand along the hiking trail which starts near the boat ramp. The trailhead is on the down-river side of the ramp, and as you hike the short trail (which more or less paral-

One of the enormous oaks that you'll find along the Abbotts Bridge trail, a short hiking trail which begins immediately downriver from the boat ramp.

lels the river) you'll pass several of these oak giants. They are truly huge, and seeing them is well worth the time it takes to do so.

Abbotts Bridge is not a major hiking destination, but what it might lack in miles of trail it certainly makes up for with those impressive trees. Be sure to check them out. ☐

Remember that it's artificials-only from GA 20 downriver to the Medlock Bridge boat ramp. This section is part of the artificials-only water, so don't use bait.

McGinnis Ferry to Rogers Bridge to Abbotts Bridge

The McGinnis-to-Rogers-to-Abbotts section of the Hooch is a good ways downriver from Buford Dam. Perhaps because it's come so far, the river seems to have settled down. The watchwords now are "slower" and "deeper" and "don't forget to bring the paddles."

Those paddles, in fact, will be important when floating here, especially if you want to move downriver any faster than the average flow of about 1.5 miles per hour. The reason: the river begins to flatten below McGinnis Ferry. That means, for the most part, that you'll be on water with less current, and less current means longer float times.

Most who float here do so in a kayak, canoe, or rowable pontoon (or in a powered boat). Is that to say that this is not float tube water? Well, it can certainly be done in a float tube. In fact, a float tube trip from McGinnis Ferry to Rogers Bridge or from Rogers Bridge to Abbotts Bridge can be a relaxing way to enjoy fishing the river.

But "relaxing," in this case, may also be a synonym for "slow."

If you're floating here in a tube, be sure you give yourself enough time to complete the float (with fishing time added, of course) and reach your takeout – and you may need more time than you think.

As noted earlier, the theoretical benchmark is about 1.5 river miles per hour on average through this section. But depending on conditions, and depending on how much time you spend fishing, experienced tubers on this section will tell you to expect your actual rate of progress to be no more than one mile per hour (or even slower). The exact rate will vary depending on how much time you spend fishing...and it might be even slower if the wind happens to be blowing from the wrong direction. This is another section of the Chattahoochee where the wind can literally

Remember that it's artificials-only from GA 20 downriver to the Medlock Bridge boat ramp. This section is part of the artificials-only water, so don't use bait.

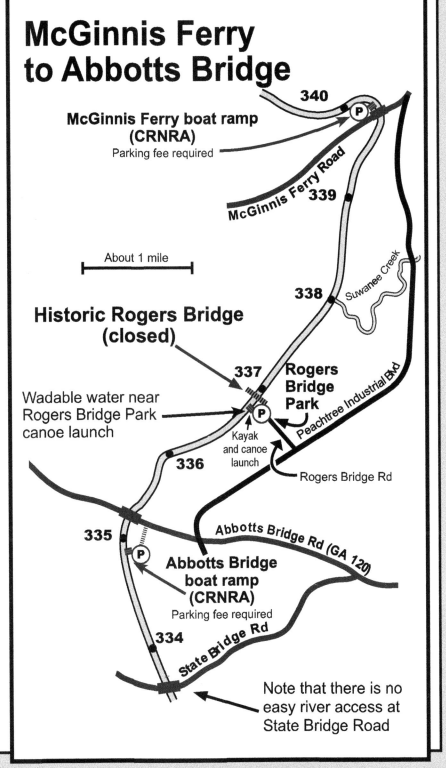

McGinnis Ferry to Abbotts Bridge

McGinnis Ferry boat ramp (CRNRA)

Parking fee required

340

339

McGinnis Ferry Road

338

Suwanee Creek

About 1 mile

Historic Rogers Bridge (closed)

337

Rogers Bridge Park

Wadable water near Rogers Bridge Park canoe launch

P

Kayak and canoe launch

Peachtree Industrial Blvd

336

Rogers Bridge Rd

335

Abbotts Bridge Rd (GA 120)

P

Abbotts Bridge boat ramp (CRNRA)

Parking fee required

334

State Bridge Rd

Note that there is no easy river access at State Bridge Road

Trout

blow a float tube upstream.

For those reasons, the general feeling seems to be that this section of the river is best suited for floating in a canoe, kayak, personal pontoon with oars, or some sort of a powered boat. Such craft give you much more freedom of movement on this water and will liberate you from total dependence on the current.

By the way, those who fish this section of river may be interested to know that the one-time state record brown, a monster weighing 18 lb. 6 oz., was caught in the stretch of water between what is now Rogers Bridge Park and the McGinnis Ferry bridge about three miles upstream. That fish of a lifetime was landed by angler Charlie Ford.

Ford's fish stood as the state record from 2001 until the summer of 2014, when angler Chad Doughty landed an even bigger one weighing 20 lb. 14 oz. It too came from the tailwater.

Reminder: It's still artificials-only...and if you're floating beyond Abbotts Bridge, note that there's no real access at State Bridge Road. ☐

McGinnis Ferry to Abbotts Bridge

Fly and lure recommendations

Flies: Small midges such as Blue Assassins, Moonshine Midges, Zebra Midges, and the like often do well here. So do big-and-ugly stonefly nymphs. Or try a two-nymph rig using a size 18 midge emerger as a dropper behind a weighted Pat's Rubberlegs...or even two stonefly nymphs.

If you're thinking dries, try the Elk Hair or Foamback Caddis or perhaps a Stimulator. They resemble the caddisflies and stoneflies that occur in much of the tailwater. Royal Wulffs or an Adams often work well too. Near grassy banks, try hoppers.

You may also have success with a dry/dropper rig with (say) a midge emerger under an Adams. It's the same sort of set-up you might use up near the dam.

Streamers resembling brown trout are as effective here as elsewhere. Fish close to cover. Big streamers tempt big fish.

Lures: The tailwater standards – Roostertails or Mepps Spinners, spoons, or small crankbaits – can all work well here, especially if they resemble a brown trout. As someone once said, any lure with the word "trout" in its name is probably going to be a good tailwater spinning lure.

Above: The canoe launch at Rogers Bridge Park provides a nice intermediate put-in/take-out point between McGinnis Ferry and Abbotts Bridge. Below: Trout anglers use the Abbotts Bridge ramp to access the tailwater for floats downriver to Medlock Bridge or beyond. This ramp also serves as a takeout for short floats starting at Rogers Bridge or at McGinnis Ferry, and it's also a good put-in for floats downriver to Medlock Bridge or beyond. Tubes work for shorter floats; for longer runs, kayaks or canoes are better.

Trout anglers use the Abbotts Bridge boat ramp to access the tailwater for floats downriver to Medlock Bridge or beyond.

Davie Crawford, founder of Deep South Fly Anglers, mans the oars near Medlock Bridge.

Talking trout
(early!)
at Medlock Bridge

There's nothing like early morning on the river, especially when you're talking about trout.

"How about we meet at the Medlock Bridge boat ramp at 7 a.m.?" says Davie Crawford, founder of Deep South Fly Anglers. It's funny how 7 a.m. never sounds like a bad idea at 1:30 in the afternoon. But when the alarm goes off at 5:45 the next morning, you might be inclined to ask the proverbial question "why?"

Actually, I've set the alarm for 5:30. I'm like that when fishing is involved. I want to be sure I get there on time. On the front end of a trip, it's all about the clock. But once on the water, it's "fishin' time." The tyranny of the alarm clock somehow seems to fade away. Fishin' time is good.

Davie Crawford began fishing the Chattahoochee around 2000 and has loved the river ever since. He works fulltime in the Geographic Information Systems (GIS) field but still maintains a busy guiding schedule. He's on the water (between guiding and fishing for fun) about 150 days each year.

"I do it because I love to do it," he says as we stand at the boat ramp at the Medlock Bridge Unit of the Chattahoochee River National Recreation Area. His boat's already in the water, and he's ready to go.

Davie's boat, outfitted with an outboard jet motor, is ideal for the upper tailwater. I climb aboard, and he points the bow upstream. The river is low, revealing obstacles that could easily ruin your day – logs, snags, and tooth-like rocks, all waiting to take a bite out of a careless boater's boat.

"It only takes a split second for one of them to tear up your motor...or worse," he says.

The plan is to run upstream and then drift and fish back down to where we started. Along the way, he adds, we'll try nymphs as well as streamers.

"I usually try to incorporate a stonefly into my nymph rigs," he says. When fishing a two-fly set-up, one will almost always be a Rubberlegs-style stonefly nymph or a Kaufmann's Stone in size 6 or 8. Sometimes he replaces one of the stoneflies with a size 14 or 16 Prince nymph.

Rainbows may hit either one, he adds, but his experience suggests that browns will go after the stonefly 99 percent of the time.

"You can throw small flies or attractors and catch a bunch of rainbows," he says. "Or you can throw something bigger and more natural looking and catch browns. It all depends on what you're after."

We run up the river for a while. Sometime later, and some distance above the ramp, Davie shuts off the motor. Our forward progress slows and then reverses as the current takes hold and the boat begins to drift downriver. We're in what he calls "soft water" – that is, water without a lot of riffles. Instead of the riffles you'd get if the river was flowing over rocks or shoals, this water is smooth. It really is kind of like a soft pillow.

Davie notes that the low flow that morning (in the neighborhood of 700 to 800 cfs) makes it easy for the fish to move around a bit, particularly along edges where there are current seams.

"Fish may be moving in and out of the main flow," he says, adding that that's good news for fishermen. During higher flows, more vigorous current can drive fish to the relatively quiet water along bank. But this morning's calm conditions give the fish the green light to move freely around the river.

Those low flows are good for nymphing, he adds. But higher flows (in the 1000 to 2000 cfs range) are the signal to put away the nymph rod and go to a big streamer – perhaps a Sex Dungeon or a Double Deceiver. Color-wise, he says, he leans toward streamers in black, white and yellow.

Davie does note that he himself will sometimes fish the river at even higher flows. At such times, he says, you may get strikes if you throw big streamers right against the bank. That calls for precision casting, however, and making surgical casts at high flows is a fast-paced undertaking that is not for the faint of heart.

Nor is it for beginning anglers.

"Personally, I will throw streamers up to about 7,000 cfs," he says. "Anything above that, though, I go to the house."

Does he keep streamers in the arsenal all year long? Yes, he says, adding that he is particularly fond of big streamers in the spring. Why is that?

"Because that's when they stock so many rainbows," he says. "A lot of anglers don't realize it, but rainbows are something big browns like to eat."

Davie acknowledges that when he fishes big streamers he will probably not catch many small fish. But the flip side of that is that a very high percentage of the fish he does catch will be large ones.

"If I'm streamer fishing, I'm going for zero or hero," he says.

Today, however, the conditions say "nymphs." Davie picks up a rod rigged with a fluorocarbon leader and two weighted stonefly nymph imitations spaced about a foot apart. He adds a small #4 shot about six inches above the top fly ("to help 'em drop," he says) and then makes the cast. The flies drop near a current seam, evident as a broken line of bubbles and leaves, and a few casts later the day's first fish (a rainbow) is in the net.

Though nymphs and big streamers are prominent in Davie's fly boxes, he

A lone angler fishes below a Native American fish trap. It's still a good place to look for fish, though these days the fish are rainbows and browns.

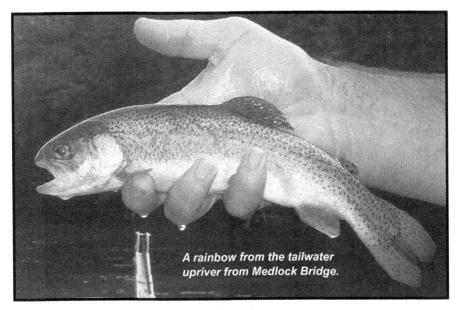

A rainbow from the tailwater upriver from Medlock Bridge.

will go with other flies too as conditions dictate.

"In April and May you get a massive caddis hatch here," he says. "At those times, an Elk Hair Caddis is the ticket –"

(The indicator, which had been drifting along peacefully while we talk, suddenly disappears. Davie sets the hook and the rod bends sharply but just for an instant. "Dang!" he says. "That felt like a good fish – probably a good brown!" But it's gone. The boat drifts on, and we are back to talking flies. He picks up where he left off.)

" – and during winter it's Blue Winged Olives and midges. Sometimes you'll find fish podded up between logs, and you can anchor up and maybe catch three or four out of a pod."

But I'm curious about something. When that fish hit a minute ago, he said it felt like a brown. How could he tell?

"Browns go to the bottom," he says. "And they like soft water and a little shade." That's what we were fishing.

Yeah, probably a brown. And since it got away, it can be as big as we want it to be.

How does Davie choose the spots where he fishes? It's a matter of learning where the fish are, he says, and that's a function of spending time on the water and remembering that good spots tend to stay good over time.

"Year after year, the fish are in the same areas," he says.

One way to find those spots is to sight-fish the water in spring and summer when the river tends to run clear. We can't do that today, since recent rains and the approach of fall have combined with minimal releases to give

---

Trout

us a somewhat murky river. It's not muddy, or even opaque, but it's definitely not crystal clear.

Davie, however, is not concerned. He knows where the fish should be, and he understands that the slight murkiness just might put the fish at ease.

He casts again. The dual stoneflies drop softly and quickly sink into the run; the white indicator drifts along above them, giving an idea of where the flies are.

Davie mends the line, moving the indicator slightly as he does. A few seconds later he mends again, causing the indicator to hop once more.

"I like to do a lot of small mends," he says, "and give the flies a little movement."

Again, he throws a slight mend into the line. Again, the indicator (along with the flies drifting unseen below it) jiggles. The rig drifts another six inches. Then the indicator dives out of sight. Davie sets the hook, and a moment later a second fish – another rainbow of about 10 inches – is in the net.

"That's why I like the little mends," he says. "I try to visualize what those flies are doing, and sometimes the fish will hammer one of them right after it moves."

In addition to thinking

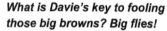

What is Davie's key to fooling those big browns? Big flies!

about where and how, Davie also factors in the level of the river and how it may be changing. It's important, he says, to catch the water just right.

"Bigger fish move a lot more when the water's going up or down," he says. "I'll throw streamers till it falls out from under me, and then I'll go to nymphing." He adds, "I like to fish the falling water myself."

We drift through a gentle little chute, and Davie nudges the oars to move the boat to one side of the run below it. Again he casts, this time to the current seam along the side of the run. Again he mends, and again the indicator disappears. He sets the hook – but this time it's not a trout but some unseen subsurface obstruction.

A gentle tug doesn't free the fly. Neither does rowing upstream to try from a different angle.

He breaks off the fly and brings in the line to re-rig. Both of the stoneflies are gone, and he ties on two more. "That was a snag," he says as he ties the knots, but he notes that a hang-up is not always a hang-up.

"I've had clients who thought they were hung, but it wasn't a snag. It was a big brown. Sometimes those fish will suck in the fly and just sit there."

What does he do then?

"I tell them *'Set! Set! Set'*" he says. "It never hurts to set the hook. And you've got to set it hard enough," he adds. "You're not going to break the rod."

I ask him about other possible fly choices – in particular, the midges that work so well farther upstream, and he tells me that he tends to like larger offerings this far down.

"As you move down the river, the bugs get bigger," he says, adding that the stoneflies "are like protein snacks for the fish...and those wild browns like protein snacks." About that time the indicator disappears again, punctuating his words with a tiny splash. This one is definitely a fish. He works it in, nets it, admires it, and eases it back into the flow.

"If you have that stonefly profile and get it in front of 'em, they're going to eat," he says.

We keep fishing and talking, and I ask Davie about the folks whom he guides. I'm interested in what advice he might give to someone thinking about booking a guided trip on the river. What is the key to getting the most out of the adventure?

"Communication," he says without hesitation. Then he explains.

"More often than not," he says, "the key is communication between the client and the guide. It's about listening to what the guide has to say."

What about casting skills, especially when it's a beginning fly caster?

"With beginners, I'll spend 30 minutes first thing going over basic casting," Davie says. But the goal, he adds, is not to master casting. The goal is to catch trout, and that's about putting the fly in front of fish.

"I tell beginners not to worry too much about the fine points of the cast," he says. "That will come with practice." Instead, he wants them to communicate with the guide because the guide knows how to get the job done.

More seasoned anglers sometimes bring a different set of challenges. For instance, when working with those who have more experience, the focus may shift to things such as drift control.

"You've got to get a good drift," he says. "I put us in position where the fish are," he continues, "and the flyfisher has to make sure that's where the fly is drifting."

Davie notes that you've also got to let the drift go on as long as you can.

"Let it drift," he says. "You get a lot of people who will let the nymphs drift only a few feet before picking up and casting again." As a result, he adds, many fish never even see the fly.

It's also important to let the nymphs swing at the end of the drift.

"A lot of fish will come up and eat on the swing," he says.

The right technique matters with streamers too. Davie underscores the need to "really work the fly around the structure you're targeting."

"You've got to vary the speed and pattern of the retrieve and actually work that streamer," he says, giving an example. Say you're casting along a downed log. In such a case, you want to quarter your cast upstream and work the fly along the length of the log rather than simply casting to the log and then pulling the fly toward you. As with the nymphs, he adds, the key is to visualize what you want the fly to do and then make it do it.

That's a lot to keep in mind. Do the folks he fishes with really take it all in? Most of them do, he says, and that makes for good trips for everybody.

"But sometimes after a couple of hours they start to slip back into old habits and I have to remind them to 'mend-that-line!' or 'pick-up-pick-up.' "

Is there anything else that helps his clients get the most out of the day? Yes, he says, there is – and it's a very simple thing.

"Polarized sunglasses," he says. "Amber or brown color polarized glasses. They help you see the fish, and that can help."

The boat has drifted back almost to the ramp. The good-sized brown that he wanted to pick up has so far eluded us. But there's time for one more stretch of soft water, and Davie has the stoneflies ready as he uses the oars to move the boat off to the side of one more run. He drops the anchor

The last fish of the day on the very last cast – a beautiful 15-inch wild brown. Davie Crawford caught this brown near the Medlock Bridge boat ramp on a large Kaufmann's Stonefly Nymph.

to hold the boat and then flicks the flies up into the flow. The first drift draws what appears to be a strike, but nothing comes of it

On the third drift, though, the indicator hasn't gone ten feet when it suddenly sinks like a stone. Davie sets the hook. Immediately it's clear that this is a fish and that it's different from the rest. The rod tip pulses as the taut line cuts the surface upriver and then down.

Davie works the fish to the surface. The fish rolls and then dives again. It is indeed a good fish – a very good fish – a very nice brown.

I get ready with the net. The fish approaches the boat but then runs again. Davie works it back within range. This time the stars align and I ease the net under the trout and lift it gently from the water.

"Nice!" I say, and it is. "Very nice!" It's a wild brown, born in the river, and it's fat and healthy and unbelievably colorful. It measures right at 15 inches – a respectable fish in any angler's book.

I can't think of a better way to end a morning on the river than that. ☐

Medlock Bridge up close

Moving on downriver, the next access point on the tailwater is at the Medlock Bridge Unit of the Chattahoochee River National Recreation Area.

Medlock Bridge Road (also known at various points as Peachtree Parkway and as 141) crosses the Chattahoochee at a point where the river makes a major zigzag. The road crosses the river at the northern end of the zigzag, and the area between the zigzag and the road is the Medlock Bridge Unit of CRNRA.

The pleasantly wooded Medlock Bridge Unit feels remarkably separate from the civilization that surrounds it, despite the fact that it's located right off Medlock Bridge Road (141), one of the busiest thoroughfares in this area. In fact, at peak traffic times, there's so much traffic whizzing by on Medlock Bridge Road that it can be difficult to get into or out of the Medlock Bridge Unit entry road. Be careful (and patient) when entering and leaving this area, especially during rush hour.

The Medlock Bridge boat ramp, suitable for trailered boats as well as kayaks, canoes and float tubes. Note that it's artificials-only from GA 20 to the Medlock Bridge boat ramp; below this ramp, bait can be used.

As at other CRNRA units, a parking fee is required.

For fishermen interested in the tailwater, Medlock Bridge offers a boat ramp suitable for tubes, kayaks, canoes and pontoons, as well as for trailered boats. Like some of the other access points profiled on the previous few pages, Medlock Bridge puts you on the water in a generally deeper and slower section of the Chattahoochee.

By the way, note that GA 20 crosses the river between Abbotts Bridge and Medlock Bridge. There's what appears to be a fisherman's parking area on the south side of the road, just east of the bridge. But remember the issues with river access at GA 20. It's possible only if you don't mind hauling up or down a slope over large and overgrown boulders.

Note that the Medlock Bridge boat ramp marks the lower end of the artificials-only water. Below the ramp, bait is okay. ☐

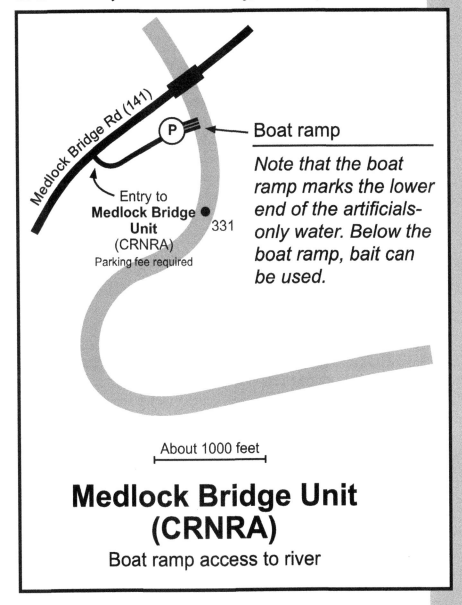

Medlock Bridge Rd (141)

P ← Boat ramp

Note that the boat ramp marks the lower end of the artificials-only water. Below the boat ramp, bait can be used.

Entry to
Medlock Bridge
Unit 331
(CRNRA)
Parking fee required

About 1000 feet

Medlock Bridge Unit (CRNRA)
Boat ramp access to river

Abbotts Bridge to Medlock Bridge (to Jones Bridge?)

For dedicated Chattahoochee tailwater trout anglers, another popular section for float fishing is from Abbotts Bridge down to Medlock Bridge and/or from Medlock Bridge to Jones Bridge. Since the current here is decidedly slower than in some other areas, this tends to be the realm of powered boats, kayaks, canoes or oar-equipped personal pontoons. This section can be floated in a tube, of course, but you will need to be prepared for a very long float and a very long time sitting in the tube. Sometimes that's not as much fun as you might think.

Because these sections are so similar, we'll profile them together, starting with a look at the float fishing possibilities between Abbotts Bridge and Medlock Bridge.

Abbotts Bridge to Medlock Bridge

The Abbotts-to-Medlock float covers a bit more than four river miles. It's a quick and easy run for knowledgeable powerboat operators. If your watercraft is non-motorized, however, you'll find that it usually takes a couple of hours in a canoe or kayak and four hours or more in a float tube. Actual times depend on those now-familiar variables including water level, wind, and fishing time.

If you're in a non-motorized craft, you'll want to keep an eye out for powerboats on this part of the tailwater. It's not unusual to see motorized boats moving up or down this section of the river. Most powerboat operators are courteous and alert, but stay on your toes. That's especially important if you're in a float tube, which can be hard to see.

If you make this trip, you'll find that there are occasional pieces of relatively shallow and wadable water. One effective strategy is to stop and wade those shallow areas and fish the edges (where shallow meets deep) as well as the deeper water itself. In some places, the shallow area is mid-river with deeper water along each bank. That allows you to take your time fishing both sides.

The river through this section has a more urban feel than in some other areas. You'll pass St. Ives Country Club (above State Bridge Road [GA 20] on river right) and the Atlanta Athletic Club (below State Bridge Road). But there are always reminders of the river's rich cultural history. For example, below the Atlanta Athletic Club, as the river bends to the right, you may be able to identify another fish weir.

Note that there is no easy river access at GA 20. Once you start at Abbotts Bridge, you're pretty much committed down to Medlock Bridge.

Note too that the current is relatively slow through portions of this float, particularly on the long and straight section as you approach Med-

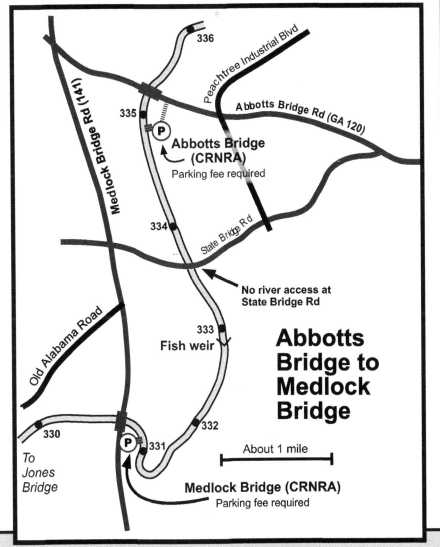

Abbotts Bridge to Medlock Bridge

No river access at State Bridge Rd

Fish weir

About 1 mile

Medlock Bridge (CRNRA)
Parking fee required

Abbotts Bridge (CRNRA)
Parking fee required

lock Bridge. Be aware of the wind, which (if it's from the wrong direction) can actually blow a tube upstream.

The takeout at the end of the float is the Medlock Bridge boat ramp on river left as you round a prominent bend in the channel.

Medlock Bridge to Jones Bridge

The Medlock-to-Jones float, like the Abbotts-to-Medlock float just up-river, is characterized by a good bit of relatively slow water. This is best thought of as canoe or kayak territory, though some float it in tubes.

Near the end of this section you'll approach Jones Bridge Shoals, where both river and fishing change significantly. We'll look at the Jones Bridge area separately later on.

It's about three river miles from Medlock Bridge to Jones Bridge. That's no problem in a powerboat. In a canoe or kayak or oar-driven

---

Abbotts-to-Medlock-to-Jones

Fly and lure recommendations

Flies: Effective nymphs include Gold Ribbed Hares Ears, Pheasant Tails and Prince nymphs, and especially large weighted stonefly nymph imitations such as Kaufmann's Stone or Pat's Rubberlegs. Small midge emergers are as effective here as elsewhere too.

For dries, try the Elk Hair or Foamback Caddis and Stimulators, Royal Wulffs or Adams (regular or parachute). Size-wise, match what's flying; that's usually something in the size 12 to 18 range. As elsewhere, try hoppers along grassy banks.

For big browns, use big streamers. You won't catch many small fish on 'em, but any you do catch are likely to be memorable.

Lures: As elsewhere on the tailwater, it's hard to beat in-line spinners such as Roostertails or Mepps Spinners or small crankbaits. Those that imitate small brown trout can be especially effective at times. Choose lure weight with deep water in mind.

Fast-sinking yellow curly-tail grubs on jig heads are often over-looked but can be effective here, too, particularly if you put some spots on the side of the grub with a permanent marker to make it resemble a small brown trout.

Note that the Medlock Bridge boat ramp marks the down-stream limit of the artificials-only section. Below the ramp, bait such as worms or crickets or corn can be used. Do not use bait here unless you're fishing *below* the Medlock Bridge ramp.

pontoon the trip should take an hour and a half to two hours (plus fishing time), while tubers should plan on two to three (or more) hours plus or minus those afore-mentioned factors such as river level, wind and of course how long you take to fish.

The Medlock-to-Jones section comes with houses, buildings and other signs of civilization along the river just beyond the tree line. But the trees make it feel a bit less "developed" than what you found above Medlock Bridge.

Though it's not there anymore, one spectacular example of riverside development stood for several years on river right about eight-tenths of a mile below Medlock Bridge. Just as the river bends left, you'll pass what was once the site of Dean Gardens, a 32,000 sq. ft. home built in the late 1980s and early 1990s. The pricetag was said to be in the neighborhood of $25 million (yes, $25 million) not surprising in light of its gold sinks and other amenities.

Eventually put on the market for $40 million, the house was finally sold (17 years later) to Tyler Perry for a bit more than $7 million. Perry, in turn, sold it to developers. The house was subsequently demolished to make way for a residential development, and nowadays the grandeur that was Dean Gardens is preserved only in photographs and memories

How did the river's trout react to such luxury? Those who fished here in years past say it didn't seem to bother the trout at all.

Conditions here are what you've come to expect on this section of the tailwater. It's deep and relatively slow-moving,and because of the depth fly fishers may need to adjust their tactics. For example, if using streamers, break out the sinking or sink-tip line. Similarly, if you're using nymphs with an indicator, be sure that you add enough weight to your tippet to get the nymph or nymphs well down into the water column.

It's a bit simpler if you're spin fishing. The key is to use deeper-running lures and to thoroughly fish the water, especially around any cover that you see.

Jones Bridge, where this float ends, is named for an old steel bridge (more precisely, for *half* of an old steel bridge) which extends out over half of the river's width from the Fulton County side (river right). The original bridge, built around 1904, was used into the 1920s. However, by that time it was showing its age. No one wanted to pick up the bill for needed repairs, so the bridge was left alone and continued to decay.

One day in the mid 1940s, some of the local residents noticed that crews were dismantling the bridge from the east side. Everybody fig-

The remains of Jones Bridge, namesake of the Jones Bridge Unit of CRNRA and of Gwinnett County's Jones Bridge Park.

ured the demolition crew was working for the government, but in actuality it was a bunch of folks who were stealing the steel to sell for scrap. No one caught on until half the bridge was gone. The thieves were never caught, and what remains there now is the portion of the bridge that the thieves left behind.

There are actually four places to exit the river at Jones Bridge. The two primary access points are a canoe launch on river right in CRNRA's Jones Bridge Unit (near the upriver end of the unit's access road and about a two-minute carry from the main parking lot) and an actual trailer-friendly boat ramp (also within the CRNRA unit on river right) about seven-tenths of a mile downstream from the canoe launch. Entering the park, you'll come to the boat ramp first.

Additionally, and also within the CRNRA unit, there's a river access point near the old bridge ruins. Because of the length of the carry to that launch point from the parking area, however, that one is best thought of as float tube access only. In fact, some Jones Bridge float tubers like to hike up to it and put in there for a float downriver to the canoe launch or (more often) to the boat ramp. Doing so lets you float and fish a section of relatively still water directly downriver of Jones Bridge, water that you would miss if you got into the river farther downstream.

It's also possible to exit (or enter, for that matter) on river left at Gwinnett County's Jones Bridge Park just below the ruins of Jones Bridge. Although there is no developed take-out site at Jones Bridge Park, steps leading down to the river make access relatively easy. But note that some boat toting will be required to get back to your car.

In any case, regardless of where you decide to exit, the sign that the takeout is drawing near is spotting what remains of Jones Bridge as it reaches halfway across the river.

As you work your way down this section, you'll notice that shoaly water becomes more evident. That in fact is what characterizes the Jones Bridge area, and (as you might expect) this shift in the prevailing conditions (that is, away from relatively calm water to water that's loaded with shoals) has a dramatic impact on how you fish. We'll look closely at fishing Jones Bridge in the next section. ☐

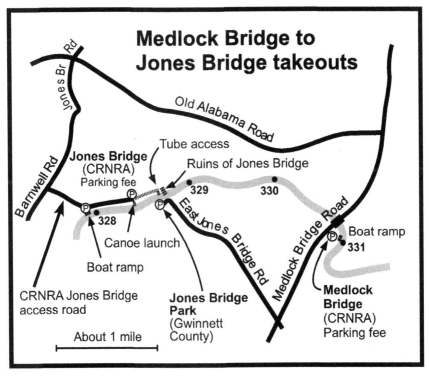

Medlock Bridge to Jones Bridge takeouts

Jones Br Rd

Old Alabama Road

Tube access

Jones Bridge
(CRNRA)
Parking fee

Ruins of Jones Bridge

Barnwell Rd

329   330

328

Canoe launch

East Jones Bridge Rd

Medlock Bridge Road

Boat ramp
331

Boat ramp

CRNRA Jones Bridge
access road

About 1 mile

Jones Bridge Park
(Gwinnett County)

Medlock Bridge
(CRNRA)
Parking fee

Wade fishing heaven

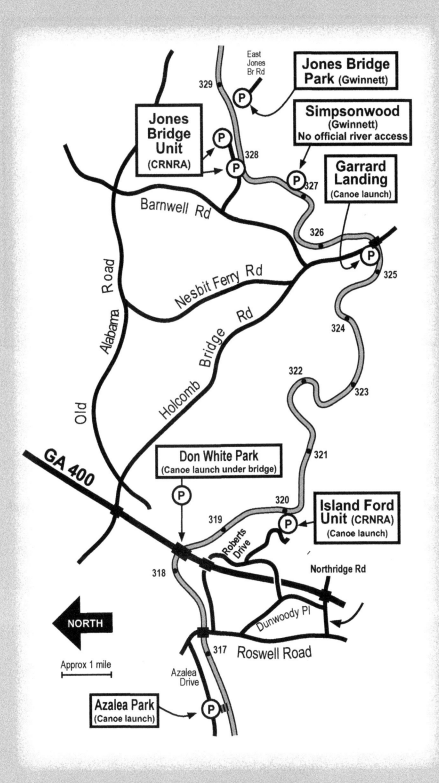

The float tube's ready to go at the Jones Bridge canoe launch.

Feet wet at Jones Bridge

Many consider Jones Bridge to offer the best wade fishing on the entire tailwater

"What do you think?"

I'm talking to Jeff Wright, manager of Alpharetta Outfitters (alpharettaoutfitters.com). In addition to managing a full-service fly shop, Jeff guides in the Jones Bridge area of the Chattahoochee, and today we're planning to spend some time fishing that water and shooting a few last-minute photos for this book.

Or at least we were until they updated the weather forecast last night.

"They're saying rain," I'd said to Jeff on the phone earlier that morning. "A 70 percent chance."

Jeff, ever the optimist, was not dissuaded.

"Let's see if we can squeeze it in before the rain gets bad," he replied. "I really want to get you out on the water at Jones Bridge. It's a great place to

---

get your feet wet with wading for browns. Would you be up for that?"

"Sure!" I reply. "Let's go for it!

I haven't fished Jones Bridge in a long time. But Jeff has fished there since he was young. Today it's some of his favorite water, and he as guided many anglers to some memorable days there fishing for the stocked rainbows and wild browns that call the Jones Bridge area home.

For some time now he has been after me to join him at Jones Bridge. "It's nice," he's been saying. "You'll like it."

So here we are at the Chattahoochee River National Recreation Area's Jones Bridge Unit parking lot. I've just pulled in, and (uh oh) I see those first flecks of moisture appearing on the windshield as I do.

Jeff's already there. In fact, he's already been to the river while waiting for me to fight my way through Atlanta's morning traffic.

"How does it look?" I ask, noting that he's wading wet. Apparently he really takes this "get your feet wet" thing seriously. Actually, you can do that in relative comfort at Jones Bridge during the summer months, at least once you get used to it. It's not as cold there as it is at the dam. But Jeff's younger than me too. One of the few advantages of being

Jeff Wright of Alpharetta Outfitters makes his way down the Jones Bridge step ramp to a delightfully wadable part of the river.

(how to put it) more seasoned is that I don't have to be cold and wet if I don't want to. So I'm going to wear waders.

"Any takers yet?" I ask.

"Not yet," he replies, "but the day is young!"

Looking at Jeff's rod, I see that he's thinking "big fish." He's got a super-sized articulated Olive Woolly Bugger tied to the end of his leader.

"Whatcha thinking about using?" he asks.

"That's what I was going to ask you," I say. It's always good to bow to the knowledge of the locals. "But I was thinking about a dry and dropper. I've got this big Chubby Chernobyl that floats really well, and..."

Jeff is already rummaging in his vest for a fly box. Finding the one he wants, he opens it and hands me three emergers. The one that catches my eye is a Walt's Worm, about size 16, with a pink tungsten beadhead.

"...and that one looks good for a dropper," I continue, picking up the Walt's Worm and tying it to the two-foot piece of 6X tippet which dangles from the eye of the much bigger foam dry.

I set my rod on the car and put on my waders. There's a sputter of raindrops, one of which lands squarely on the end of my nose. I don't think I've ever had that happen before. Maybe it's an omen of good things to come.

A moment later we're on our way to the water, bound for the step ramp near the main parking lot. Literally a series of steps leading from the trail to the water, it provides an easy way to get into the river. For float tube fishermen, it's ideal. This ramp also serves as a good canoe or kayak launch. The carry from the parking lot to the steps is a short one, though you don't

You know it's got to be a good spot when the heron manages to beats you to it!

see many boats launched there.

There are a few more drops of rain, but – still undeterred – Jeff enters the river and I follow. The bottom is a mix of gravel and smaller boulders with sandy spots, grassy patches, and a few ledges thrown in too. There are shallows, deeper runs,

A pair of float tube anglers drifts downriver from the Jones Bridge boat ramp.

channels through the grass, and long and flowing glides.

"There's some of everything," I say to no one in particular and then, to Jeff, I say, "You're the expert. What's your recommendation?"

"That looks like a good run to your right," he says, pointing out a piece of water where a distinct channel cuts through the gravel. I flip the dry-and-dropper combo into the flow and it drifts through untouched.

"Try putting it more along the edge," Jeff advises, explaining that in that kind of water the browns in particular often seem to hold along the very edges of the channel.

I pick up and cast again, following his advice. The flies land softly and drift about three feet, and the Chernobyl disappears. I lift the rod, setting the hook on a beautiful wild brown of about seven inches.

Yes, it's always good to listen to the professionals.

The sputters of rain are getting more frequent and more assertive, but I'm focused on fishing the rest of the run and don't really notice. Harder to ignore, however, is the distinct sense that my right foot is no longer dry and toasty warm. Is that water I'm feeling? Has the leaky wader syndrome caught up with me again?

I don't have long to think about it, though, because the Chubby Chernobyl disappears again. I feel the tug for just a second and then it's gone.

"Got another one?" Jeff calls over the sound of the river.

"Had him," I answer, and then add my favorite missed-fish mantra: "Since he got away, he can be as big as I want. Right?"

"Sure!"

"Then it was probably a two-footer," I continue.

Who's to say? Works for me!

While I continue to play at seams and edges, Jeff has moved out into the river and has positioned himself near an incredible-looking run, working it with the big articulated Woolly. It's a textbook example of the kind of place that a big brown would hang out. A few casts later he has a strike and feels the tug, but the fish comes unbuttoned. Jeff goes back to casting.

Meanwhile, the browns continue to appreciate that Walt's Worm. Like all browns in the upper tailwater these days, they're wild streamborn fish. Some a big, but others are small. My biggest that day is that seven-incher.

I manage to fool a rainbow, too, a stocked fish of about 10 inches. It also takes the Walt's Worm, and it's nice to be able to say that I've managed to catch both species on this rainy Wednesday morning.

But I'm particularly interested in the smallest of the browns that I en-

counter – a brave little fish about three inches long. It's actually smaller than the streamer that Jeff is casting, but its significance is profound. To find such

Above: A very nice wild brown landed by Jeff Wright on the Chattahoochee tailwater. Right: Big browns often prefer larger flies such as this articulated Olive Woolly Bugger.

Jones Bridge offers plenty of good wading water accessible either from the CRNRA Jones Bridge Unit (on the Fulton County side of the river)or from Gwinnett County's Jones Bridge Park.

a tiny little trout this far down the upper tailwater is proof positive (as if any more proof was actually needed) that brown trout are solidly established in the reborn Chattahoochee River.

By this time, the spatters of rain have turned into a steady soaking drizzle. I look over toward Jeff and see that he's moved to a different part of the run, though it's getting harder to see through the increasing rain. He makes a cast and begins the retrieve, and I think I see what looks like a hookset. His rod appears to bend briefly, but then it goes slack again.

Through the rain-filled air I see him move a little more and then go back to casting. I decide to move a bit too and ease about 10 yards downstream.

With every step, that right foot squishes.

I line up with another good-looking spot, picking water that resembles the kind of run which Jeff had pointed out earlier. I make the cast. There's a splashy strike on the Chubby Chernobyl, and I miss it clean.

I cast again, and then again, and then the top fly once more disappears. I set the hook. Another brown has taken the Walt's Worm.

I shift my right foot as I bring in the fish. The foot has graduated from squising to sloshes. Leaky waders for sure.

Getting my feet wet at Jones Bridge? You bet I am (in more ways than one). And I don't mind at all.   □

Wade fishing heaven

Jones Bridge offers some of the best wade fishing on the entire tailwater

Jones Bridge, with its great combination of trout habitat and easy access to extensive areas of wadable water, is the hands-down wading-water star of the upper tailwater. Whether you prefer to fish with a fly rod or with spinning gear, Jones Bridge has the fishing (and the wading) you're looking for. In many ways, it really is a trout angler's dream come true.

Accessing the water

There are two ways to access the Jones Bridge area of the tailwater – from the Fulton County side (from CRNRA's Jones Bridge Unit) or from the Gwinnett County side (via Jones Bridge Park).

Via Jones Bridge Park (Gwinnett County): This county park is located on the east side of the river just downstream from the ruins of old Jones Bridge. It's accessible from East Jones Bridge Road via Peachtree Parkway/Medlock Bridge Road and has plenty of parking.

There is no formal canoe or tube launch at Jones Bridge Park. However, steps lead down to the river in places and make access relatively easy – if you don't mind a walk and a carry to get to the water. You'll find plenty of wadable water around Jones Bridge Park.

It's also possible to put in there with a float tube and then float and fish your way down to the boat ramp at CRNRA's Jones Bridge Unit on the Fulton County side. But note that if you do this you'll be starting and finishing on opposite sides of the river. You'll have to wade back across to return to your car – or go with a friend and take two cars, leaving one at the take-out as a shuttle.

Via the Jones Bridge Unit of CRNRA: CRNRA's Jones Bridge Unit is directly off Barnwell Road. From GA 400, take the GA 140 (Holcomb Bridge Road) exit and go east for about 4.3 miles to Barnwell Road. Turn left on Barnwell and go 1.6 miles to the Jones Bridge Unit entry on your right. You'll find very limited parking at the boat ramp (be sure to observe the parking restrictions) with more parking in the main lot at the far end of the road.

Most anglers park at the main lot and access the river from the

Jones Bridge up close

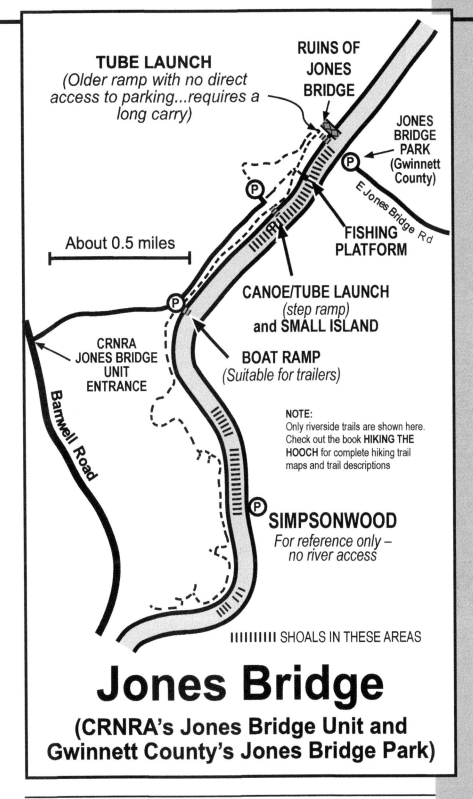

TUBE LAUNCH
(Older ramp with no direct access to parking...requires a long carry)

RUINS OF JONES BRIDGE

JONES BRIDGE PARK
(Gwinnett County)

E Jones Bridge Rd

FISHING PLATFORM

About 0.5 miles

CANOE/TUBE LAUNCH
(step ramp)
and SMALL ISLAND

CRNRA JONES BRIDGE UNIT ENTRANCE

BOAT RAMP
(Suitable for trailers)

Barnwell Road

NOTE:
Only riverside trails are shown here. Check out the book **HIKING THE HOOCH** for complete hiking trail maps and trail descriptions

SIMPSONWOOD
For reference only – no river access

IIIIIIIIII SHOALS IN THESE AREAS

Jones Bridge
(CRNRA's Jones Bridge Unit and Gwinnett County's Jones Bridge Park)

Fly fishers Justin Couch and Caitlin Gentry get ready to enjoy some good wading near CRNRA's main Jones Bridge Unit parking area.

stepped canoe launch directly opposite. That puts you in the water near a small island, and the area around that island can be productive. Those using float tubes may hike further upstream to an older boat ramp (not accessible to vehicles) located just downriver from the old bridge ruins and put in there, gaining access to a section of relatively flat water and especially to the upper portion of the shoals above the fishing platform. Some even float and fish from that upper ramp downriver all the way to the boat ramp at the lower end.

On the Fulton County side, note that the land upriver from the ruins of the old bridge is private and posted. Respect the posted signs.

How's the wading?

There's a lot of good wading in the Jones Bridge area, and in many places you can wade and fish all the way across the river. Much of it is easy wading, too, with a bottom that tends toward easy-to-walk-on gravel. But there are also quite a few angled flat rocks and some deeper areas to contend with as well. A wading staff will provide that extra third point of stability that sometimes comes in so handy.

As you explore the wadable areas here, you'll encounter shoals, runs, shallows, grassy patches, ledges, holes, and just about every other stream configuration you can imagine. There's a lot of variety in terms of structure, and that means more chances of finding the situation that the fish are liking on any given day.

Can we say anything about specific wading areas? Let's start at the primary canoe launch near the parking area at the end of Jones Bridge access road.

Upstream from the launch site you will find shoals that frequently hold fish. Since there may be deeper water between the canoe launch and those upriver shoals, however, those shoals are most easily accessed by walking upriver along the riverside trail and then entering the river at the desired spot.

What's downriver from the canoe launch? Just downstream from the launch you'll see a small island, and around that island is broad and expansive area of wadable water with deeper runs interspersed with grassy patches in some of the shallows. It's possible to work your way upstream, downstream, and across the river. There is plenty of water in that one area for a very full afternoon of fishing.

If you wade downstream far enough, you'll eventually find water that's too deep for further progress. But a float tube can get you through those deep spots and lets you float and fish all the way from the canoe launch to the boat ramp.

What lies beyond the boat ramp? As shown on the map on page 249, portions of CRNRA's Jones Bridge Unit hiking trail network provide down-river access below the boat ramp and take you toward additional wadable shoals. The trail follows the river for a while and then climbs a ridge to detour

At Gwinnett County's Jones Bridge Park, sets of steps provide access to the river.

around some private land (be sure that you honor the "posted" signs and stay on the CRNRA trail) before dropping back to the river in an area that promises additional wadable shoals. Because these downstream shoals are a bit off the beaten track and require some effort to get to, they don't receive nearly as much pressure as the shoals near the canoe launch. For that reason, they're popular with fly fishers who don't mind making the hike.

Again, a float tube can help you access those lower shoals. In fact, some anglers will float and fish from the upper canoe launch downriver beyond the boat ramp and on to those lower shoals, exiting the river there and then hiking back up along the CRNRA trails.

Here, as elsewhere, it's a good idea to scout the river from land before making any sort of float. That lets you familiarize yourself with take-out points as well as with the access trails that you'll use to reach them. CRNRA's Jones Bridge Unit trails make such pre-fishing scouting easy too. Basic trail info is included in the map on page 249, but you can find much more detailed info on those and other CRNRA trails in the book HIKING THE HOOCH. Available from Chattahoochee Media (chattahoocheemedia.com), it's an excellent resource for any angler with an interest in accessing the Chattahoochee through the various Chattahoochee River National Recreation Area units. I recommend it.

Fly fishing at Jones Bridge

One key to fly fishing happiness at Jones Bridge is to realize that this an area with varied and abundant aquatic life. Your fly box should reflect that diversity and should contain a variety of different patterns (dries and nymphs, streamers, and junque flies) to allow you to find the one you need on that particular day. Make sure it holds some scuds, too, for they're common in the grassy or weedy areas and appear to be very popular with Jones Bridge trout.

Another key is to adjust your offerings based on the time of year. Remember that what worked in the middle of summer may not be effective in winter. For that reason, let's take a season-by-season look at how to strategize your fly fishing at Jones Bridge.

Spring: This is the time of year when caddis hatches are likely. Shake a branch as you get into the river; if the caddis hatch is on, you'll dislodge dozens of the little bugs, sending them fluttering through the air and out over the river. Some will likely make water landings, and should that happen don't be surprised if you see fish start to hit them downstream. Seeing this take place is usually enough to increase the heart rate of any trout angler, especially a fly fisher!

When the caddisflies are hatching, try a gray or brown size 14 Elk Hair or Foamback Caddis, or perhaps a Stimulator, with a mid- to dark-toned body.

Traditionally, such dries are fished dead-drift and without drag. But one technique worth trying here is to "skitter" the fly across the surface as if it's an adult struggling to escape into the air. Trout sometimes respond with explosive strikes.

At such times, subsurface fishing with caddis emerger patterns can also be effective. Try a beadhead Soft Hackle Emerger tied on a curved-shank hook. Flies with mottled hackle seem to have the edge. You might try that emerger as part of a dry-dropper combo, too, especially in shallower riffle areas with rocky bottoms.

Whether using nymphs alone or in a dry-dropper rig, let the flies hang in the current below you for a moment at the end of the drift. They will appear to be struggling toward the surface and often draw strikes. Fish apparently don't like to see dinner getting away!

Here's one more thing to think about during the caddis hatch. When the insects are actively coming off, there will be large numbers of emergers in the water. Small minnows will be chowing down on those emergers, and some of the bigger fish will in turn be chowing down on minnows. That's a good time to try a streamer.

Summer: Summertime, with its warmer temperatures, usually causes the fishing to slow during the midday hours. Early and late become the times to target. You might see mayfly activity, but caddis hatches will become sporadic and irregular.

You'll also see increasing numbers of terrestrials such as beetles and grasshoppers. The "plop"of a hopper or beetle as it falls into the river is like a dinner bell for nearby trout. Runs near brushy banks can be great places to fish something big and meaty like a Chernobyl Ant or a hopper, and foam spiders work surprisingly well too. So do (of all things) small popping bugs, especially green and yellow ones resembling hoppers. They're unorthodox, but the work.

Try ants too. At Jones Bridge, ants are definitely among the summer superstars. I remember one summer outing at Jones Bridge when I'd entered the river at the main canoe launch and then picked my way upriver to a point where I could fish a smooth run that flowed near a section of grassy shoreline. I eased into position and dropped a size 16 ant so it drifted slowly down the run. I saw the flash an instant before the fish (a nice rainbow) took the fly. It was the first of several rainbows (and two browns) that would fall for that ant over the next hour or so.

What's the best ant pattern? Almost any floating ant will work. I like high-visibility parachute-style ants in size 14 or 16; they do a good job of imitating the carpenter ants that are everywhere at that time of year. But don't overlook smaller ant imitations – and certainly try some subsurface ants. Hard-body "drowned" ants work well here, and I'm especially fond of Ken's Crazy Ant, a "Shelf Liner" ant pattern created by Ken Walrath. Especially when fished wet, it rarely fails to draw attention from nearby trout.

If it's hot, try targeting deeper areas with traditinoal nymph patterns such as Pheasant Tails, Gold Ribbed Hare's Ears, Princes, and so on. It's often productive to pair such a pattern with a weighted Rubberlegs-style stonefly nymph.

Fall and winter: With the coming of fall, stocking ends. The remaining holdover rainbows become more picky about presentation and about what they eat – and the browns, of course, are already selective. Smaller insects become much more significant. Dry fly enthusiasts often go with a size 16 or 18 Adams or Blue Winged Olive to mimic the midges you'll see this time of year. But since most feeding takes place subsurface, make sure you have plenty of small midge emergers and midge larvae imitations too. Favorites include Zebra Midges, Blue Assassins, and Rainbow Warriors in size 18 or 20. A Walt's Worm can be a good producer too.

A word on streamers

One fly type that can work at Jones Bridge all year long is the streamer. That's no secret, and experienced Jones Bridge fly fishers usually carry streamers in a variety of patterns, sizes, and colors.

Is there a favorite streamer for use in this area? There are several. One is a size 6 or 8 black or olive Beadhead Woolly Bugger, fished as if it's a minnow by stripping it actively on the retrieve. Flies tied with sparkle-chenille bodys, extra-soft hackle, large bead heads and additional weight tend to have the edge with wild browns as well as with stocked rainbows.

A popular variation on the basic Woolly Bugger is an olive, brown or black Articulated Woolly, again with a heavy bead head. These big and bulky flies are especially good choices if you're specifically targeting big fish.

When fishing for recently-stocked rainbows, try a flashy streamer such as a silver-over-gold Rolex. Another pattern that works in that situation is a size 6 or 8 chartreuse and white Clouser Minnow.

Yet another streamer that has worked well for me at Jones Bridge over the years is the flank-winged Hudson Streamer. Tied with guinea fowl or barred grizzly feathers for wings, it sinks quickly and presents a nice profile. On some days it's the only fly I'll use – unless (and this happens pretty often) I've given them all away and have none left in my flybox! It is effective on browns as well as on rainbows and can also be tied with mottled hen wings to imitate sculpin-type minnows.

Spinning tactics

Spin fishing is a great way to fish at Jones Bridge. In shallow areas, a floating crankbait can be effective. Cast so that the lure swims near good holding areas (behind rocks, near ledges, and so on) or, if you're not sure, simply try blind-casting in a fan-like pattern to thoroughly cover the water around you. The fish can surprise you as they come out of nowhere to smash the lure.

Another effective spinning technique for Jones Bridge is to cast a floating plug upstream and then let it drift downstream with no additional action beyond what the current imparts. Let it float past you and then below you... and as soon as your line starts to tighten, give it a *pop* and immediately begin your retrieve. Strikes sometimes come at the very instant you pop the lure. Growing up, I used this technique all the time in warmwater streams for bass. It's just as effective nowadays on trout as it was on those redeyes back then.

Plugs are not the only spinning lures that work well in the shallow runs. In-line spinners are as effective here as they are elsewhere. Fish them across or across-and-down and with a retrieve that's fast enough to keep them from hanging up on the bottom. They also work when cast upstream and retrieved just fast enough to maintain contact with the lure. Again, a pattern that presents trouty colors is often most effective. In fast water, of course, be sure that you select a lure that's heavy enough to sink to the desired depth.

What about fishing deeper places? Those are the realm of deep-diving crankbaits or (as elsewhere) of deep-running spoons. When spin fishing here, don't overlook those deep runs.

Similarly, be sure to make a few casts to the water just above shoals. The river gets shallower it approaches a shoal, squeezing the current and concentrating food. That in turn concentrates fish. It's a pattern worth looking for anywhere you go on this section of the river.

Though most spin fishers will be using artificials, bait is legal to use at Jones Bridge. Corn is popular, especially for recently-stocked rainbows. But a nightcrawler or red wigglers rigged with enough weight to sink into the depths can be particularly effective. ☐

Rainbows and rock shelters

More wade fishing (and some fascinating history) awaits you at Island Ford

A river like the Chattahoochee is rich in a lot of ways. There's the trout fishing, of course, and the scenic beauty too – not to mention the chance that it offers to get away from technology (especially that perpetually annoying cell phone, the bane of modern living) and into the great outdoors.

There's a lot of history along the river too.

Some of that history is relatively recent – for example, the building at the end of Island Ford Parkway, a venerable structure which now serves as the headquarters and visitor center for the Chattahoochee River National Recreation Area.

A distinctive building it is, too. Constructed in the 1930s by Atlanta attorney Samuel D. Hewlett as a family retreat, it was built using cypress logs from property that Hewlett owned in the Okefenokee Swamp and from rock said to have come from Stone Mountain. It's one of the few Adirondack-style structures in the south.

Hewlett sold the building to the Buckhead Century Club in 1950; when the club disbanded in 1955, it was sold to the Atlanta Baptist Association for use as a retreat center.

The National Park Service acquired the building after the Chattahoochee River National Recreation Area was established in the late 1970s. Today, this classic old structure is listed on the National Register of Historic Places. It's a much-photographed favorite of those who visit the park.

But there's other history to be found here, too – including some that dates back possibly as far as 1000 BC. This comes in the form of a number of ancient rock shelters which were used ages ago by some of the earliest peoples to inhabit this region.

Native Americans frequented this area for many centuries, long before the Europeans came. During what archaeologists call the Woodland period from 1000 B.C. to about 900 A.D., those original inhabitants hunted and fished in this area. Archaeological evidence suggests that they used the naturally occurring rock shelters as places in which to take refuge from

Looking at the top end of the upstream island at Island Ford. There's calm water before the island, but then the shoals begin.

Above: As you hike the Riverside Trail, you'll usually see canoe and kayak enthusiasts)enjoying the river. Below: One of the prehistoric Native American rock shelters along the Riverside Trail. Archaeologists say they were used during the "Woodland" period from 1000 BC to about 900 AD.

storms or to set up overnight camps.

That's the kind of history you find when you walk the riverside trail at Island Ford.

I remember one afternoon many years ago. My daughter was just a little girl, and we were hiking that very trail. I was on a mission, looking for fishing access points on that section of the river.

But the child was a lot smarter than me. She was in it purely for fun – and for adventure!

Adventure? You bet. She and I had been talking about the ancient rock shelters, several of which were easily accessible and located right beside the trail. We'd been talking about the people who might have called them home, and about what their kids liked to do, and about the many and varied adventures that they might have had all those many centuries ago.

Now, as we explored those shelters together, imaginations (hers as well as mine) were running at full speed.

It was perfect daddy-daughter time.

All at once (you know how it is in the summertime) a sudden thunderstorm opened up right on top us. In an instant, we went from clear blue skies to a deluge of near-Biblical proportions.

We had no rain gear – but was that an ancient rock shelter up ahead?

Indeed it was. We dashed for the shelter, where we waited out the storm accompanied only by faint shadows that flickered and danced every time a lightning bolt split the sky. Were they the shadows of long-ago Native Americans?

Imagination –

"Daddy," I remember her saying, "do you think some other daddy and some other little girl might have hidden out here a long time ago?"

"Could be," I said. "Yes, it very well could be."

The child is grown now and lives far away. But a few weeks ago, hiking that same trail yet again to check a few details for this book, I thought back to that day years ago with my daughter. And then...

Not really considering exactly why I did so, I wandered up the side trail to the very rock shelter that had saved us from the storm. And as I did, I realized (though I hate to admit it) that I had one thing those Native Americans did not have – a cell phone.

I decided that my return to the rock shelter was a perfect excuse to give Daughter of Mine a call.

So I did. I told her where I was, and she remembered.

"Aw, Dad," she said, "that's sweet that you called me from there!"

Okay. So sometimes maybe technology is not so bad after all. □

Accessing and fishing Island Ford

Thoughts on finding trout fishing near the lower end of the upper tailwater

Island Ford is an interesting piece of the Chattahoochee trout fishing picture. To look at it, the water appears spectacular – riffles, shoals, pools, and more, with a riverside trail that provides straightforward access. Parking is convenient. Getting in the water is easy. There's plenty of room for plenty of anglers. It seems like the ideal place for some trout fishing, and sometimes it is.

But there will be times when Island Ford can be challenging. Located toward the lower end of the upper tailwater, it tends to be a bit warmer than sections of the river farther upstream. During the summer, the fishing at midday may slow as the sun warms the water. For that reason, some anglers choose to fish elsewhere during the warmer months. But as summer gives way to fall and cooler temperatures return, Island Ford can once again become a destination of choice.

Anglers typically access Island Ford either from the parking lot new Hewlett Pond (from which a foot path leads down a moderately steep hill to the river) or from the parking area in front of the park headquarters and visitor center. From either parking area, the goal is to access the "Riverside Trail" which parallels the river through the length of the Island Ford unit. This trail ends at Beech Creek on the downstream end, where the parkland ends at private property.

There's another piece of CRNRA land beyond that private property further downstream. It's accessed from the "Sandy Springs" trail which begins at the first parking area as you enter the Island Ford Unit on Island Ford Parkway. However, there's no easy river access from that section of trail. Thus, trout anglers focus on the section of river which flows alongside the Riverside Trail.

Let's assume that you're starting at the visitor center. Follow the paved path around the left side of the building, passing a soft drink machine, and then take the dirt steps down the hill past a picnic pavilion until the trail deadends at a crosstrail. Turn right. You'll quickly come to the Riverside Trail. Then turn left (downstream), cross a footbridge over a small creek, and you're on your way.

As you look out across the water, you'll actually be looking at

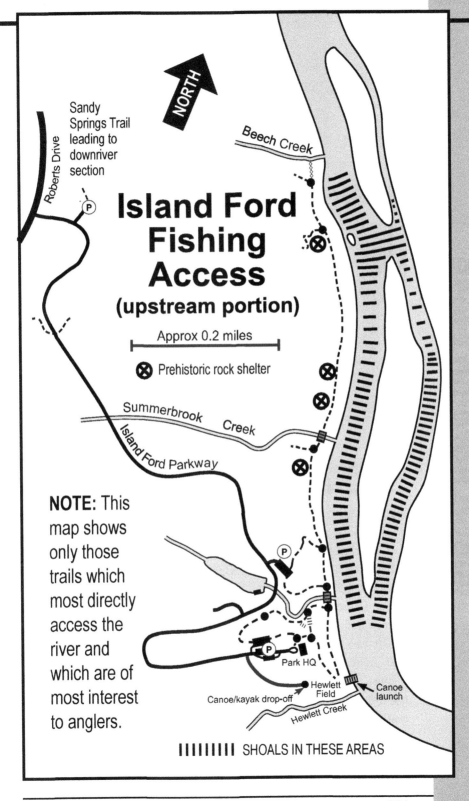

Sandy Springs Trail leading to downriver section

Roberts Drive

Beech Creek

NORTH

Island Ford Fishing Access

(upstream portion)

Approx 0.2 miles

⊗ Prehistoric rock shelter

Summerbrook Creek

Island Ford Parkway

NOTE: This map shows only those trails which most directly access the river and which are of most interest to anglers.

P

Park HQ

Hewlett Field

Canoe/kayak drop-off

Canoe launch

Hewlett Creek

|||||||||| SHOALS IN THESE AREAS

The Riverside Trail at CRNRA's Island Ford Unit parallels the Chattahoochee for quite a ways and provides good access to a great deal of wadable water. The trail is popular with hikers and anglers alike.

the near side of the first of the Island Ford islands. There's plenty of good-looking shoal water between where you stand and the island. In fact, the area near that first little footbridge is a good one, with shoals and good runs. The promising water continues as you move downriver, too, offering more shoals interspersed with additional deeper areas. Sometimes it's hard to decide where to begin, though many start right there near the footbridge and work their way downstream.

On warm summer days, expect plenty of company at Island Ford. The exposed rocks that punctuate the shoals are popular with river visitors, and you'll often find folks enjoying the sunshine on rocks far out toward the island. Recreational boaters frequently float through on their way to one of the takeout points further downriver at Don White Park or Azalea Park. It's a popular area.

It's popular with trout fishers too. You'll often see anglers either wading (there is a lot of wadable water) or working their way down through the shoals in float tubes.

Float tubes, incidentally, offer a good way to explore the water along the Riverside Trail. Some Island Ford float tubers like to start at the upper end, perhaps putting in at the canoe launch at Hewlett Field near the upriver end of the Island Ford Unit. They then float and fish their way downriver toward the lower end of the unit, taking out at one of the many places where trail access is easy. At that point they either return to the car and head for home – or, if the fishing's been good, perhaps they hike back upriver and do the float again.

Should you decide to fish from your float tube, walk the trail first to familiarize yourself with the general lay of the land and also with possible takeout points. One popular takeout for float tube anglers ers who want to fish a lot of water is the small island that sits just a few yards from the bank on river left near the downstream end of the Riverside Trail. This island is a little ways above the point where Beech Creek enters the river, and it signals the approach of the lower end of the wading and tubing water Island Ford.

The most impressive islands here, however, are the big ones far across the water. Actually, it's not the islands themselve that draw an angler's attention; rather, it's the extensive shoal areas that lie between the islands and the mainland. Those shoals offer an abundance of holding water, and it will take you some time to thoroughly explore it all. But wade carefully. The footing can be a little on the tricky side.

Eventually, you may decide you want to explore the channel on the far side of the upstream island too. Dries or dry/dropper combos are often the flies of choice there. But if you fish the back side of the island, remember that this puts you a long ways (all the way across the river, in fact) from where you started. Be sure that you plan with the water release schedule in mind. Also note that the far bank (beyond the islands) does not offer public access to the river.

Fly fishing strategies

Many of the anglers you see at Jones Bridge or Island Ford will be fly fishing, and it's easy to see why. The biggest reason, aside from the fish, is all that wadable water combined with the fact that the water is varied enough to offer a variety of good fly fishing options.

As at Jones Bridge (we'll say "as at Jones Bridge" a good bit in this section, but that's only because the two areas are so similar in terms of what works), the time of year is a major factor in determining how you approach the water.

Spring: Here, as elsewhere on the tailwater, springtime is caddis-time. Try a gray or brown size 14 Elk Hair or Foamback Caddis with a mid- to dark-toned brownish body. A Stimulator will also do a good job, especially if you use one with darker body tones. Subsurface caddis emerger patterns work well too.

Indicator-based nymph rigs (or indicator-free "Euro" style nymphing set-ups) will also do the job during the caddis hatch.

During spring, dry-dropper combos are a good call at Island Ford. Try pairing an Elk Hair or Foamback Caddis or a Stimulator with a caddis emerger. I sometimes use emergers with glass beads since they aren't too heavy to use as droppers with small dries.

Put the dropper about 18 inches below the dry – and whether using nymphs and emergers alone or as part of a dry-dropper combo, remember to let the flies hang in the current below you for a moment at the end of every drift. When you do this, they appear to be struggling toward the surface and often draw strikes.

As at Jones Bridge, don't hesitate to try streamers during a caddis hatch. Sometimes that will tempt one of the larger fish.

Summer: With the arrival of summer, the water at Island Ford will tend to warm up. Once that happens, the fishing will slow down, particularly at midday. Early morning and late afternoon become the preferred times, and you'll probably have the most success in deeper runs or pools as trout look for shady places where it's cooler. Try fishing such spots with deep-running nymphs such as beadhead Pheasant Tails or beadhead Gold Ribbed Hare's Ears. Woolly Buggers and big stonefly nymphs can also work; again, fish them deep.

Summer's higher temperatures mean that caddis hatches slow down, but they also mean that terrestrials such as ants and grasshoppers become much more active. To imitate terrestrials, think "big and chunky" when choosing a fly. If you find a good run near an overgrown bank, probe it with something substantial like a Chernobyl Ant, a hopper, or some other terrestrial imitation. Here, as elsewhere, the *plop* of the fly's landing is a signal to any trout within earshot to come and take a look.

But even with terrestrials, big isn't always best. Be sure to try some smaller terrestrials such as ants during the summer too.

Fall and winter: As fall moves into winter, it's time to break out the smaller flies. Dry fly enthusiasts often switch to a size 16 or 18 Adams or Blue Winged Olive, good imitations of the midges that you may see. You'll want to be equipped with plenty of midge emergers and midge larvae imitations. Favorites include Zebra Midges, Blue Assassins, and Rainbow Warriors in size 18 or 20. In early winter, stonefly nymphs can be effective.

Spinning tactics

When spin fishing, as when fly fishing, the rig you use will depend on the nature of the water you're fishing as well as on the time of year.

Island Ford has a good bit of shoal water, and the drift/jerk/retrieve technique described in the section on Jones Bridge can also work well here. Another good approach, especially if you're not sure where in the shoals the fish might be, is to simply fan-cast with a floating or shallow-diving crankbait. That lets you cover a lot of water and can put you on a surprising number of fish.

What about areas of greater depth? In such places, go with deeper-running lures. A slowly-wobbling spoon can draw strikes from winter-chilled fish and is a favorite of many colder-weather trout fishers.

Bait is permitted here, too, and can also be a good choice during the cooler months. Try drifting a nightcrawler through some of the deeper pools, using a sinker that's heavy enough to take your offerings to the desired depth.

Spin fishing (either while wading or, as here, from the bank) is a popular activity at Island Ford, where numerous near-shore shoal areas create good holding water for trout

Here, as elsewhere on the river, pay particular attention to the water on the upstream side of shoals. Remember that as the water approaches a shoal, it often tends to concentrate whatever food it might be carrying. Trout know this and often hang out in such places waiting to see what might come along. If it's your spinner or crankbait, the result could be a very good day. ☐

Trout 265

What's between "JB" and "IF"?

Are there trout? Sure. But what about access to the river?

For trout anglers, Jones Bridge and Island Ford are certainly among the stars of the upper tailwater.

But if you look at the map you'll notice that there are several other public spaces between those two major access and fishing points. Do they have anything to offer to trout fishermen?

Simpsonwood

One of the more recent additions to the list of public access spots is Simpsonwood Park. This 223-acre Gwinnett County park was for years a conference center owned by the North Georgia Conference of the United Methodist Church. The property was given to the church in 1973 under the condition that it not be divided or developed. But faced with mounting costs, the church began to consider its options – including the possibility of selling the site. To make a long story short, Gwinnett County eventually purchased the Simpsonwood tract for $14 million. Today it's Simpsonwood Park.

Simpsonwood Park offers a nice riverside trail and restful benches where you can sit and enjoy the view of the river – but there's no direct river access.

Besides amenities such as a pavilion, grills and restrooms, the park is also

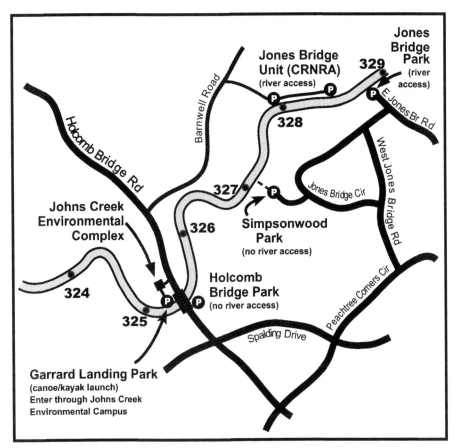

the site of a chapel that's in demand as a wedding venue.

This park is popular with hikers, too, offering about three miles of hiking trails traversing upland terrain or following the river. In fact, Simpsonwood Park has about 2,100 feet of river frontage.

River frontage, eh? Does Simpsonwood provide river access too? Alas, no. There's no formal river access here, though the water bordering the park is just downriver from the Jones Bridge parks and definitely holds fish.

According to the Gwinnett County Parks and Recreation Department, there are no plans to add river access at Simpsonwood. A spokesperson for the department noted that the river's banks are extremely steep, making river access difficult. Anglers who have fished this area in the past agree and point to much easier river access just upriver at Gwinnett County's Jones Bridge Park or, on the Fulton County side, at CRNRA's Jones Bridge Unit.

Long-range plans for Simpsonwood Park call for two overlook platforms (assuming availability of funding to build them). According to the master plan for the park, at least one of those is designated for "[p]ole fishing from [the] deck area." However, according to Gwinnett County's parks and recreation department, there are no plans for direct river access at Simpsonwood.

Holcomb Bridge Park

Just upriver from Garrard Landing – in fact, directly across Holcomb Bridge Road on river left and just upstream from the Holcomb Bridge Road bridge – is a small Gwinnett County park, Holcomb Bridge Park. This 12-acre site features a playground, restroom, picnic tables and other amenities, including two river overlooks and some short hiking trails.

This park does not offer any direct river access. However, you can find canoe access on the other side of Holcomb Bridge Road at the canoe launch in Garrard Landing, another Gwinnett County park, as described below.

Garrard Landing

About three river miles below Jones Bridge is Garrard Landing, a City of Roswell park. Garrard Landing is named for the family which owned the land before it became a park. The family was interested in preserving this land for the future and did not want to see it developed.

The park is adjacent to the site of a covered bridge which once crossed the Chattahoochee just downriver from modern-day Holcomb Bridge Road. Known as McAfee's Bridge, it was built in 1834 by Robert McAfee, who

owned the land there.

Before the bridge, the only way across the river was via a ferry operated in the 1820s by Charles Gates, an early settler. This ferry was located about 200 feet downstream of the current Holcomb Bridge structure, and it's said that traces of the original ferry road can still be seen.

The Garrard Landing canoe and kayak launch (top) is suitable for canoes and kayaks but is not accessible for trailered boats and is not a recommended take-out for tubes. As you approach from upriver, the actual ramp will be tucked in behind some vegetation (as shown at left) on the right side of the river. Look for the Garrard Landing sign, and don't miss the ramp.

Modern bridges sit on supports built of concrete or steel, but this one would be held up by nothing but stacked native rock. No cement or mortar was used. Instead, the supports were constructed simply by stacking large flat rocks until the column reached the desired height.

Eventually, the 220-foot-long bridge was completed, and for many years it was the only structure (except for a Western & Atlantic railroad bridge) to cross the river in the area. That gave it some significance during the Civil War, and on July 5, 1864, retreating Confederate troops burned it in an attempt to stop their Union pursuers. Union forces soon rebuilt it. But Sherman burned again a few weeks before Atlanta fell, and that time it was not rebuilt.

Instead, ferry service eventually resumed at the crossing site. Later, in the early 1900s, a single-lane steel truss bridge was constructed at the site – still utilizing those original stacked-stone columns. Later still, in the 1960s, the first modern two-lane concrete bridge was built nearby.

What's there now? In addition to that original stone column, you'll find (in the nearby park) a modern-day reconstruction of a very short covered bridge built in the style of the original.

Though you won't find wading in this area, you will find a paved canoe launch. This launch is easy to get to, but the ramp itself is often very muddy.

Mud notwithstanding, is this a viable river entrance or exit point for persons paddling or floating this part of the river? Maybe, though some potentially tricky navigation is required below Holcomb Bridge in order to exit here. If you have the skills, it's do-able in a canoe or kayak.

But it's a very poor choice as an exit spot for float tubes. That's unfortunate, since the next possible float tube takeout is the canoe launch at Island Ford – an additional 5.2 river miles below Garrard Landing. That would be a lo-o-ong trip in a tube – too long to recommend it. This underscores the fact that some of the lower parts of the upper tailwater are better suited for more mobile watercraft such as canoes or kayaks and are not a good choice for those using tubes.

It is, however, a potential put-in for canoe or kayak floats to Island Ford.

The Garrard Landing canoe launch is accessed through the Johns Creek Environmental Campus, a building designed in the style of a late 19th century textile mill but actually a sewage treatment facility. Enter the Environmental Campus complex and turn left in front of the building. When that road ends, turn right and continue to the parking area. The canoe launch is behind the playground area, and there is limited parking at the launch site.

By the way, the view across the river from the launch is (how to put it) a bit "industrial," but that's just the way it is. It's still access to the river. □

Float fishing possibilities –
Jones Bridge to Island Ford (and beyond)

Between Jones Bridge and Island Ford is about eight miles of varied and sometimes surprisingly scenic (and productive) river. This can be interesting water to float and fish from a kayak or canoe.

There are several float-trip possibilities which start at Jones Bridge. The floats described here assume you're starting at the boat ramp at the downriver end of CRNRA's Jones Bridge Unit; if you start at the upper end of Jones Bridge, extend the expected duration of the trip.

Jones Bridge to Garrard Landing (Holcomb Bridge): One possibility is to float from Jones Bridge down to the canoe launch at Garrard Landing. The paved takeout at Garrard Landing is on river right directly opposite the water plant just downriver from the Holcomb Bridge Road bridge. The take-out is often muddy. Additionally, as noted on the previous pages, some potentially tricky maneuvering is required to get to the takeout, which is tucked in behind some trees on river right just below Holcomb Bridge. If you plan to take out here, scout from shore first.

Because of the tricky navigation required to reach the ramp, this is not a recommended takeout for float tubes.

This float covers not quite three river miles and takes you through Judge's Shoals (about a half mile below Jones Bridge) and a couple of other shoal areas as well. Fishing can be good, but those shoals can eat up a boat if you're not careful.

Garrard Landing to Island Ford: At almost five river miles, this one is a nice canoe or kayak float that lets you see and fish water which many folks never see. But it's long. Trip time varies depending on paddling vs. fishing.

Jones Bridge to Island Ford: If you're in a kayak or canoe, it's also possible to float from Jones Bridge all the way to the canoe launch on river left at the upper end of CRNRA's Island Ford Unit. This float covers about 8 river miles. You'll encounter shoals above Garrard Landing, but below Garrard Landing the river is generally easy to the Island Ford takeout.

Note that this is a kayak or canoe float. It's not one to consider if you're using a float tube.

Island Ford to Don White Park: Beyond the Island Ford shoals, you'll enjoy slow-flow conditions down to the next takeout at Don White Park (directly under the Georgia 400 bridge), where you can beach your boat at the

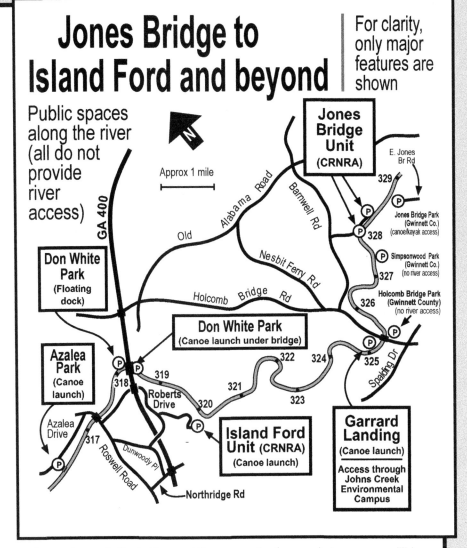

Jones Bridge to Island Ford and beyond

For clarity, only major features are shown

Public spaces along the river (all do not provide river access)

Jones Bridge Unit (CRNRA)

E. Jones Br Rd

329

328

Jones Bridge Park (Gwinnett Co.) (canoe/kayak access)

Simpsonwood Park (Gwinnett Co.) (no river access)
327

Holcomb Bridge Park (Gwinnett County) (no river access)
326

325

Don White Park (Floating dock)

Don White Park (Canoe launch under bridge)
322   324

GA 400

Old   Alabama Road

Barnwell Rd

Nesbit Ferry Rd

Holcomb Bridge Rd

Spalding Dr

Azalea Park (Canoe launch)
318   319

Roberts Drive
320   321

323

Azalea Drive
317

Roswell Road

Dunwoody Pl

Island Ford Unit (CRNRA) (Canoe launch)

Garrard Landing (Canoe launch)

Access through Johns Creek Environmental Campus

Northridge Rd

Approx 1 mile

park area beneath the bridge and then carry it a few yards to your car. This is canoe or kayak water, and wind can be a major factor.

What about a mega float from Jones Bridge to Azalea Park? The National Park Service estimates that the float time from Jones Bridge all the way down to Azalea Park (Chattahoochee River Park) should be in the neighborhood of 6 to 8 hours in a canoe. That's a long float and a lot of paddling! You won't have a lot of time to stop and savor the fishing, but at least you'll get to see a lot of the river.

By the way, the Park Service also estimates that this mega float would take 9 to 12 hours in a raft This one is *definitely __not__ a float for anglers using float tub*es.   ☐

The last of the upper tailwater

Below Island Ford you approach the waters of Bull Sluice Lake. Are there trout?

If you continue downriver beyond Don White Park, the last on-the-river takeout is about two more miles down the river at the paved boat ramp at Azalea Park (a.k.a. Chattahoochee River Park). Actually, at that point, you've

Don White Park (above) is located beside and beneath the Georgia 400 bridge. It offers some parking and an informal access point for canoes and kayaks. . Just below the bridge, another portion of the park features a floating dock (left).

moved solidly onto the relatively placid waters of Bull Sluice.

In between, what happens to the fishing?

Not surprisingly, if you start asking around about the fishing below Don White Park, you'll hear a lot of talk about warmwater species. Certainly the water there warms up during the summertime. Bull Sluice Lake is not very deep (it's filled with sediment over the years) and thus makes a dandy warming basin through the sunshine-rich months of late spring, summer and early fall. The resulting balmy water is apparently very hospitable to a variety of warmwater species such as sunfish and perch. Carp like it, too, and the warm shallow flats draw carp and carp enthusiasts alike.

But trout? Is there a secret trout fishery as you move below Island Ford?

Yes...or no. Or maybe. The answer depends on who you ask and on where, exactly, you're asking about.

Certainly there are trout at the bottom end of Island Ford. And trout move around...so it stands to reason that they will be

What about fishing Island Ford's lower shoals?

The shoals below Island Ford include some very trouty looking water. Are those shoals fishable? Yes, they are – but only if you can get to them.

In a canoe, it's possible to float downriver from Island Ford, fish the shoals and then continue on to a take-out somewhere further downstream.

But because of the potential for damage to motors and hulls, it's very risky to try that in a powered boat. Those shoals are not known to be friendly to boats and motors, and some of the most experienced river runners I know won't even try 'em.

A discussion of running boats through shoals is well beyond the scope of a fishing guide like this one, but the short version is this: it's probably not a good idea to try it.

If you do want to use a powered boat to explore this water but don't want to worry about shoals, one option may be to put in at the paved ramp at Azalea Park (Chattahoochee River Park) and then run upriver toward Island Ford as far as you're comfortable. When you reach your limit, simply turn around. Then drift and fish your way back downriver at the pace that you choose without having to fret about running afoul of those bothersome rocks.

found downriver of Island Ford too.

But that raises a question: Just how far below Island Ford might you reasonably expect to find them?

For the sake of discussion, let's consider a particular spot along this stretch. Let's consider the bend in the river just below the Georgia 400 bridge. It's not quite two river miles below the Island Ford Unit of CRNRA. Might we reasonably expect to find trout there?

> ## River access below Island Ford
>
> Beyond Island Ford, the next potential take-out is at Don White Park (directly under the Georgia 400 bridge). From the Island Ford canoe launch to Don White Park is about two river miles. Alternately, you can continue just a little bit further to the floating dock on river right just beyond the 400 bridge.
>
> If you decide that you want to go even further, then paddle for another couple of miles beyond Don White Park to the paved boat ramp on river right at Azalea Park (Chattahoochee River Park).
>
> Except for an informal take-out back in a slough off Willeo Road, these spots are the last river access before Morgan Falls Dam.

Years ago, I had an aquaintance who used to do a little guiding on the river. He had his "client" spots, places to which he would take his customers, but he also had his "day-off" spots where he would go if he wasn't working.

One day a good many years back, in a moment of weakness and perhaps while suffering from insufficient morning coffee, he started talking about that very part of the river. He didn't get too specific. He was a guide, after all. But I remember that he kept mentioning Georgia 400.

The other day I happened to be driving south on Georgia 400. As I crossed the river, I saw (for perhaps the thousandth time) the broad sandbar on the inside of the bend where the river curves left below the bridge.

Bends tend to be shallow on the inside and deeper on the outside, and every time I cross that bridge I tell myself that someday I'll have to fish that outside bend. But I still haven't gotten around to fishing that particular spot. So if you ask *me* whether there's a trout fishery in that spot, I'll have to say "maybe." There are trout just a little ways upriver, so there should be trout there too. But lacking proof positive, "maybe" is all I can say.

And yet even though *I* have not fished that particular spot, I know of others who have. One day, curious, I asked one of them (a buddy of mine and a serious and very intense trout fisher) about that water.

"How's the fishing below the 400 bridge?" I asked in my most innocent voice. "Are there trout in there?"

He didn't hesitate an instant.

"NO!" he said. "There are NO trout in that water! Just a few little perch and a bunch of people in kayaks and canoes. But no trout. Not a one. Don't waste your time."

Interesting. A definite "no." *Very* definite. But he had answered quickly. Too quickly? And then he changed the subject...

So we have a "maybe" and a "no."

And yet sometimes you hear stories...

One of those stories is told by my brother Daniel, who some years ago encountered an enormous trout while fishing that area with his daughter Anna, then about six years old. Anna had a brand new kid's rod, which had come with a cheap plastic reel loaded with line of indeterminate test. To the end of that line, Daniel had tied a three-inch-long rainbow trout-patterned Rapala.

"She made a beautiful cast with that little rod," he recalls, "and the second the Rapala hit the water the river ex- ploded."

It was a big fish – a *really* big fish.

Young Anna managed to get a couple of turns of line back onto the reel, Daniel recalls, before the rod finally gave up and broke.

Did they land the fish? Alas, no.

"It had to be a big one, probably a big brown," Daniel says.

I think that means we can put him down for a "yes." ☐

The launch at Azalea Park (Chattahoochee River Park) on Azalea Drive can handle trailered boats as well as canoes and kayaks. It puts you on water that's more like a lake than a river.

Lower Tailwater

5

Exploring the
lower tailwater

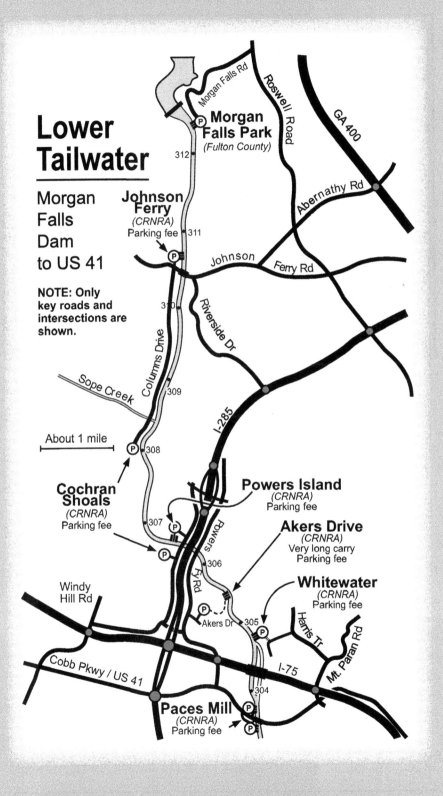

A lower tailwater overview

The lower tailwater is two different fisheries in one, and one of 'em is good for trout.

"**D**o you fish a place called Morgan Falls?"

Morgan Falls! It's a placename that somehow kind of rolls off the tongue. Hearing the words sparks visions of thundering cataracts, pounding whitewater, icy cascades, and movie-worthy battles with trout of epic proportions.

The person who asked that question was visiting from across the pond – from England, to be precise.

"Morgan Falls? Well, yes, I do," I replied. "Why do you ask?"

"Well, I was reading in an old magazine about how great it is for trout," he said. "Sounds like the kind of place I'd like to do some fishing. Do you think I might do well there?"

"That depends," I said at last. "You see, it's like this..."

Morgan Falls Dam, located about 35 miles downriver from Buford Dam, is considered to be the dividing line between the upper Chattahoochee tailwater (which extends from Buford Dam down through Bull Sluice Lake) and the lower Chattahoochee tailwater (which begins at the foot of Morgan Falls Dam).

Completed in 1904, the dam and its accompanying powerhouse were built to provide electricity to power Atlanta's streetcars. At that time it was the largest hydroelectric power plant in the south, with a generation capacity of about 10.5 megawatts. A 1924 reconstruction effort upped its capacity to 15 megawatts. Some 33 years later, in 1957, the dam's height was increased to allow re-regulation of water released from Buford Dam. Today's version of the dam is 896 feet long and 56 feet high.

When Buford Dam was completed and began to release cold water from Lake Lanier, the upper river became a coldwater river almost overnight. The water stayed cool down through Bull Sluice Lake and below Morgan Falls, too, where trout were eventually stocked – and those trout thrived. In fact, until about the

There is some beautiful and very "fishy" looking water on the lower Hooch tailwater – for example, this shoally water above the I-75 bridge.

mid 1980s, the river below Morgan Falls Dam was revered as good trout water. Dry-fly anglers were especially fond of its afternoon mayfly hatches, though folks who fished it often said that the fish could sometimes become extremely selective. But if you had the right fly on the end of your leader, you might have a banner day. Reports from that time are more than enough to fire the imagination of any fly fisher who loves dry flies.

As recently as the early 1990s, there appears to have been good trout fishing below Morgan Falls Dam. Though development was beginning to have an impact, the river below that dam still provided a good home for the large numbers of fingerling trout which were stocked there. Those fingerlings dined on the abundant insect life and soon grew to catchable sizes.

But still development continued. Concrete and asphalt covered more and more of the landscape. All that pavement heated up under Georgia's summer sun – and during summer, every time it rained, hot runoff poured into the river. The resulting "thermal spikes" bumped up the river's temperature, sometimes significantly, and it doesn't take a lot in the way of warm water to have a really bad impact on trout.

Striped bass in the trout water?

At the risk of getting off-topic, it's worth noting that stripers appear to be reproducing in the lower tailwater. Baby stripers reportedly began to show up in the late 1990s, and there is now a resident population of striped bass in the river below Morgan Falls Dam. But most of the stripers you encounter in the lower tailwater have migrated up from West Point Lake, arriving sometime around May and sticking around until the water cools in the fall. That can sometimes make for interesting fishing whether you encounter any trout or not! But this is a book about fishing for trout, so we'll save the striped bass saga for another time.

Something else was happening too. Striped bass migrating up from West Point Lake found those rainbows to be the culinary equivalent of a well-crafted pepperoni pizza. That made it tough to be a rainbow, but it did make for some happy and very well-fed striped bass.

Does that mean that there is now no trout fishing below Morgan Falls Dam? You might think so, given all of that. But you'd be wrong.

In reality, it's like this:

During the traditional fishing months (that is, from late spring through early fall), there really are better trout fishing options farther upriver (that is, on the upper tailwater). For when the weather is warm, the lower tailwater heats up and is not at all suitable for trout.

However, things change once the weather begins to cool off with the arrival of fall. Lower air temperatures help keep the water in the lower tailwater from becoming too warm, and at some point the river below Morgan Falls will actually become cool enough for trout.

So trout fishing possibilities on the lower tailwater are as much as question of *when* as of *where* – and the *when,* as we'll see in a minute, is primarily during what's known as the Delayed Harvest trout season from Nov. 1 through May 14.

But we're getting ahead of ourselves. Before we consider the "DH" fishing possibilities on the lower tailwater, we've got to take a look at one very important factor which affects the fishing there: the impact of what goes on at Morgan Falls Dam. ☐

The lower tailwater is really two fisheries in one. During warm months, the focus is on bass (inset). But come winter, the water from Sope Creek to US 41 is managed for Delayed Harvest trout fishing. Sure, it's cold. But the fishing can be more than enough to keep you warm. Here, fly fisher Laura Nichols pauses for a photo before releasing a Hooch DH rainbow. Both fish came from the same place on the river near I-75 – just at different times of year.

Morgan Falls Dam marks the upper end of the lower Chattahoochee tailwater.

The impacts of releases from Morgan Falls Dam

The conditions you encounter on the lower tailwater are directly affected by what happens at Morgan Falls Dam.

One thing to keep in mind when planning any trip on the lower tailwater is that the stretch of river below Morgan Falls (which includes the Delayed Harvest water) is affected by two different dams – Buford Dam and Morgan Falls Dam.

Earlier, we looked at Buford Dam's impact on the *upper* tailwater. Its impact on the *lower* tailwater (that is, below Morgan Falls Dam) is less direct, of course, because Morgan Falls Dam acts as a buffer. But Buford Dam must always be considered since everything released from Buford Dam must eventually flow through Morgan Falls Dam too. Always keep that in

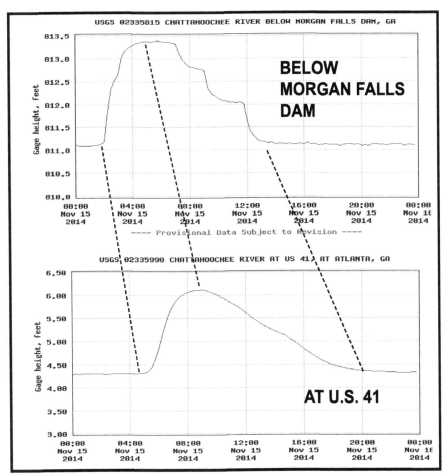

Here's how water released from Morgan Falls Dam might impact the lower tailwater. The top graph shows a water release from the dam; the bottom graph shows that it takes about 3 hours for that water to reach the bottom of the lower tailwater near US 41.

mind, and plan accordingly.

The most direct impacts on the lower tailwater, however, come from Georgia Power's Morgan Falls Dam. Water released from that dam will impact the bottom end of the lower tailwater (about 8.5 miles downriver) within about three hours; obviously, impacts will be felt sooner closer to the dam.

As an example, take a look at the USGS streamflow charts reproduced above. They show how the water level "BELOW MORGAN FALLS DAM" (that is, at the top of the lower tailwater) relates to changes in the river's level "AT U.S. 41" (the bottom of the tailwater).

Using Morgan Falls release data to plan lower tailwater trips

Clearly, the first step is to check the water release schedule for Morgan

Falls. As of the time this was written, here's where to access Morgan Falls flow info online:

www.georgiapower.com/in-your-community/lakes-and-recreation/lake-levels-dynamic.cshtml

Once on the page, check the current release amount (in CFS) as well as the tentative release schedule for the very near future.

During periods of heavy release, Morgan Falls Dam may pass as much as 10,000 cubic feet per second of water into the river. To be fishable, however, the amount of water being released should not exceed 1300 CFS. Less is better.

As of this writing, it's also possible to get this information on your cell phone by calling the Georgia Power "Land Management Lakes and Recreational Information Line Including Hydrogeneration Schedules and Lake Elevations" at 888-472-5253. But you'll have to do some button pushing to get the info you need. Here's how:

- **Call** the info number at 888-472-5253.
- Following the welcome announcement, **press "2"** to access "Hydrogeneration Schedules and Lake Elevations." Then...
- **Press "1"** for info on lakes on the Chattahoochee. Then...
- **Press "5"** for info on Morgan Falls Dam. Then...
- **Press "2"** for info on the current generation schedule, and...
- **Press "7"** for the "future" tentative schedule.

Remember that for the lower tailwater portion of the river to be fishable, the amount of water being released from Morgan Falls Dam should not exceed 1300 CFS.

Here's one more thing to always keep in mind. As the disclaimers on the automated messages say, all of that predicted release data is tentative and subject to change. Sometimes it does change, too, and unexpected releases are not unheard of. Always plan with the idea that the unexpected could possibly happen. Give yourself an exit strategy, and remember that *you* are the only one responsible for your safety on the river.

In addition to checking water releases from Morgan Falls Dam, you will also want to check on releases from Buford Dam by calling 770-945-1466. At the risk of repetition, remember that anything that happens at Buford

Dam (that is, any water that is released there) will eventually affect what you have to deal with when you're fishing below Morgan Falls. Yes, they're two separate dams with separate operators. But info on releases from Buford Dam is definitely something to consider in your long-range planning.

The bottom line, of course, is to make sure that the river's level on the lower tailwater is low enough for safe fishing. You can determine the level from publicly available information which is provided by a series of river level gauges operated by the USGS.

The first relevant gauge is located below Morgan Falls Dam, and you can directly access the data that it provides via the following web address:

APPROXIMATE TIME TO IMPACT OF WATER FROM MORGAN FALLS

Estimates only. Actual times depend on many factors including river conditions and the magnitude of the release

Location on the river	Miles from dam	Minimum time to impact (hh:mm)
Morgan Falls Dam	**0**	**Immediate**
Johnson Ferry N.	**2**	**0:45**
Cochran Shoals	**6**	**3:00**
Paces Mill	**8.5**	**4:00**

Times are only estimates of approximate time to impact following a release. Actual downriver impact times may vary depending on factors such as precipitation, river level, and quantity of water being released.

waterdata.usgs.gov/ga/nwis/uv/?site_no=02335815

On that gauge, a water level reading of about 811 tells you that the river level is good for fishing. Readings approaching 812 tell you that the river is too high (which usually means it's too muddy as well) for fishing. When the gauge reads above 812, forget it and fish elsewhere.

The "below Morgan Falls Dam" gauge tells you what's going on at that one spot at the dam. But for Chattahoochee Delayed Harvest anglers, the most useful gauge may be the one at the U.S. 41 bridge at the lower end of the DH stretch. Here's the web address for real-time data from that gauge:

waterdata.usgs.gov/ga/nwis/uv/?site_no=02335990

On that gauge, a water level reading of 4 to 4.5 is ideal and tells you that conditions for wading should be good. The turbidity is usually good at those levels as well. Determined anglers who really know the river will sometimes wade parts of the Hooch DH when this gauge reads 5 feet or even a little more, but it's definitely more challenging under those conditions. It's better to wait for lower readings and safer levels. □

Access and fishing tips:

Are there trout possibilities in the "upper" lower tailwater?

Is the section from Morgan Falls to Sope Creek fishable? Sure. For trout? Well...

Though these days it's best known as bass water, the upper section of the lower tailwater – that is, the four-mile stretch of the Chattahoochee from Morgan Falls Dam down to the mouth of Sope Creek – was once impressive trout water with amazing insect hatches and good numbers of trout. It was a "put-grow-take" fishery of the first order, and it was the site of many a great trout fishing adventure.

Alas, the eventual warming of the river (not to mention major flooding brought on by a hurricane) eventually brought those halcyon days to an end. The river below Morgan Falls simply became too warm for trout, and that was the end of that.

Pat Snellings, fisheries biologist for the Georgia Department of Natural Resources, knows a great deal about the Chattahoochee tailwater, including the area below Morgan Falls Dam.

"What's holding it back," he says, echoing the common refrain,

The boat ramp directly below Morgan Falls Dam is a popular access point for those interested in fishing the upper portion of the lower tailwater.

"is the fact that toward summertime the water there becomes too warm."

In the fall, however, cooler water temperatures (and the approach of Delayed Harvest season) set the stage for trout to be stocked in the river below Morgan Falls Dam. Most will go into the river at Cochran Shoals or in the vicinity of Paces Mill upriver of US 41. But only a limited amount of stocking is done above Sope Creek.

"Some trout are stocked at Morgan Falls," Pat says, "and some

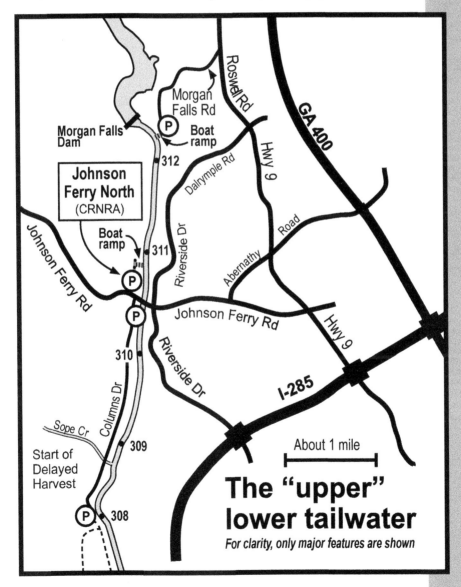

The "upper" lower tailwater

For clarity, only major features are shown

A raft parked at the Johnson Ferry boat ramp, a popular intermediate access point on the lower tailwater.

are stocked at Johnson Ferry." Both of those locations are upstream from the DH water's upper limit, he notes, explaining, "We try to sprinkle some in there so they can wash down." He adds that some other stocking points have been considered, too, but the problem is that there would be little or no public access to the stocked water.

What happens next depends, among other things, on "what the water year is like," Pat says.

A high-water year helps disperse those fish, he says, washing them down into the upper part of the DH stretch (but, alas, out of this upper water nearer to Morgan Falls). However, if the high water is not *too* high, it's also possible that some of the DH trout stocked farther downriver might eventually make their way upstream and into the water closer to the dam. In other words, during the winter at least, you *might* find trout in the upper-lower tailwater.

Another factor might pull trout toward the upper end of the DH water too. With the coming of spring, some DH rainbows may try to move into the mouth of Sope Creek in an attempt to spawn.

As spring moves ahead and this section of the river begins to warm, some DH trout may try to move upriver in search of cooler water. A few of them might find some spring-fed hole where they can hunker down and wait out the warm water of summer. As River Through Atlanta's Chris Scalley puts it, "If they find just the right scenario, a few of them might make it." It could happen.

But for most of those trout, the warm water means the end of the line – that and the fact that striped bass prowl those waters too. Weakened by the warming water, the trout become easy prey for stripers, who apparently love to dine on trout for dinner.

The bottom line? Except for a few early-DH stockers and a few fish which wander in from the DH water below (and, possibly, except for a few holdover fish) you should not expect to find a lot of trout action between Morgan Falls Dam and Sope Creek.

Accessing the water: In order to most effectively explore this upper part of the lower tailwater, you're going to need a boat of some sort as well as a place to put it into the water.

I can't help you with the "boat" part, but I can definitely point you toward two good launching points.

There's a ramp suitable for trailered boats at the far end of the park just below Morgan Falls Dam. This park is accessible from Morgan Falls Dam Road, which turns off Roswell Road (GA 9). The ramp is at the far end of the parking area, not far beyond the dog parks. No parking fee is required.

Another trailer-friendly boat ramp is located on river right at the Johnson Ferry North Unit of the Chattahoochee River National Recreation Area. You'll see this ramp soon after you turn into the Johnson Ferry North Unit. Remember that this is a CRNRA site, so a daily parking fee is required to park here.

There's no further trailer-accessible access until you reach the lower end of the Delayed Harvest water near the US 41 bridge, which we'll look a little later in this guide.

What about wading? You'll find only limited opportunities between the dam and Sope Creek. There is some wadable water near the dam, but getting to it can be complicated. Some who know the area well will start at the boat ramp and pick their way across the channel to access the wadable area below the dam. But you really do have to know the bottom contours well to cross the channel (which is borderline too deep for wading) – and you'll have to deal with significant current in the channel too, even at low river levels.

Other anglers use a boat to shuttle across the deep water by the ramp to the shallows across the channel. That's also a possibility.

But especially during the warmer months, if trout are the target, it's better to look elsewhere.

And that brings us at last to take a close look at the theory and practice of fishing for Delayed Harvest trout. ☐

The "lower" lower tailwater and Delayed Harvest

Here's how "DH" turns part of Atlanta's urban Hooch into a wintertime trout fisher's dream come true.

"You do know it's the middle of winter," says my friend Ed. "Do you really think we'll catch fish?"

It is indeed wintertime – about 11 a.m. on a mid-January Tuesday, to be precise. The air is cold – somewhere between 41 and 44 degrees, depending on which bank's thermometer is to be believed. The sky is that certain metallic gray that you see sometimes on cold mid-winter days, and now and then a little gust of wind slices through like an ice-cold blade (as if to remind us that we might be nuts to be here instead of someplace warm), and our breath forms icy little clouds with every exhalation.

"Really," Ed says again. "Are you sure this is a good idea?"

We are in the parking area at the Paces Mill Unit of the Chattahoochee

River National Recreation Area. Just a few yards away is the cold water of the wintertime Hooch. You know that look that rivers get during the middle of winter? Kind of like ice-cold flowing steel? That's what we see when we look at the water.

Winter-cold water...gray, leaden skies...gusts of icy wind...

All in all, it might seem an unlikely setting for a day of trout fishing. But in fact it is just about ideal. It's the middle of Delayed Harvest season, you see, and this is prime Delayed Harvest water.

Things are about to get good.

What is Delayed Harvest? Delayed Harvest streams are streams which are too warm for trout during the summer but which are cold enough to make trout (and trout anglers) happy during the colder months of the year. During the Delayed Harvest season, which in Georgia runs from Nov. 1 through May 14, designated DH waters are managed under special catch-and-release regulations which specify artificials-only (no bait, in other words) and also limit anglers to single-hook lures.

The special regulations help to keep the fish population up through the course of the DH season, even though herons and striped bass and (let's be realistic) the occasional poacher will pull some out along the way. But speaking broadly, your chances of catching trout in the Chattahoochee during Delayed Harvest season usually remain high.

Georgia presently has five designated Delayed Harvest fisheries – portions of Amicalola Creek and Smith Creek and parts of the Chattooga River, the Toccoa River, and the Chattahoochee River. They are scattered across the northern part of the state from Rabun County (in Georgia's extreme northeastern corner) down to the Chattahoochee DH in Atlanta.

How are these sections of stream chosen for inclusion in the Delayed Harvest program?

When considering a section of a creek or river for DH designation, fisheries professionals look for good water quality, low wintertime water temperatures, and good public access. The lower Chattahoochee tailwater from Sope Creek down to the US 41 bridge meets those criteria. It's a five-mile stretch of river that has become very popular with wintertime trout anglers over the last several years.

DH fishing on the Hooch began in 2000. Today Georgia DNR stocks about 50,000 trout (mostly rainbows but also browns) throughout the DH season at various points along that stretch. Occasionally, in the past, some brook trout have been stocked too. That creates a mix of newly-stocked (easy to catch) and more experienced (streamwise and harder to catch) fish

---

Trout   293

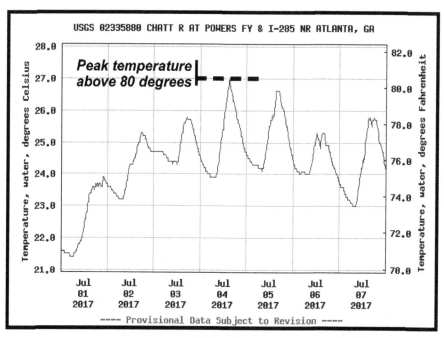

Why DH works: Here's how water temperatures change in the Delayed Harvest portion of the lower tailwater from summer to winter. The top graph shows temperatures for seven days in midsummer (July 1-7, 2017) at Powers Ferry and I-285, just downriver from the start of the DH water. With peaks topping 80 degrees Fahrenheit, it's too warm for trout during Georgia's summer. But six months earlier (Jan. 1-7), the temperature at that same site ranged from about 43 to 53 degrees Fahrenheit – plenty cool enough to make for happy trout (and happy anglers).

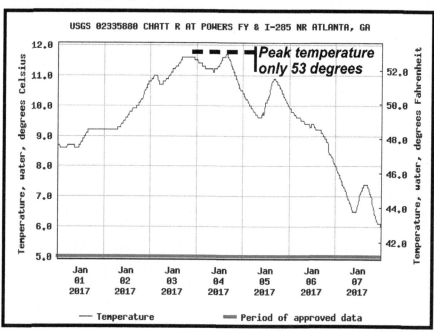

Delayed Harvest trout fishing on the Chattahoochee can bring a smile to your face faster than you can say "fish on!"

from late fall through winter and early spring. The result can be some very enjoyable fishing – if you don't mind being a little cold.

If there's anything that is true these days, it's this: You have to go fishing when the opportunity comes along.

For Ed, opportunities to fish had been scarce of late. He had a new job, and he and his wife had just moved to Florida, bought a house, and had a baby too. But now the baby was settling into a routine, and when Ed had called the week before, he'd shared that his wife had told him he needed to take a break.

"She basically said I had to get out of the house and go fishing," he told me, "so I'm calling you. Even though it's the middle of winter," he added.

Winter or not, trout fishing on the Chattahoochee Delayed Harvest water can be a perfect antidote for even the worst case of new-baby-new-house-new-job cabin fever. So now Ed has come north for a couple of days, and that's how we found ourselves there on that frosty January morning, standing in the Paces Mill parking lot, drinking those last few sips of hot coffee as we pump up the float tubes and put on our waders and get the fishing rods ready to go.

"Got your gloves?" I ask, knowing we will need them to keep hands warm for the next few hours.

"Right here," Ed says, patting his pocket. "Got my hat too. Man, it's cold!"

Our plan is to fish the Chattahoochee DH from float tubes, using the tubes to give us access to more water than we would be able to reach if we were wading.

My float tube trip categorization system for the Chattahoochee DH water is utterly unscientific and totally informal, but it works. It breaks the river into "upper" floats and "middle" floats and "lower" floats, and I choose the one to do based on available time and inclination. Thanks to the many access points along the DH stretch, it's possible to start and end a float tube adventure at many different points. That makes lots of different floats possible (we'll take a closer look at some of them starting on page 310). If you're feeling really ambitious, it's even possible to float almost the entire DH stretch in a day, starting at Cochran Shoals and floating down to the takeout at Paces Mill (I call that one the "big float") though you'll want to start early to squeeze it in and still have time to stop for fishing.

The float I have in mind for us on this particular morning is one of my favorites and also one that's especially good for newcomers to Delayed Harvest float tube fishing.

"Let's do the 'lower' float," I suggest as we hike up the concrete-paved pathway leading up the river from the Paces Mill parking area. The path closely parallels the water, making the going easy, and as we move upriver I explain that we will be starting near the I-75 bridge and then floating and fishing downriver to the Paces Mill boat ramp near US 41."

"So we're starting by that bridge there?" Ed asks, pointing with his rod tip toward the looming concrete structure which is now coming into view. "Somehow that doesn't sound very woodsy. In fact, it sounds kind of...well, kind of urban. Does urban bother the fish?"

"Don't think so," I answer as we reach the getting-in point. I step into my float tube and then ease into the flow. Ed follows, and the current tugs us gently downstream.

The first clue that this is going to be a good day comes about four minutes into our float. Ed, who is fishing with spinning gear, casts a silver and gray Roostertail towards a run near one of the concrete bridge supports as he drifts downstream.

"You know," he says, "I think –"

I never learn what he is thinking because the tip of his spinning rod suddenly bends as something grabs the little lure. Ed instinctively pulls back to set the hook.

"Well, well!" he declares as the fish takes to the air for the first of two jumps. It is a rainbow that turns out to be about 12 inches long when he slips his net under it a moment later.

"How about that!" he adds, unhooking the fish and easing it back into the cold river.

Before Ed can cast again, it's my turn to feel the tug. One minute my indicator is drifting along a current seam to the left of my tube; the next the indicator has disappeared.

"Fish!" Ed yells even as I set the hook, and it isn't long until I too net my first DH trout of the day. Like Ed's, it is a rainbow.

And that's how it goes. Ed hooks one, and then I hook one. We catch some in the water near the bridge. We catch a few more drifting through the runs below. We catch still more in shoals a bit farther downriver, with one particularly memorable fish falling for the spinner after Ed drops it inches from a partly submerged rock ledge.

We catch fish, all right. Oh, do we ever catch fish.

The clock ticks on, and our tubes carry us downriver Ed keeps throwing in-line spinners, and he catches fish. I stick with nymphs or streamers, and I catch fish. The river is good to us that day.

That's not to say that every day on the Chattahoochee Delayed Harvest water will be a many-fish day, for DH fishing (like any fishing) is always at the mercy of things beyond your control.

But it's not unusual to leave the Chattahoochee DH water with a smile on your face. You'll have one of those kind of days when the universe aligns and everything seems to click. The company is good, nobody falls in, and the fish cooperate too.

That's how it was that Tuesday in January right in the heart of winter.

Urban fishing? Yes indeed. Sometimes there's nothing like it. ☐

Fishing the DH section of the Chattahoochee, here literally in the shadow of the I-75 bridge.

Flies and lures for DH trout

Even though they're stocked fish, it's important to use the right fly or lure

When it comes to gear for the DH, you'll do fine using the same basic set-ups (a 9-ft. 6 wt. fly set-up or a 6 ft. 6 in. medium-light spinning rig) that you used on the upper tailwater. What may change, however, is your choice of flies or lures. Let's look at flies first.

Flies for Delayed Harvest trout

Earlier, we mentioned the distinction between newly stocked fish and more seasoned fish in various parts of the Chattahoochee. That distinction becomes especially significant on the Delayed Harvest section of the lower tailwater below Morgan Falls Dam. There, it's not at all unusual to have fish that were stocked that morning swimming alongside other fish that have been in the river for weeks or months.

When that's the case, what should you have in your fly box? To answer that question, you need to understand something of the nature of Delayed Harvest trout.

At the heart of DH fly selection is what I like to call the "DH Conundrum." The dictionary defines a conundrum as a challenging question of some sort, and when you're picking out flies for use on Delayed Harvest water that question is, "Do I want flies that will let me target freshly-stocked fish (like the ones stocked yesterday) or do I want flies which will target more experienced fish (like the ones stocked two weeks or a month or two ago)?"

Why is there a difference in the flies you'd choose for one class of trout versus the other? Because fresh stockers are running pretty much on instinct and will be more likely to hit things that instinct says are good to eat.

One such instinct-approved food form is the lowly fish egg. A roundish egg imitation in a shade of pink or orange often works well on freshly stocked fish. Flies such as the Y2K, 3-D Suckerspawn, and Yarn Egg all fall into that category.

Streamers can also work well on such fish. When actively stripped, they imitate a fleeing minnow – and trout seem predisposed to chase down and eat things that are trying to swim away. The Rolex in silver and gold or red and gold is a good pattern; a Woolly bugger stripped minnow-style will also do a good job. Other good bets include small Clousers as well as two streamer patterns developed especially for the Hooch DH, the Chebaw Fly and the Hudson Streamer.

Another factor that seems to be a trigger for freshly stocked fish is "bugginess." It's a little hard to define, but you will know it when you see it. A "buggy" nymph will have a nymph-like profile and should be a bit (sometimes a lot) on the shaggy side. In fact, the bugginess of the fly often seems to matter more to fresh DH fish than does the specific pattern.

If you are getting the idea that newly stocked Delayed Harvest fish are fairly easy to catch, you might be right (at least sometimes). However, those new stockers don't remain "newbies" for long. They very quickly begin to wise up, showing more and more interest in the many food forms which naturally occur in the stream. As they make that shift your fly choice will need to shift a bit too. More traditional flies will come into play as the fish increasingly take on the feeding characteristics of more streamwise trout.

As noted earlier, the challenging thing about all of this is that you can have both classes of fish (that is, fresh stockers and seasoned veterans) swimming together in any given place at any given point in time. Essentially, that challenges you to choose flies for two different types of fish.

One effective strategy in such cases is to fish two subsurface flies at a time. Make one of them a gaudy "junque food" pattern such as a Y2K; for the other, go with a more natural looking nymph of some sort – perhaps a Soft Hackle Pheasant Tail in size 14 or 16. That allows you to give the fish a choice. New stockers will probably choose the Y2K, while veterans may prefer the nymph. That's a very good way to deal with the "DH Conundrum."

The matter of weight: Most Delayed Harvest trout will be caught on subsurface flies, so let's take a moment here to review what is probably the

Flies for Chattahoochee DH
(DH season is Nov. 1 - May 14)

Right after fish are stocked	**Eggs:** Y2K, Sucker Spawn, etc., (12-16) **Worms:** San Juan Worm in pink, red or chartreuse (12-14) **Streamers:** Rolex, Hudson Streamer (6-8) **Mop Flies:** Try pink, orange or chartreuse in size 10-14
Soon after fish are stocked	**All of the above** plus... **Small nymphs:** Pheasant Tails or Hare's Ears in sizes 14-18 **Soft-Hackle Emergers:** Try flies with bright as well as drab body colors in sizes 14-18 **Woolly Buggers/Leeches:** Olive, brown or black...and pink or orange!...in sizes 6-12
All season	**All of the above** plus... **Suitably sized dries:** Try dries if you see significant bug activity, especially in spring
Winter	**All of the above** and... **Midges:** Dry or emerger versions, size 16-20 – favorites include Blue Assassin, Rainbow Warrior, and Griffith's Gnat
Spring	**Elk Hair or Foamback Caddis:** Try it in sizes 14-16 during caddis hatch in March. **Terrestrials:** In April and May

most important key to successful DH subsurface fishing.

And what is that key, you ask? Simply making sure that your flies run deep enough to get down to where the fish are. Trout typically hang out near the bottom. But sometimes DH anglers don't add nearly enough split shot, and as a result they're never actually putting flies in front of fish.

I recall one early-season outing near US 41 last year. I was getting plenty of fish on a Y2K with a size AB shot on the leader 8 inches above the fly.

About 50 yards downstream, another angler was also fishing a nymph-style rig. However, he hadn't hooked a single fish. Even at a distance, his body language said he was getting frustrated.

It bothers me when I see someone on the river who's not having a good day, so over the next little while I eased down toward him.

"How's it going?" I asked.

"Not good," he replied with a rueful grin. "I'm still pretty new at this, and I must not have it figured out yet because I haven't caught a thing."

"Uh-oh!" I said. "Mind if I asked what you're using?"

He stripped in his line and showed his set-up to me. To my surprise, he was using the same fly I was – a beadhead Y2K.

But I saw right away that he wasn't using nearly enough added weight on the end of this leader. Whereas I was using that size AB split shot to quickly sink my fly, he was using what appeared to be a single piece of size 6 shot.

Ahh. There's your problem.

"Mind if I make a suggestion?" I asked. You have to be careful asking that question of someone who's not catching fish. Some take offense. But this angler was open to help.

"Sure," he said. "I'll take all the help I can get."

We spent a couple of minutes working on his set-up. I removed the tiny little size 6 shot, replacing it with a much larger one in size AB a few inches above his Y2K.

"Try that," I said. "Sometimes that little bit of extra weight can make all the difference."

I turned then and started back upriver. I hadn't gone 30 feet before I heard an excited yell.

"Hey, buddy!" he said as I turned to see his rod bent and his line tight. "That's all it took! Thanks!"

Moral of the story? Be sure you use enough weight!

Streamers for DH trout: There's no doubt about it. DH fish love streamers. An eye-catching streamer can be impossible for a Delayed Harvest trout to resist.

To fish a streamer, cast it across the current. Then do an upstream mend, lower your rod tip so it's pointing down your line toward the fly, and strip the fly back to you in 8- to 12-inch strips. As you strip the fly, the current will carry it downstream, so follow the line with your rod tip to make sure that you have a tight line to the fly. Strikes are unmistakable.

Dries for DH? Dry flies can indeed work on Delayed Harvest trout. Early in the DH season, a dry with a large body profile (for example, a Humpy) can be effective, possibly because it resembles the food pellets that the fish were used to eating in the hatchery. Later, during winter, especially on seasonsed fish, small midges such as Griffith's Gnats or BWOs can work too.

Some of the most exciting DH dry fly action comes in spring when caddisflies begin to appear on the lower tailwater. This typically happens in March when small (size 14 or 16) caddisflies start to appear. You'll see them everywhere, particularly on streamside branchs. The hatch lasts several weeks, and it can be an exciting time to fish the river's DH water.

During the caddis hatch, a dry-dropper rig consisting of a tan or gray Elk Hair or Foamback Caddis and a caddis emerger can be extremely effective. I've had very good luck with this in March and April above the I-75 bridge.

Spinning lures for Delayed Harvest

When choosing spinning lures for DH fishing in the lower tailwater, remember that you're limited to *single-hook lures* on all of Georgia's Delayed Harvest streams. Either barbed or barbless is okay (I'd go barbless) but each lure can only have a single hook.

It's possible these days to purchase single-hook versions of many lures. If you can't find them, you can convert treble-hook models to single-hook by either replacing the treble hook with a single hook or by using wire cutters to cut away two of the three hooks on the treble.

Note that if your chosen lure has multiple trebles, you'll have to remove one of them completely and then modify the other one. In other words, the goal to have but one "point" on each lure.

Aside from the matter of hooks, you'll find that the same spinners you used above Morgan Falls Dam will also work on the DH water. "Bright" and "flashy" usually seem to be the key, though "a little less flashy" can be good if the water is super-clear. Color-wise, try a white-bodied in-line spinner with a silver or gold blade. On cloudy days, go a bit darker.

There are also times when more elaborately colored spinning lures seem to have the edge on the Delayed Harvest water. One of my favorite color schemes for DH lures is a "rainbow trout" or "firetiger" pattern. A solid pink or orange lure can work surprisingly well, too, perhaps because the color makes the trout think of eggs! ☐

Float tubing on the Hooch DH

The Chattahoochee Delayed Harvest section is great water to fish from a float tube (also known as a "belly boat). The tube makes it easy to get through some of the river's deeper spots and thus allows you to fish areas that wading anglers might not be able to reach.

A tube can be particularly useful later in the Delayed Harvest season once the fish have had a chance to spread out. Early in the season, the trout may be concentrated near stocking points. But later on they'll disperse all across the river. A tube gives you the mobility you will need to get to them.

With its many pockets, a float tube makes it easy to gear up for wintertime fishing on the Hooch DH too. Use those pockets to carry things you might need. That includes extra fly boxes, extra split shot, and spare leaders and tippet. I store these in the side pockets where they're easy to get to.

In one of the larger pockets (say, for example, the one that forms the back rest) I might stash an extra sweater in case I get chilly or

Fly fisher Amanda Hoppers gets ready for a float on the Hooch DH water.

even a breathable rain jacket in case an unexpected shower comes along.

I also like to carry a spare set of gloves in case the ones I'm wearing get soaked. There's no faster way to cold hands than via a pair of wet gloves.

Finally, I'll make sure that somewhere in one of those pockets is some water and a snack of some sort – possibly homemade chocolate chip cookies!

A number of great float tube trips are possible on the Chattahoochee DH water. We'll take a close look at several of them starting on page 310.

By the way, whatever route you choose, here's something to remember if you plan to end your float near the Paces Mill boat ramp. Some of the water near the ramp can be quite shallow, particularly on river right. If you "bottom out" in a float tube it can be very difficult to stand up!

As always keep safety in mind when float tubing. Wear your PFD. ☐

Exploring the Hooch DH water

How to get in on this great wintertime trout fishery at the lower end of the lower tailwater

Starting at the mouth of Sope Creek, and continuing down to the US 41 bridge, the Chattahoochee's DH stretch offers what can be some very exciting wintertime trout fishing. Whether you're wading or floating, and whether you fish with a fly rod or prefer spinning tackle, you'll find it has something just for you.

Access points within the Chattahoochee River National Recreation Area (CRNRA) make it simple to get to the water. One favorite is CRNRA's Paces Mill Unit off US 41 near Cumberland Mall near the lower end of the DH water. It provides access to wadable water as well as to two boat launch sites. Depending on the river level, the downstream ramp is usually best for trailered boats.

Another popular access point is CRNRA's Whitewater Unit. This one provides more wading access (though wading can be tricky) as well as a canoe or float tube put-in or takeout.

Other popular access spots include Cochran Shoals (for wade fishing or to put in a tube) as well as the Sandy Point access from CRNRA's Akers Drive parking area (which requires some hiking).

Bank fishing

There are several ways to fish the Chattahoochee DH water; we'll start with a look at bank fishing. Fishing from shore can be easy here if you're using spinning gear, and that can be a great way to approach things if you've brought your kids along. They'll love it.

To locate good bank fishing areas, look for places where trails or clearings provide access to holding water where fish may be congregated. That might be a pool, a run, a ledge, a brushpile, or some other fish-holding area.

There are many suitable bank fishing spots along the DH section. Here are some areas to check out. It's not an exhaustive list, but it'll get you started:

- Along the riverside portion of the Cochran Shoals Unit Fitness Trail

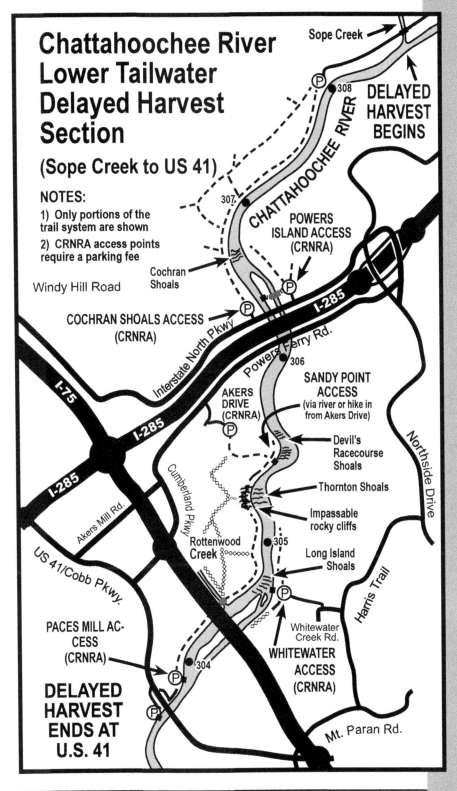

Chattahoochee River Lower Tailwater Delayed Harvest Section

(Sope Creek to US 41)

NOTES:

1) Only portions of the trail system are shown

2) CRNRA access points require a parking fee

Sope Creek

DELAYED HARVEST BEGINS

●308

307

CHATTAHOOCHEE RIVER

POWERS ISLAND ACCESS (CRNRA)

Windy Hill Road

Cochran Shoals

COCHRAN SHOALS ACCESS (CRNRA)

Interstate North Pkwy

I-285

Powers Ferry Rd.

●306

SANDY POINT ACCESS (via river or hike in from Akers Drive)

AKERS DRIVE (CRNRA)

I-75

I-285

I-285

Akers Mill Rd.

Cumberland Pkwy

Rottenwood Creek

●305

Devil's Racecourse Shoals

Thornton Shoals

Impassable rocky cliffs

Long Island Shoals

Northside Drive

Harris Trail

US 41/Cobb Pkwy.

PACES MILL ACCESS (CRNRA)

●304

Whitewater Creek Rd.

WHITEWATER ACCESS (CRNRA)

DELAYED HARVEST ENDS AT U.S. 41

Mt. Paran Rd.

- Around the mouth of Rottenwood Creek above the I-75 bridge
- Downriver from the I-75 bridge via the paved multi-purpose trail
- Beneath (literally!) the I-75 bridge.
- At CRNRA's Whitewater Unit near the canoe launch area.
- At Sandy Point, accessible by hiking in from the Akers Drive parking area.

It's not at all uncommon to see anglers fishing the Hooch DH from shore. Most bank fishers will be using spinning gear since casting a fly rod under such conditions can be difficult due to a lack of room for the backcast.

Wading

A good bit of the Hooch DH water is wadable – good news for all anglers. Wading puts you on wide-open water with few obstructions and plenty of room to make those long casts.

What about waders? Neoprene, while warm, can cause you to overheat (as you'll see in a minute). Instead, consider going with breathable chest waders with layered clothing underneath.

Can we pinpoint specific spots for good wade fishing? Maybe. But remember that bottom contours change every season. Every time the river rises, high flows may resculpt things. The gravel bar I enjoyed two months ago might have completely disappeared by the time you get there two weeks hence. This happens more often than you'd think, and that's why it's impossible to say "wade here" with any certainty that the advice will be accurate at some future time.

What we can do, however, is note general areas. Let's start at the top of the DH section and work our way downriver, looking at some promising wading areas along the way. The map on page 305 will keep you oriented as we go.

Below Cochran Shoals

Cochran Shoals, with its loop fitness trail, is popular with joggers and cyclists – and the shoals are popular with wading anglers. At low water, wading there is not too difficult. The river is accessible from CRNRA units on both banks (either from the fitness loop trail or from the Powers Island side). On Powers Island, check out the canoe/raft launch on the river side of Powers Island, accessible by crossing a foot bridge near the Powers Island parking lot.

What about wading above Cochran Shoals? Alas, it's deep and

not suitable for wading. Similar conditions are encountered for some distance below the I-285 bridge. Those stretches are the realm of anglers with a kayak, canoe or float tube.

At Sandy Point near Devil's Race Course Shoals

Some wading is possible at Devil's Race Course Shoals, the first significant shoals below I-285.

One way to access this areas is by floating down from upriver in a kayak or canoe or float tube, beaching your craft on river right at Sandy Point and then wading the area before returning to your boat.

Another way to access this part of the river is to park at CRN-RA's Akers Drive parking area and then follow the trail down the hill to the river.

Whitewater

The Whitewater parking area, part of the Chattahoochee River National Recreation Area, provides good access to the main river on river left and to side channels along Long Island. Whitewater is also the site of volunteer-assisted Delayed Harvest stocking events several times a year.

How's the wading there? Directly in front of the Whitewater canoe

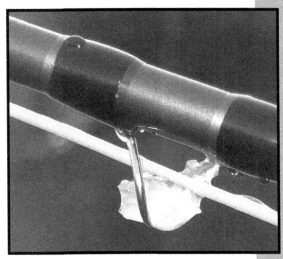

An occupational hazard of wintertime Delayed Harvest trout fishing – ice forming on your rod's guides!

launch is a relatively shallow gravel bar; beyond it is deeper water with a rough bottom well blessed with rocks and ledges. Some anglers wade to the edge of the gravel zone and then cast to the deeper water, though others wade farther out. But wading here is tricky (lot of rocks and ledges) and not for the faint of heart.

The channel between Long Island and the main bank also offers interesting wading possibilities and will remind you of a creek. Note, though, that the bottom is soft in spots. Near the lower end you'll find some deep holes, and the side channel's bottom becomes rough and tricky as you near the lower end of the island.

A favorite wading spot is the area around the Paces Mill boat ramp.

Above the I-75 bridge

At low water levels it may be possible to enter the river near the bridge over Rottenwood Creek and then work your way out into the flow. Most of the time, you'll find a channel near the mouth of the creek; it's got a lot of rocks in it, and those rocks can trip up the careless or the unwary. But if you can cross the little channel, you'll find yourself in a fairly large area of wadable water. By picking your way around deeper spots, you'll have access to at least an afternoon's worth of DH fishing.

Downstream from the I-75 bridge

If you hike upriver (toward the I-75 bridge) along the paved trail which starts at the Paces Mill parking area, you'll notice many spots where well-worn spur trails lead from the main path down to the river. Often, they lead to an access point where bank fishing is possible or where it's relatively easy to enter the river and wade.

Once in the river, look for those deeper areas of holding water. Fish them as if they were small creeks. Good fishing can be found all the way across the river, especially later in the DH season. Just be realistic about your wading abilities.

Upstream from the Paces Mill boat ramp

It may be possible (at low water) to wade a good ways upriver from the boat ramp toward I-75. Like any approach that takes you any distance from the most easily accessible water, it's likely to put you on fish that others may not have bothered too much.

Above the boat ramp, the river is shoally in places with ledges, runs, and pool-like places to explore. All can be good waters to fish. But wade carefully, because the same features which create those good fishing areas also make for tricky wading conditions. For example, the sloping underwater rocks that create nice riffles and holes also make for tricky wading. To make the going easier, most who fish this area frequently carry and use a wading staff.

In front of the upstream boat ramp at Paces Mill

This may be the most heavily fished part of the Chattahoochee DH, and it's easy to see why. A broad, paved boat ramp makes access easy, and beyond the end of the ramp is a wide gravel bar extending into the river toward a number of promising runs. For another thing, it's a major stocking point that usually holds good numbers of fish.

One of the most obvious of these runs is the large channel adjacent to the prominent rock that you'll see in front of you from the bottom of the ramp. It seems that everybody has to make a few casts there. Fish not only the deep parts of the many channels in the area but also the heads and tails of runs.

There are many other similar runs in this section of the river. Keep your eyes open for them as you explore. Some are large; others are smaller and more subtle. But all share one characteristic: they're at least a little bit deeper than the water around them, and thus they are potential holding water for trout.

Georgia Department of Natural Resources personnel stock trout directly beneath the I-75 bridge, one of several DH stocking points.

Remember: the farther from the ramp you're willing to walk, the more likely you are to find more lightly fished water.

Floating the Hooch DH water

Anglers who enjoy fishing from canoes, float tubes or pontoons will find much to like on the Hooch DH. Floating provides mobility that lets you fish areas which might be inaccessible otherwise. However, floating must be done safely. A complete discussion of floating safety is beyond the scope of this guide, but it is critical that you know how to safely use your personal watercraft before taking to the river. We'll say it again: Your safety on the river is solely your responsibility.

If you're ambitious it's possible to float and fish from Cochran Shoals all the way to the downriver end of the DH water at US 41. That's a long float, however. Most prefer shorter trips that are less tiring and provide more time to thoroughly fish the water.

Here, starting at the upper end of the DH water and working our way down, is a look at several popular floats on the Chattahoochee DH. These can be combined to create a variety of different float fishing adventures. Consider your abilities and skills when selecting any float on a river like the Hooch.

Sope Creek to Cochran Shoals?

As noted earlier, the water above Cochran Shoals is too deep for wading. However, float trips can provide access.

Where can you start? There are two put-ins above Sope Creek – one at the ramp near the foot of Morgan Falls Dam and one at the ramp at CRNRA's Johnson Ferry Unit. From either, you can float down to the start of the DH water.

How's the fishing in this extreme upper portion of the DH? Early in the season, it won't be very good. You're quite a ways from the nearest DH stocking point (Cochran Shoals), and it takes time for those first stocked fish to make their way upriver.

As the season moves on, however, the fish spread out a bit and some will move into the water nearer to Sope Creek.

Come spring, boat-equipped DH anglers might want to check out the lower portion of Sope Creek. Rainbows with spawning on their minds may move into that water.

Remember, too, that this can be striped bass water at certain times of year. But that's another story.

Cochran Shoals to Sandy Point (Akers Drive parking area)

Another area that's mostly too deep for wading but that's good for floating is the stretch between Cochran Shoals and Sandy Point. It's popular with those who have tubes, pontoons, kayaks, canoes or even drift boats. It gives floating anglers a shot at fish that wading anglers never see. Being between the stocking points at Cochran Shoals and at Whitewater, it may hold decent numbers of fish too.

There is some potentially good water through this stretch. One spot that many anglers like to fish thoroughly is the area along the rocky bluffs on river left, not far downriver of the I-285 bridge. When fishing the deep water near the bluffs, use a lot of weight (if fly fishing) or relatively heavy or deep-diving lures (if spin fishing).

Making this float requires two vehicles (one at each end of the trip) plus a willingness to make a very long uphill carry back to your car at the Akers Drive parking area.

Sandy Point (Akers Drive parking area) to Paces Mill

This float, or some subset of it, is a popular one. There are some complicating factors, however. Reaching the put-in at Sandy Point requires a sig-nificant hike from the Akers Road parking area (and a second car at float's end at Paces Mill). Al-ternately, it's pos-sible (but fairly strenuous) to hike with a float tube

On the Hooch DH, a canoe or kayak offers great mobility upstream as well as down.

from Paces Mill to Sandy Point and then float and fish your way back to your starting point.

On the plus side, this gives you access to water that gets less pressure. On the other hand...

If you make this hike, don't make the mistake I made years ago, early in my DH fishing career. I'd decided to park at Paces Mill, hike from there to Sandy Point and then float in my tube back to my truck while fishing all the way. I'd made that hike many times, and while it's definitely a leg-stretcher it was nothing I couldn't handle.

But I'd never tried it while wearing waders and toting a tube.

To make a long story short, I attempted the hike on a very cold day, wearing neoprene waders (a serious mistake) and carrying the tube and my PFD on my back.

I was (how to put it) uninformed about the best way to do that.

What I should have done, of course, was stuff my waders into the big pocket on the back of my tube, make the hike, and then put on the waders once I got to my starting point.

Unfortunately, on that long-ago day when I made that first trip, I wasn't yet wise in the ways of the Hooch DH. The problem was that I was hiking while wearing what was, in effect, a personal, portable sauna. I overheated on the hike in, and then (and to no one's surprise) I got cold and clammy floating back.

I'll be honest. I was a truly miserable person by the time I returned to the truck. In fact, my fishing buddy (who had the good sense to do what I should have done and carried his waders in a day pack) said I looked so bad he was about to call 911!

This DH rainbow fell for a Hudson Streamer stripped through a run.

Bottom line: don't do heavy hiking in waders.

But I digress.

What's it like once you're on the water? Between Sandy Point and Thornton Shoals, expect a section of relatively calm water. Then comes Thornton Shoals and, beyond there, an even longer section of the calm-and-deep. It's great water, but it fishes better later in the season once the trout have spread out.

If you're fishing with a fly rod, try drifting a heavily weighted nymph rig alongside your tube as you float through the deep areas. Alternately, use a sink-tip line and work a streamer near cover as you drift through those deep spots. Spinning enthusiasts sometimes do well with deeper-running crankbaits and other minnow imitations. In either case, pay special attention to the cover along the banks. Fallen trees provide great cover for trout, and you may be able to coax one to come out and nail a well presented fly or lure.

Paces Mill – the short, middle, and long floats

Sometimes I'll only have a few hours to fish the Hooch DH. When that's the case, it's hard to beat one of the short-and-easy floats which you can enjoy using the parking area at Paces Mill as your base of operations.

There are actually three possible short floats – from I-75 down to the Paces Mill boat ramp, from near the shoals opposite White-water down to I-75, and from the end of the river-right trail (which continues upriver as a dirt trail beyond the bridge over Rottenwood Creek before eventually ending a rocky cliffs) down to the shoals opposite Whitewater. These short floats can be enjoyed individually, combined to make a couple of medium floats, or (if you have time) experienced all together for a longer fishing adventure.

Things to be aware of along the way include (1) possible slow going in the relatively slack water above Whitewater, particularly if there's wind blowing upriver, plus (2) the possibility of obstructions lodged against bridge pilings at the I-75 bridge. Also be aware of (3) submerged, tilted rock ledges in the vicinity of Whitewater and of additional ledges as you approach the ramp at Paces Mill. Finally, be aware of (4) very shallow water near the Paces Mill takeout. If you end up in the shallows while still in your float tube, you may find it difficult to get your feet under you so that you can stand up.

You will notice a number of intermediate river access points throughout this stretch. As you learn the river, you may be able to use those alternate access points to further customize your Chatta-hoochee DH trips.

To find good fishing, follow the fish

One thing you'll notice on the Hooch DH is that the quality of fishing will vary in any given area as you move through the DH season. One day you may hook dozens; the next day (or week or month) you may hook nothing...or you may do even better than before.

To understand why, consider this. First, assume you're fishing early in the season. The fish you're encountering have come from early DH stockings, typically in the Cochran Shoals or Paces Mill area. After any DH stocking, there will be a high concentration of fish near the stocking point but fewer fish elsewhere until those trout spread out. They do this naturally, and (depending on things like flow) sometimes very quickly. Dispersal is aided by anglers too, for as anglers wade near the stocking points, they'll disturb close-in fish and get 'em moving out into the rest of the river.

Since the DH water is stocked several times during the season, this stocking and dispersal of trout is an ongoing process. Early in the season, the number of fish present will be greatest (and thus the fishing will likely be best) nearest the stocking points. But as the season moves along and fish spread out, you'll increasingly find trout throughout the Chattahoochee Delayed Harvest water.

Surprises on the Chattahoochee DH

One of the nice things about the Chattahoochee Delayed Harvest water is that it's fairly predictable. On most of your outings during

Is there trout fishing near Morgan Falls Dam? Sometimes. But there's other fishing there to keep you busy there, too, as these two upper-lower tailwater fish (a carp and a striped bass) suggest. The striper went for a streamer fished on a sinking tip line; the carp grabbed a size 12 Y2K fished under an indicator.

the DH season, you can usually expect to catch at least a few trout. But sometimes the DH water will surprise you.

I remember one late afternoon in early March. I was fishing near the I-75 bridge, using a streamer on 4x tippet to probe the water for rainbows. I'd picked up a couple – and then I had a strike that nearly took the rod out of my hands.

I'll cut to the chase. It took a solid half hour, but I finally got in enough line that I could see the line/leader connection. And then I glimpsed the fish. It was a striped bass, 2 or 3 or maybe 10 feet long. I could see the streamer hanging in its jaw.

About that time the bass saw me, too, and with one flick of its tail it popped what was left of the tippet and was gone.

Another day, another year: I was in the float tube, drifting a Y2K a few feet beyond the tube as I floated slowly through the deep water below I-285. Suddenly my indicator stopped – it simply stopped – and my first thought was that I'd hung up on the bottom.

I tightened the line to see if it would pull loose, and then the line started to move.

It wasn't moving like a trout, and it wasn't moving like a bass. What I finally learned, about a quarter mile downriver when I finally brought the fish to my totally inadequate net, was that it was moving like a carp...a really big carp. The fish took the barbless Y2K and somehow stayed on. A nearby fishermen took a photo for me, and I look at it now and then to remind me that on the river, as in life, you never know what's about to come your way. □

> What happens below US 41? There's an additional 3 miles of river administered by the National Park Service from the 41 bridge down to the mouth of Peachtree Creek. It sometimes yields trout during the DH season (especially later in the season as the fish spread out) as well as bass, including stripers.
>
> Unfortunately, there's no good public access to the river through that stretch. If you have a boat and can fish down from Paces Mill and then paddle or motor back upriver to the take out, however, you'll almost certainly have the water to yourself. Because of the access issues, it is fished by very few anglers.

Have some fun... stock some trout!

Be part of volunteer-assisted stocking on the Chattahoochee Delayed Harvest water. It's a great way to support trout fishing in Georgia – and it's fun!

Georgia's Department of Natural Resources does a great job of stocking Georgia's rivers and streams, but every now and then even DNR needs a little help.

Let's say that there's a need to stock a section of the Hooch DH that the hatchery truck can't reach. That's where you and I come in.

Several times a year, DNR invites members of the fishing community to get personally involved in the Delayed Harvest program by helping stock a Georgia DH stream. These volunteer-assisted stockings take place on several different streams, but one of the most popular is at Whitewater on the Hooch DH water not far from US 41.

Stocking dates are announced several weeks ahead of time at

fishing club meetings and on websites such as North Georgia Trout Online (ngto.org). An effort is made to schedule these events so they coincide with school holidays, too, which makes it easy for kids to participate as well.

Here's how it works. Folks arrive at the designated stocking site at the specified time (typically about 10 a.m.) bringing 5-gallon buckets and waders. Everyone signs a release form.

Then, once the hatchery truck arrives, it's all business as volunteers line up with buckets. DNR personnel transfer fish to buckets, and the buckets are then carried straight to the river. The fish are placed into the water, and then it's back to the truck for another load...and another... until, pretty soon, several thousand trout have a new home in the river.

What sort of trout are stocked? Mostly rainbows and browns. They range from "SNITs" ("standard nine-inch trout") up to larger fish.

"Helping stock is a great way to support trout fishing," said one father of two at a recent volunteer-assisted stocking at Whitewater on the Chattahoochee Delayed Harvest section. His kids were there, too, sharing the experience.

"And it is *fun!*" said the youngest as she and her sister joined forces to haul a bucket of trout from the truck to the water. "But they sure do *splash* a lot!"

Once stocking is done, the volunteers often stay and fish for a while. That's a great time to introduce a beginner to trout fishing, and there are usually plenty of people on hand to help beginners get the hang of things. ☐

Appendix 1:

Distances and float times

UPPER TAILWATER	From here ———→ To here		Miles	From Morgan Falls
	Lower Pool Pk (Buford Dam)	Hatchery	1.8	1.8
	Hatchery	GA 20	0.7	2.5
	GA 20	Settles Bridge	2.2	4.7
	Settles Bridge	Chattahoochee Pointe	2.5	7.2
	Chattahoochee Pointe	McGinnis Ferry	1.8	9
	McGinnis Ferry	Rogers Bridge	2.7	11.7
	Rogers Bridge	Abbotts Bridge	1.8	13.5
	Abbotts Bridge	Medlock Bridge	4	17.5
	Medlock Bridge	Jones Br (Gwinnett or upper CRNRA)	2.5	20
	Jones Br (Gwinnett or upper CRNRA)	Jones Br (CRNRA/lower)	0.5	20.5
	Jones Br (CRNRA/lower)	Garrard Landing	2.5	23
	Garrard Landing	Island Ford	5.2	28.2
	Island Ford	Don White Park	1.7	29.9
	Don White Park	Azalea Drive Ramp	2.1	32

LOWER TAILWATER	From here ———→ To here		Miles	From Morgan Falls
	Below Morgan Falls Dam	Johnson Ferry	1.9	1.9
	Johnson Ferry	Cochran Shoals (I-285)	4.3	6.2
	Cochran Shoals (1-285)	Sandy Point (via Akers Dr)	1	7.2
	Sandy Point (Akers Dr)	Whitewater	0.8	8.0
	Whitewater	Paces Mill boat ramp	0.8	8.6
	Paces Mill boat ramp	US 41 bridge	0.2	8.8

This chart provides **rough approximations** of float times for canoes/kayaks or float tubes.
Distances were **measured from topo maps.**
Estimates may be on "long" side; on average, **figure 1-1.5 river miles/hour in a float tube.**
Actual float times vary depending on water level, time fishing, wind direction, etc.
Water below Garrard Landing is not ideal for float tubes and is better for canoes or kayaks.

This chart does NOT address time for water released from Buford Dam or Morgan Falls Dam to reach the indicated areas!

Canoe/kayak	Float tube	Comments
No takeout	1.5-2 hours	Tube exit only at hatchery
Rough exit	0.5-1 hour	Rough exit at GA 20
1-1.5 hours	2-3 hours	Rough entry at 20
1-1.5 hours	2.5-3 hours	Exit river right
1-1.5 hours	2-3 hours	Enter and cross to avoid eddy
1-1.5 hours	2.5-5 hours	Exit river left
1 hour	1.5-2 hours	Exit river left (tube/kayak/canoe)
1.5-2 hours	4-5 hours	Exit on right, before bridge
1-1.5 hr	2.5-3 hours	Allow plenty of fishing time
0.5 hour	0.5-1 hour	Allow LOTS of fishing time!
1-1.5 hours	2.5-3.5 hours	Tricky exit in a tube Muddy ramp
2-3 hours	Not recommended	Some slo-o-ow water
1 hour	2+ hours if windy	Best as canoe/kayak water
1-1.5 hours	Not recommended	Flat water, may be windy

Canoe/kayak	Float tube	Comments
1-1.5 hour	2-3 hours	Exit on river right
1.5-2 hours	3.5-4.5 hours	No ramp, exit right near 285
0.5-1 hour	1 hour	Put in near I-285 bridge; very long carry from river to Akers Dr parking
0.5 hour	1 hour	Very long carry from Akers Dr parking area to river; exit on river left
0.5 hour	1 hour	Exit on river right
Just a few minutes	Less than a half hour	Exit ramp on right just below 41

Appendix 2:

Selected fly recipes

W e've mentioned a number of flies in this guide, and you'll find many of them well described in the literature. There are, however- er, a number of patterns or pattern variations are particularly popular on the Hooch or have evolved to suit the river's fish. Here are recipes for 23 of those patterns, along with notes on using them.

3-D Sucker Spawn (egg)

Hook: 12-16 nymph hook
Bead: Pink or orange, optional
Thread: Red 3/0 or 6/0
Body: Fuzzy pink or orange yarn, looped

Notes: This simple egg imitation works well on the Delayed Harvest section and other stocked portions of the river. Body is 4-5 loops of pink or orange fuzzy yarn. Loops should be about the size of the hook gape. Fish like a nymph.

Articulated Woolly Bugger (large streamer)

Rear hook: Nymph or woolly bugger hook, 10-12, 2XL
Thread: 3/0 or 6/0. match body color
Tail: Marabou with flash strands
Rear body: Chenille
Front hook: One or two sizes larger than rear hook

Connection: 19-strand Beadalon with 2-3 beads
Bead: Gold or silver
Front hackle (back): Grizzly
Front body: Chenille
Front hackle (forward): Grizzly
Collar: Red dubbing

Notes: An effective fly for large browns in the upper tailwater. Tie in various colors. Black or olive work well. So do "brown trout" colors. There are many ways to tie the Articulated Woolly Bugger; this approach is easy and versatile. This fly is a favorite for large trout and works well on bass too.

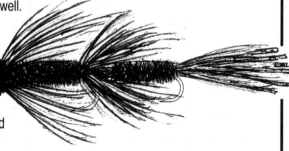

Beetle (Deer Hair) (terrestrial)

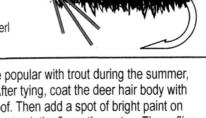

Hook: 10-18 dry fly hook
Thread: Black
Body: Black deer hair, folded over
Underbody: Black dubbing or peacock herl
Sight spot: Dot of red or yellow paint

Notes: Terrestrials such as beetles are popular with trout during the summer, and deer hair beetles are easy to tie. After tying, coat the deer hair body with head cement to make it more waterproof. Then add a spot of bright paint on the back (a sight spot) to help you better track the fly on the water. These flies can be particularly productive when fished near grassy or overgrown banks – in other words, near places where beetles might be crawling.

Blue Assassin (midge emerger)

Hook: 16-20 curved shank nymph
Bead: Silver tungsten bead
Thread: Gray 6/0 or 8/0
Tail: A few strands of Z-lon
Ribbing: Extra fine silver wire
Abdomen: 2-3 strands of pearl flas wrapped forward from ben
Thorax: 2-3 turns of blue dubbed thread directly behind bead

Notes: An outstanding midge emerger fine-tuned for the river by guide Chris Scalley. Use wherever midges or small mayflies are present, especially on the upper tailwater or above Upper Chattahoochee River Campground.

Chebaw Fly (streamer)

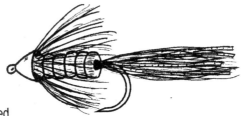

Hook: Woolly hook, 3xl, 6-8
Bead: Gold or silver conehead
Hackle: Orange, pink, or grizzly
Body: Glass craft beads
Tail: Marabou with flash added

Notes: The Chebaw Fly was developed for use in Delayed Harvest waters and was featured in the book "Tying Flies for Stocked Trout." It is a flashy and fast-sinking streamer that is effective on stocked as well as wild trout (and bass too). Match body and tail colors. Pink, orange, white and light blue have proven to be effective. Fish it like a streamer.

Double Deceiver (large streamer)

Rear hook: Size 2
Rear tail: Schlappen
Rear body: Bucktail
Connection: 19-strand Beadalon with 2-3 beads
Front hook: One or two sizes larger than rear hook
Front tail: Schlappen
Front body: Bucktail
Eyes: Medium or large eyes glued to head
Head: Cover with clear finish for durability

Notes: Use this large articulated streamer when fishing for large fish such as the big browns on the upper Chattahoochee tailwater.

Foamback Caddis (adult caddis or stonefly)

Hook: Dry fly hook, 12-18
Thread: Tan, gray or black, 6/0-8/0
Back: Narrow strip of thin closed-cell foam
Body: Tan, black, or sparkle dubbing
to match color of naturals
Wing: Stacked elk hair
Collar: Coarse dubbing

Notes: The Foamback Caddis is high-floating dry for use on the Chattahoochee, particularly in the spring when caddisflies are emerging. It is especially effective on the Delayed Harvest water during the massive caddis hatches that occur there during March. Try pairing it with a Soft-Hackle Emerger dropper.

Gold Ribbed Hare's Ear (beadhead) (nymph)

Hook: 12-18 nymph hook
Bead: Brass bead
Thread: Black 6/0 or 8/0
Tail: Bundle of guard hairs from hare's mask
Ribbing: Fine gold wire
Abdomen: Hare's ear blend dubbing
Wingcase: Section of turkey quill
Thorax: Coarse hare's ear dubbing

Notes: The Gold Ribbed Hare's Ear is effective where thicker-bodied nymphs are found. It works throughout the Chattahoochee trout water. Don't hesitate to try very small (size 18) versions of this fly...and try an *all-pink one* during DH!

Hudson Streamer (flank wing streamer)

Hook: Size 8 2XL or 3XL streamer or woolly hook
Bead: Brass bead
Thread: Red 3/0
Tail/body: 8-10 strands of flash tied in to form tail and wrapped to form body
Wings: Grizzly (shown) or guinea fowl
Hackle: 2-4 turns of grizzly, guinea or hen
Collar: Red dubbed thread

Notes: Works well throughout the season in stocked as well as wild-fish water. Count down to depth, and then actively work the fly with 8- to 12-inch strips.

Island Park Special (midge)

Hook: 12-18 nymph hook
Bead: Copper- or gold-colored tungsten
Thread: Black 6/0 or 8/0
Ribbing: Extra fine wire
Body: 2-3 strands peacock herl
Tail: (Optional) 1-2 strands flash
Hackle: Brown dry-fly hackle

Notes: Essentially a tiny Woolly Bugger with no tail, the Island Park Special is fished like other midge patterns. Note that the hackle is *dry fly* hackle, even though the pattern is fished subsurface. An optional tail (not shown) can be added with a strand or two of flash material.

Ken's Crazy Ant (Shelf Liner Ant)

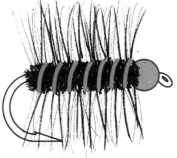

Hook: 16-18 dry fly hook
Thread: Black 6/0
Body: Prepared from non-slip shelf liner material
Wing: White Antron
Hackle: Grizzly or black, tied in at waist

Notes: Use anytime and anywhere that ants are present. Works well during late spring through fall on headwaters as well as the upper tailwater, especially where vegetation overhangs the water. Use floatant to fish this one as a dry, but note that it's very effective fished subsurface.

Moonshine Midge (midge emerger)

Hook: 16-18 curved shank nymph hook
Bead: Copper-colored tungsten bead
Thread: Black 6/0 or 8/0
Body: Black thread
Tail: Short tag of flash left when flash is tied in
Ribbing: Single strand of copper-colored flash
Thorax: Black dubbing or peacock herl

When to use: This midge emerger, developed by Stephen Tomasovich for the upper tailwater, works wherever midges or small mayflies are present. The **"Prowler variation"** on the Moonshine Midge uses vinyl rib for the body and a single strand of copper flash wrapped between the vinyl rib wraps as ribbing.

Mop Fly (egg/worm/larva)

Hook: Size 6-10 nymph or scud hook
Bead: Black (or match body color
Thread: Black 6/0 or 8/0
Body: Chenille tendril cut from dust mop
Collar: Spiky/flashy dubbing in contrasting color, especially black

Notes: One of the simplest flies you'll ever tie, the Mop Fly uses a chenille tendril from a dust mop as the body. Try pink, chartreuse, red, orange or cream color mop tendrils for the body. The dark dubbed collar adds refinement and seems to make it even more effective.

Pat's Rubberlegs (stonefly nymph)

Hook: Size 2-8 woolly bugger hook
Weighting: Lead-free wire on hook shank
Thread: Black 6/0
Tail/antenna: Rubber leg material
Body: Chenille is usually used to form the body, though dubbed thread can also be used and gives you a lot of flexibility.
Legs: Rubber leg material

Notes: An effective and easy-to-tie (at least by stonefly nymph standards!) imitation of the stonefly nymphs that are present in much of the Chattahoochee. Very effective in the tailwater. Also try these in the headwaters, where they can be surprisingly effective.

Kaufmann's Stone is another good stonefly nymph imitation for the Hooch.

Pheasant Tail Nymph (with or without bead) (nymph)

Hook: 12-18 nymph hook
Bead: (Optional) gold-colored brass
Thread: Black 6/0
Tail/abdomen: Pheasant tail fibers
Ribbing: Fine gold wire
Thorax: Peacock herl
Wingcase: Section of pheasant tail feather

Notes: This great all-around nymph imitation is especially effective where slender-bodied nymphs are present. Check under rocks to see what's moving, and use this pattern to imitate slender nymphs. A great fly for the mountain headwaters...and on the lower tailwater, try a pink one (really!) for DH.

Royal Wulff (attractor dry)

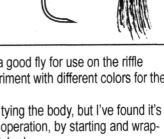

Hook: Dry fly hook, 1XL, 12-18
Wing: White calftail or Antron yarn, divided
Tail: Moose body hair, stacked
Body: 2-3 strands of peacock herl
Midbody: Red, chartreuse, or orange thread
Hackle: Brown dry fly hackle

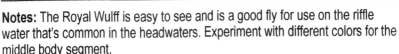

Notes: The Royal Wulff is easy to see and is a good fly for use on the riffle water that's common in the headwaters. Experiment with different colors for the middle body segment.

Some tyers add the mid-body thread while tying the body, but I've found it's easier to add it at the very end, as a separate operation, by starting and wrapping red thread over the middle of the peacock herl.

Rolex (streamer)

Hook: Size 6-8 streamer/woolly hook
Eyes: Molded eyes, red
Thread: Red 6/0 or 8/0
Tail and upper body: Silver flash
Lower body: Gold flash

Notes: With its bright mylar body, wing and tail, this is the fly fishing equivalent of the in-line spinner.

Popular color combinations include silver/gold, silver/red and gold/red. Because of the way it's tied, this fly tends to ride hook-up in the water. Especially effective on recently stocked fish.

Scud (Flashback)

Hook: 12-18 curved scud hook

Thread: 6/0 to match body color

Weighting: Lead-free wire wrapped around mid portion of shank

Antenna: A few strands of dubbing material

Tail: Tips of mottled hen or partridge

Ribbing: 5X monofilament

Back: Approx 1/8-inch wide scud back material or strip of flash material

Body: Generously applied scud dubbing (orange, rust, brown)

Notes: Fish the scud like a nymph. It can be effective near patches of aquatic vegetation. It's good to try on the tailwater near grass beds. Try it in pink for DH.

Soft-Hackle Emerger (caddis emerger)

Hook: 12-16 nymph or scud hook

Bead: Gold, or small glass bead for lighter weight

Body: Fuzzy yarn, dubbed thread, or flash

Ribbing: Small copper or silver wire

Hackle: A couple of turns of mottled hen feather

Collar: Coarse red dubbing on tying thread

Notes: Here's an all-purpose pattern that works in a variety of settings and on all parts of the Chattahoochee trout water. It's especially effective in spring when caddisflies are beginning to appear.

Walt's Worm Variation (larva/worm)

Hook: Size 12-16 jig hook (so fly rides hook up)

Bead: Tungsten (silver or black)

Weight: Extra-fine lead-free wire

Thread: Orange

Ribbing: Single strand of fine flash

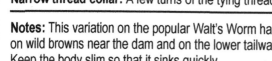

Body: Hare's mask and antron dubbing blend

Narrow thread collar: A few turns of the tying thread

Notes: This variation on the popular Walt's Worm has proven to be effective on wild browns near the dam and on the lower tailwater during caddis season. Keep the body slim so that it sinks quickly.